D1606113

Gardening for
Flower Arrangement

BY ARNO NEHRLING AND IRENE NEHRLING

DRAWINGS BY

Charlotte D. Bowden and Charles A. Mahoney

DOVER PUBLICATIONS, INC.
NEW YORK

Published in Canada by General Publishing
Company, Ltd., 30 Lesmill Road, Don Mills,
Toronto, Ontario.
Published in the United Kingdom by Constable
and Company, Ltd., 10 Orange Street, London
WC 2.

This Dover edition, first published in 1976, is an
unabridged, unaltered republication of the revised
(1969) edition of *Flower Growing for Flower Arrangement,* originally published in 1958 under the
title *Gardening, Forcing, Conditioning and Drying
for Flower Arrangement.* The present edition is
published by special arrangement with Hearthside
Press, Inc., Publishers, 445 Northern Boulevard,
Great Neck, New York 11201, publisher of the
previous editions.

International Standard Book Number: 0-486-23263-8
Library of Congress Catalog Card Number: 75-20966

Manufactured in the United States of America
Dover Publications, Inc.
180 Varick Street
New York, N.Y. 10014

CONTENTS

CONTENTS

ACKNOWLEDGMENTS

This book owes much of its content to horticulturists and experienced amateurs all over America. Our long questionnaires dealing with the gardening aspects of flower arranging were promptly and enthusiastically answered by the following, to whom we are deeply grateful: Prof. Henry P. Orr of Alabama; Mrs. H. Jeff Davis of Florida; Mrs. Jim Peterson of Georgia; Mrs. Howard Buery of Kansas; Mrs. H. W. Farmer of Kentucky; Mrs. N. Martone of Louisiana; Mrs. John W. McNair of Maryland; Mrs. Marie Cook and Mrs. Emily Seaber Parcher of Massachusetts; Mrs. W. H. Barton of Michigan; Mrs. Peggie Schulz of Minnesota; Mrs. Robert J. Hamel of Montana; Mrs. Morgan P. Gilbert of New Hampshire; Mrs. Clement Bowers of New York; Mrs. Paul Kincaid of North Carolina; Mr. Arnold M. Davis and Mrs. Zelda Wyatt Schulke of Ohio; Mrs. Allen Henry of Oklahoma; Mrs. C. F. Gregg of Oregon; Mrs. Maxwell W. Steel of Pennsylvania; Mrs. Luther Burriss, Mrs. J. S. O'Brien and Mrs. Walter Pond of South Carolina; Mrs. R. E. Day and Mrs. L. W. Hillam of Utah; Mrs. J. M. McCabe of Vermont; Mrs. James H. Donohue Jr. of Virginia; Mrs. Fred W. Gordon of Washington; Mrs. Ernest J. Adams of West Virginia; and Mrs. Fred C. Marquardt of Wisconsin. We appreciate the help of the many state presidents of garden clubs who selected the men and women in each state who could be most valuable in supplying regional information.

We are particularly grateful to Mr. George Taloumis, editor of *Horticulture*, for advice, to Prof. Clark L. Thayer, former head of the department of Floriculture, University of Massachusetts, for a critical reading of the manuscript, and to Mr. Bernard Harkness, Bureau of Parks and Recreation, Rochester, New York, for reading the chapter on forcing branches.

ACKNOWLEDGMENTS

Horticulture permitted use of material from its columns. Miss Dorothy Manks, librarian of the Massachusetts Horticultural Society, has been most helpful in making research material available; Mrs. Charlotte Bowden and Mr. Charles A Mahoney are responsible for the clear drawings; Miss Ann B. White was most helpful in many ways; and Mrs. Bennett Levine typed the manuscript.

This would be incomplete if we did not record our deep appreciation to Nedda Anders for her good judgment, enthusiasm, counsel and untiring assistance in planning, organizing and editing the book.

ARNO and IRENE NEHRLING

Needham Heights,
Massachusetts.
January 1958

For Dorothy, Warren and Pamela

1

GARDEN DESIGNS FOR FLOWER ARRANGERS

Design principles govern landscaping as well as flower arranging. Each type of composition must have these characteristics: good balance, a proper size relationship of all parts to each other and to the composition as a whole, contrast for the sake of interest, rhythm or repetition which creates a visual path through the design, and harmony or unity.

These principles have been covered in many landscaping books, and if you are designing your first garden, we suggest that you read at least one of the many good basic ones which have been published. It should help you lay out a garden to fit the needs of the family, dividing the lot into areas planned for welcome, service, and recreation. The basic outline should be drawn on graph paper, with house and lot indicated in scale.

After the overall plan is laid out, the actual plant material should be selected. Unfortunately, many otherwise perfect plantings overlook the homemakers needs indoors. This is a great pity because even the smallest garden, hedge, or edging strip can be made practical for cutting purposes. To guide you in selecting suitable material, the following lists were prepared with landscape effect only one of the considerations. Floriferousness, lasting quality when cut, fragrance, availability during otherwise barren seasons, and good form and color viewed at close range (as flowers indoors are likely to be) were some of the characteristics we looked for in compiling the data for this book.

LANDSCAPE DESIGNS
Offering Color, Succession of Bloom, Varied Forms

Cape Cod Cottage
Climbing roses frame door, cover fence. Boxwood either side of entrance. Flowering
shrubs at corners. Flower border inside fence

Ranch Type House
Clipped Yews define entrance.
Window view unobstructed by
flower border. Flowering shrubs
near corners. Long, low line re-
lieved by tree

Small City Garden
Green and white predominate.
Crab apple, white rhododendron.
Solomon's seal and ivy. Potted
white geraniums, petunias

Backyard Garden
Screen of evergreens good background for shrubs and flower
border. Edging repeats primrose
border around pool

Patio Garden
Fern leaved foliage of Wisteria over door
lovely all season. Pyramidal arbor-vitae
accent plant at far right. Floribunda
roses bloom all summer

Naturalistic Planting
Lilacs to left, rhododendron under
trees on right with flower border
enhance natural setting

C. E. Bowden

SHRUBS AND TREES FOR LANDSCAPE EFFECT

Choose shrubs and trees first, for they are the background of every garden. Only specimen shrubs should be planted singly— the others are more effective in groups of three or five.

Filler shrubs are the quieter types used between accent plants such as Chaenomeles (Japanese Quince), Cotoneaster, ground covers (like Pachistima, Pachysandra or Vinca), Ilex (dwarf hollies), Leucothea, Spirea thunbergi and Viburnum burkwoodi.

Accent shrubs for contrast include the colorful evergreen Azaleas, Enkianthus with its outstanding autumn foliage, Ilex (the dwarf American holly with its rich, dark green leaves), Kalmia (Mountain Laurel), Pyracantha with its showy orange-red berries and the upright Taxus (dark green of the yews offer wonderful contrast to the silvery-gray of dwarf junipers).

Excellent hedge shrubs include Buxus (Korean Box), Deutzia gracilis, Chaenomeles (Japanese Quince), Euonymus alatus compactus, Forsythia, Ilex crenata convexa and I. c. bullata or convexa, Junipers (dwarf), Lonicera (Bush honeysuckle), Philadelphus (Mock-Orange), Pyracantha, Rosa hugonis and R. rugosa (for the seashore), Spirea in variety, Syringa (Lilac), upright Taxus group (Yews) and Viburnum in variety. Crataegus (some of the Hawthorns, especially oxyacantha), Acer campestre (Hedge Maple) and Acer ginnala (Amur Maple) are good trees for hedges.

There are many excellent specimen plants for drama such as the birch with its outstanding bark, the flowering cherries, crabapples, dogwoods and magnolias, Ilex (American Hollies), rhododendrons and Sciadopitys (Umbrella Pine).

ANNUALS AND PERENNIALS IN THE GARDEN

When shrubs and trees are selected, you will want to add annuals, perennials, and bulbs for variety of form and color, and to insure an abundant supply of material through most months. For small lots, one single broad interrelated composition—perhaps a border at least 4'-5' wide and 10' long—would be most effective. Plan so that you have something in bloom early in the spring until frost. Do not plant only one annual, perennial, or bulb, use at least 5 plants, enough to make a distinctive oval or mass of color.

Repeat the mass at intervals the length of the border. In between the masses, use flowers with complementary hues, or if you want a one-color garden, use lighter or darker values of the same color. Be sure to have contrasting forms and lines for accent and interest, not only in the garden, but also later for adding variety to bouquets.

SPIKE FORMS: Select for height, line and accent interest in border and floral arrangement.

Campanula, Canterbury Bell
Canna
Celosia (Plume), Cockscomb
Clarkia
Delphinium, Larkspur
Digitalis, Foxglove
Gladiolus
Hollyhock
Kniphofia, Torch Lily (usually offered as Tritoma)
Lathyrus odoratus, Sweet Pea (if long stemmed)

Lavandula officinalis, Lavender
Lupinus polyphyllus, Lupine
Pentstemon, Beard Tongue
Physostegia virginiana, False Dragonhead
Polianthes tuberosa, Tuberose
Salvia, Sage
Snapdragon
Stock
Thermopsis
Veronica, Speedwell

ROUND FORMS: Select them for center of interest.

Anemone
Aster, Michaelmas Daisy
Calendula officinalis, Pot Marigold
Centaurea cyanus, Bachelors-Button
Chrysanthemum, annual and perennial
Chrysanthemum coccineum, Pyrethrum (Painted Daisy)
Chrysanthemum maximum, Shasta Daisy
Coreopsis, Calliopsis
Cosmos
Daffodil
Dahlia
Dianthus barbatus, Sweet William

Dianthus chinensis, Garden Pinks
Felicia
Gaillardia
Geum, Avens
Helianthus, Sunflower
Hemerocallis
Ipomoea purpurea, Morning Glory
Lathyrus odoratus, Sweet Pea (short stemmed)
Paeonia, Peony
Papaver, Poppy
Pelargonium, Geranium
Petunia
Phlox
Ranunculus, Buttercup
Rosa, Rose

Salpiglossis
Scabiosa
Stokesia
Tagetes, Marigold
Tithonia

Trachymene caerulea, Blue Lace Flower
Tropaeolum, Nasturtium
Zinnia

TRAILERS: To relieve severe lines, obscure undesirable objects, cover high walls and to blend architectural masses into the garden picture. Equally useful for graceful and softening effects indoors. To relate floral design to containers or to other accessories in the room.

Calonyction aculeatum, Moonflower
Clematis
Cobaea scandens, Cup and Saucer Vine
Dolichos lablab, Hyacinth Bean
Hedera helix, English Ivy
Ipomoea purpurea, Morning Glory
Lonicera halliana, Honeysuckle

Parthenocissus quinquefolia, Virginia Creeper
Parthenocissus tricuspidata, Boston Ivy
Quamoclit pennata, Cypress Vine
Thunbergia alata, Clock-Vine
Tropaeolum, Nasturtium (tall)
Wisteria

FILLERS: The smaller, fluffier blossoms of plants commonly used for edging in the border are used as fillers in indoor arrangements.

Ageratum
Anchusa capensis, Summer Forget-me-not
Cynoglossum amabile, Chinese Forget-me-not
Dianthus chinensis, Garden Pinks
Gypsophila, Annual Babys-Breath
Iberis, Candytuft
Lobelia siphilitica, Blue Lobelia

Lobularia, Sweet Alyssum
Nigella damascena, Love-in-a-Mist
Petunia
Phlox—annual
Reseda odorata, Mignonette
Tagetes, Pot Marigold
Torenia, Wishbone Flower
Verbena
Viola tricolor, Pansy

2

SHRUBS AND TREES FOR
EASY UPKEEP

Fortunately, trees and shrubs require a minimum of care and those with pleasing growth habits give wonderful effects throughout the year. To choose and place them wisely, you must know the plants in all their seasons. Check on hardiness, freedom from pests and disease, and ease of growth. All of the ones listed are valuable for the arranger, so select them with other requirements in mind. Occasional feeding and pruning will be sufficient care for most shrubs. Generally, they will flower more profusely if cut when they are in bloom.

Blooming dates of plants and length of blooming period will vary, of course, with location and type of season. Magnolias, azaleas, and rhododendrons may bloom almost two months earlier in the far south than in New England. This must be taken into consideration when studying descriptions which give New England blooming dates. The dates may also vary with mild or severe, wet or dry seasons.

Unless otherwise specified, shrubs listed are hardy as far north as New York and Boston.

A list of small flowering trees, shrubs and hardy vines useful in landscaping and for cutting will help you select material to suit your needs.

RECOMMENDED TREES AND SHRUBS

Abelia grandiflora—Glossy Abelia. A lovely deciduous shrub three to four feet, but can be kept more dwarf by pruning. Bears

SHRUBS IN THE GARDEN

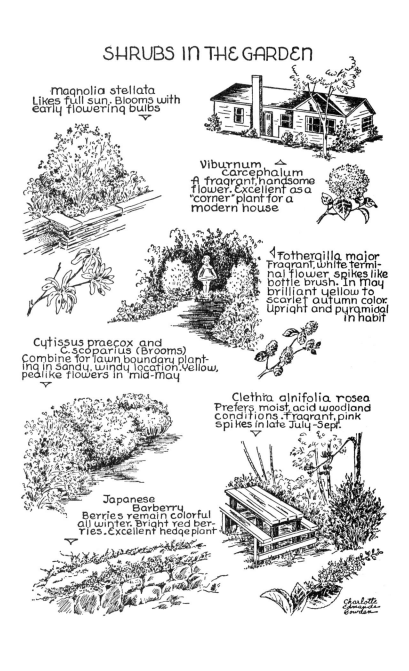

magnolia stellata
Likes full sun. Blooms with
early flowering bulbs

Viburnum
carcephalum
A fragrant, handsome
flower. Excellent as a
"corner" plant for a
modern house

Fothergilla major
Fragrant, white termi-
nal flower spikes like
bottle brush. In May
brilliant yellow to
scarlet autumn color.
Upright and pyramidal
in habit

Cytissus praecox and
C. scoparius (Brooms)
Combine for lawn boundary planting in sandy, windy location. Yellow,
pealike flowers in mid-May

Clethra alnifolia rosea
Prefers moist, acid woodland
conditions. Fragrant, pink
spikes in late July-Sept.

Japanese
Barberry
Berries remain colorful
all winter. Bright red berries. Excellent hedge plant

Charlotte
Edmonds
Bowden

a continuous supply of small white and pink arbutus-like flowers from midsummer until frost. Flowers appear on new wood. Small foliage so glossy it sparkles in sun, turns rich lustrous bronze in autumn. Excellent for the small garden. Extremely popular in south. Cut for foliage and flowers from midsummer till frost. Fall foliage is highly decorative. Treat as you would any cut woody branches. North of New York plant in a protected location.

Albizzia julibrissin rosea—Hardy Silk Tree. One of the few summer-flowering trees, with small pink flowers in slender-stalked, compact heads. Excellent cut. Treat as any woody material.

Azalea of the genus Rhododendron. Winter-hardy species excellent for cutting with wealth of bloom and splendid color. Range from white through yellow-orange, scarlet, soft rose-pinks to purple. Many fragrant. Bloom from May through July, primarily in May. Mostly deciduous but attractive branching habit has year-round appeal. Flowers most profusely with several hours of sun daily. Some varieties color richly in the fall. Cut for arrangements when three or four flowers are open on each stem or cluster. Buds open well in water. A lovely line design may be made with one well-chosen branch effectively staged.

A. ARBORESCENS—Smooth Azalea. Upright and tall, 8-20 ft., white, fragrant flowers $1\frac{1}{2}$-2″ across, in June. Flower is more open, somewhat larger and blooms two weeks earlier than R. viscosum.

A. CALENDULACEUM—Flame Azalea. Picturesque oval, upright shrub 8-15 ft. or more. Beautiful good-sized flowers $1\frac{1}{2}$-$2\frac{1}{2}$″ from light yellow through orange shades to vermilion about first week in June. Flowers are occasionally borne in round rhododendron-like trusses of 20-30. Interplant with R. catawbiense, which is evergreen and blooms at the same time.

A. CANADENSE—Rhodora. Low round shrub grows to 3 ft. tall with gray-green leaves and spreading habit. Light rosy-purplish flowers in early or mid-May, will not take vivid competition. Delicately attractive. Use with white, light yellow or green.

A. CUMBERLANDENSE—Cumberland Azalea. Medium sized azalea valuable for late bloom and rich color, orange vermilion to scarlet. Blooms about third week in June.

PRUNING FLOWERING TREES AND SHRUBS
To Keep Within Bounds

Eliminate branches
that cross and
rub

Thin dense
growth to
let in sun
and air

To Emphasize natural Beauty

Cut out suckers,
water sprouts
and old canes

Cut out dead,
weak or dis-
eased wood

A. KAEMPFERI—Torch Azalea. Picturesque upright shrub 3 to 6 ft. tall, makes a colorful display. Reddish-orange flowers about 2" across. Tend to fade in sun.

A. POUKHANENSE (R. yedoense var.)—Korean Azalea. Broad shrub —4-6 ft. tall with small winter leaves and larger summer leaves retaining a semi-evergreen character. Well covered with bloom down to the ground. Flowers fragrant, 2" across, light purplish-violet. Attractive with white, light yellow or green; brighter colors dull it. Blooms with flowering dogwood.

A. ROSEUM—Roseshell, Mountain or Mayflower Azalea. Medium-sized. Blooms about May 25. Flowers clear rose color, 1¾" across with spicy, clove-like fragrance.

A. SCHLIPPENBACHI—Royal Azalea. Beautiful 5-6 ft. shrub with clusters of big showy flowers, white flushed with rose or delicate pink. One of first to bloom. Distinctive leaves in whorls of five.

A. VASEYI—Pinkshell Azalea. Rapid grower of rare and delicate beauty, upright and tall, 6 to 12 ft. Dainty flowers which come before leaves are fully out in early May. Bright pink in bud but merely tinged like an apple bloom when open. Stamens prominent. Combine superbly with tulips and dogwood. Has bronze fall foliage. Var. album a pure white form.

A. VISCOSUM—Swamp Azalea. Not as showy as R. arborescens but valuable for lateness of bloom, coming in July. Flowers white suffused with pink, strong clove fragrance, somewhat smaller than R. arborescens, 1-1½″ across but with extra long tube. Bluish green leaves partially obscure flowers. Foliage orange-bronze in autumn.

A. YEDOENSE—Yodogawa Azalea. Colorful spreading bush 4 ft. high, green leaves to 3″ long are hairy beneath. In early May bears rosy-magenta flowers. Good with wisteria and dogwood. Avoid reds, yellows, oranges and any blue-free color as they clash with magenta.

Berberis—Barberry. To use fresh, treat like any woody plant material. For dried arrangements cut as soon as berries are fully developed and, at best color and form. Use clear plastic spray or shellac to lessen shrinking and falling of berries. Brilliant berries and bright leaves.

B. KOREANA—Korean Barberry. Attractive upright shrub 5-7 ft. with broad, bright green leaves, dense yellow flower clusters in May. Vivid red persistent fruit. Deep red in autumn.

B. MENTORENSIS—Mentor Barberry. A hybrid between evergreen and deciduous species. Has rich, leathery green leaves which turn bronzy in winter. Leaves fall only when new ones come out in spring.

B. THUNBERGI—Japanese Barberry. Deciduous, most widely grown for both trimmed and untrimmed hedges. Pale yellow flowers in April and May followed by deep red fruit and brilliant orange-red autumn foliage.

B. THUNBERGI ATROPURPUREA—Redleaf Japanese Barberry. Grows 3-6 ft. Purple red leaves.

Buddleia. Summer Lilac or Butterfly Bush. Grows 3-7 ft. Valuable summer flowers in sweetly scented spikes of white, pink, lilac, purple and wine. Graceful sprays bloom in July and August. May be winter killed to ground north of Philadelphia. In the spring they send up new shoots. Cut when $\frac{1}{2}$ flowering spike is open but before flowers begin to fade. Will last about a week. When conditioning, if spikes are not turgid, place in hot water (100° F.) a second or even third time if necessary, so panicles will be fresh and filled with water. Excellent cut flowers when properly conditioned. Some varieties bloom in July, others August, until frost. Cut flowers and keep faded blooms removed to prolong blooming season.

Buxus—Box. In great demand during the holiday season for wreaths, kissing balls, tiny assembled trees and many other decorations. When a delicate green form is desired only short cuttings are necessary and in skillful hands beautiful arrangements are achieved. Furnishes excellent short-stemmed greens the year round.

B. MICROPHYLLA (Japan and Korea). Compact shrub with lighter colored foliage. Hardier. Var. japonica grows to 6 ft., has fairly large leaves. Var. koreana upright growth to 2 ft. with smaller bright green leaves. Var. compacta less than 12″ high.

B. SEMPERVIRENS—Common or European Box. The tree "edging box." Evergreen with small, dark lustrous green leaves.
    arborescens—Tree Box. Grows to 15 ft. Open not dense.
    glauca—dull, bluish-green leaves.
    handsworthi—somewhat erect, densely bushy, leaves large and broad.
    myrtifolia—leaves somewhat narrower.
    rosmarinifolia—leaves long and narrow.
    suffruticosa—Dwarf Box. In greatest demand. Most fragrant. Can grow it from cuttings.

Calycanthus floridus—Sweetshrub or Carolina Allspice. Dense shrub with glossy foliage. Grows to 8 ft. Fragrant dark reddish-maroon to dark brown flowers in May. Beg from a neighbor for division can be made by roots, surest way to get true fragrant type. Cut branches when $\frac{1}{4}$ to $\frac{1}{2}$ flowers are open. Split stem end and condition overnight. Remove some foliage to better display flowers. Lasts a week cut.

Campsis—Trumpet Vine or Creeper. Likes sunny location. Cut branches when 1 or 2 flowers are open in a cluster. Some buds will drop off but many will adhere to open in water and serve your decorating purpose. Bright orange flowers last 3 or 4 days. Excellent trailing form for arrangements.

C. GRANDIFLORA—Chinese Trumpet Vine. Does not climb as high, not quite so hardy but showier flowers than C. radicans.

C. RADICANS—Scarlet Trumpet Vine. Popular for years. Orange with scarlet funnel form flowers in August. Fine foliage.

YELLOW TRUMPET. Golden yellow flowers.

Caragana arborescens—Siberian Pea-Shrub or Tree. Tall shrub or small tree, 15-20 ft. Bright green leaves, small, bright yellow pea-shaped flowers in June. Good background shrub. Cut for arrangements when a touch of yellow is needed.

Caryopteris—Hardy Blue Spirea. Plant in perennial border, good as foreground filler. Grows 2'-3'. Flowers from late August until frost. Valuable to arranger at time when blue flowers are scarce. Flowers form on wood of current season's growth.

Blue Mist. Charming low growing rounded shrub 18-24" tall and 2 ft. across. Covered from August till autumn frost with clusters of powdery blue, fringed flowers. Foliage silvery grayish-green.

Heavenly Blue. Beautiful deep blue flower spikes in autumn. Plant measures 18" across, 18-24" tall. Likes sandy soil and full sun. Cut when $\frac{1}{2}$ flowering spike is open but before opened flowers begin to fade.

Cedar (Canaert Red-Cedar)—Juniperus virginiana canaerti. Retains its rich dark green coloring through the winter. Abundant blue-purplish berries. Burk Red-cedar has steel-blue foliage which turns reddish in fall.

Celastrus—Bittersweet. Fast growing twining vine much prized for its yellow fruits which split open showing crimson seeds inside. Cut before heavy frost when fruits are most brilliant. Spray with clear plastic to lessen shriveling and dropping off of berries. Arrange immediately or store for later use. When dried arrangements get dusty clean with a fine mist spray of warm water, then let dry. C. scandens—American species. Must keep pruned to keep within bounds. C. orbiculata. Oriental species. Two species differ only slightly.

SHRUBS AND TREES FOR EASY UPKEEP 25

Cercis canadensis—Redbud. Shrub or tree with rosy-pink flowers in clusters, in spring before leaves, creating an airy quality. Charming combined with spring flowering bulbs. Var. alba, white; plena, double flowers.

Chaenomeles—Japanese Quince. About 3′ high. All varieties are valuable for cutting and forcing into bloom indoors in early spring. Cut when ¼ of buds are open on branch. Buds will continue to open in water for 2 weeks. Orange-red to red flowers come mostly before leaves.

c. JAPONICA var. alpina Dwarf Japanese Quince. Low spreading nearly prostrate shrub 1½ ft. high with spiny branches. All have interesting dark green foliage. Flower clusters in white, deep red, scarlet and bright red 1½″ across, come in late April or early May. Fruit yellow. Give plenty of room and place in background.

c. LAGENARIA—Common Flowering Quince. Many var. Shrub 5-7 ft. and same width. Stiff growing branches and thorns. Flowers in April or May are scarlet red, varying to pink and white, 2″ across. Single and semidouble. Lustrous dark green leaves. Fruit greenish-yellow.

Chamaecyparis—False-Cypress. Of the pine family. Handsome evergreen, slow growing with drooping foliage in fan-like sprays much used by arrangers, especially at Christmas.

Chionanthus virginicus—Fringe Tree. One of the most striking of small trees to 30 ft. Handsome oblong leaves turn a bright golden-yellow in autumn. In June large masses of loose panicles of feathery petaled, fragrant, snow-white flowers make it an outstanding garden plant. Needs plenty of room to fully develop. Comes into leaf very late in season. Fragrant snow-white panicles excellent in arrangements and combine well with most any color. Hardy north with some protection.

Clematis. Beautiful flowering vine grown on trellises, arbors and pergolas. Endless varieties, dwarf and tall, small and very large flowered with color range from white through pink, to crimson and purple. Wonderful hybrids of rare beauty. Some bloom on old wood, others on new. Those which flower from new wood should have all growth cut back in early spring while still dormant. For arrangements, cut just before petals are ready to unfold, those blooming in small clusters when only $\frac{1}{4}$ of cluster is open. Cut some old wood with each spray (applies to most flowering vines). Flowers last well when cut, about a week, and lend themselves to many unique arrangements. Most flowers open wide and flat. Varieties cover a blooming period from May to September. Vines and tendrils attractive in arrangements fresh or dried. Hang to dry. Like alkaline soil. Need some sun and well-drained soil.

C. MONTANA. Fragrant white anemone-like flowers 1 to 2″ across in May and June. Var. rubens has flowers rose or pink and young growth reddish.

C. PANICULATA. One of hardiest and easiest to grow. Conspicuous in late summer, with many flowered panicles of small white fragrant flowers. Dense shiny leaves. Decorative when flowers are gone with fluffy silver seed heads which remain into winter, interesting curving tendrils. Excellent for the arranger looking for a trailing form.

Clethra alnifolia—Summersweet, Sweet Pepperbush. One of most delightful of the late flowering shrubs. Good for any but the smallest garden. Spikes of fragrant white flowers from late July through September, when few other shrubs are in bloom, excellent for cutting. Combines well with most anything. Var. rosea pink flowering variety. Propagate by division. Cut when $\frac{1}{4}$ to $\frac{1}{2}$ cluster is in flower but before open flowers start to fade. Good seashore plant.

Cornus florida—Flowering Dogwood. No tree or shrub is more attractive. It offers something for the arranger throughout the year. In early spring, as soon as the buds swell, cut branches caring for the shape of tree. Forced indoors, flowers will last a week or more. In summer, the attractive foliage and in the fall, the red berries and colored leaves, make handsome arrangements. Condition as for any woody material. Colorful foliage may be pressed or dried for winter decoration or given glycerin and water treatment, see page 178. In winter, if you have a sufficient supply, branches with the tight unusual buds are ornamental.

C. FLORIDA. Not over 20 ft., of equal spread. White flowered, one of most valuable of small deciduous flowering trees. Floral

CHOOSING A TREE FOR A SMALL GARDEN

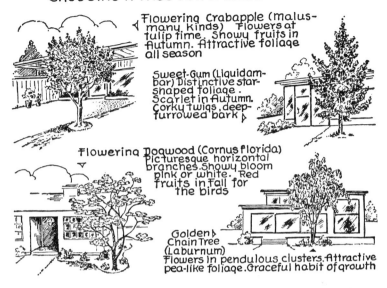

Flowering Crabapple (malus—many kinds) Flowers at tulip time. Showy fruits in Autumn. Attractive foliage all season

Sweet-Gum (Liquidambar) Distinctive star-shaped foliage. Scarlet in Autumn. Corky twigs, deep-furrowed bark

Flowering Dogwood (Cornus florida) Picturesque horizontal branches. Showy bloom pink or white. Red fruits in fall for the birds

Golden Chain Tree (Laburnum) Flowers in pendulous clusters. Attractive pea-like foliage. Graceful habit of growth

display in May and autumn color of foliage and red fruits unsurpassed. Tracery of budded branches form one of winters most exquisite patterns.

Var. plena or pluribracteata is double-flowered.

Var. xanthocarpa bears yellow berries in fall.

C. KOUSA CHINENSIS—Chinese Dogwood. Grows to 15 ft. Flower heads extremely large, 5-6″ across, white bracts overlapping the button-like mass of real flowers in the center. Flowers in June. Fruits like large strawberries, red autumnal foliage.

Cornus mas—Cornelian Cherry. Round, densely branched shrub about 12 x 12 ft. or more. Small stalked clusters of tiny light yellow flowers appear all over shrub in April before the leaves come. Branches easily forced. Large decorative, shiny green foliage to 4″ long, turns orange to scarlet in autumn. Scarlet fruit size of olive in August. Blooms with narcissi and crocuses.

Cornus sibirica—Coral Beauty. Compact, neat grower to 5 ft. Foliage excellent. Pale blue berries follow flowers in autumn. Outstanding and beautifully colored in winter months. Stems green during summer. In autumn branches take on a lovely salmon-pink which persists until spring. For winter coloring in the garden and for cutting there is nothing finer.

Corylopsis spicata—Winter Hazel. One of the earliest flowering shrubs producing clusters of soft yellow before the leaves appear. Rather coarse foliage resembles that of witch hazel.

Cotinus coggygria—Smoke Tree. Good accent plant, irregular and oval in shape, grows 6' to 12'. In June becomes entirely covered with a filmy, pinkish envelope of flowers that last a long time and produce a "smoky effect." Still conspicuous and attractive as they dry and turn brownish. Dried branches may be purchased from a florist supply or "greens" house for arrangements. The foliage takes on good red-orange coloring in the fall. Attractive with orange and apricot mums.

Cotoneaster. A group of shrubs grown for their gracefully arching branches and showy fruits in autumn. Excellent for line arrangements. Since difficult to transplant insist on getting pot-grown plants. Foliage of many brilliant fall colors.

C. DIVARICATA—Spreading Cotoneaster. Grows 6 to 8 ft. Excellent specimen for corners of house. Good for medium sized hedge 4-5 ft. or border. Pink flowers in June. Bright red berries in autumn. Foliage small and round, highly polished dark green. Turns in fall.

C. HORIZONTALIS—Rock Cotoneaster. Dwarf horizontal spreading branches 1½-3 ft. high. Half evergreen. Tiny leaves and fruits. Small pinkish flowers in June. Bright red fruit in September and October.

C. MICROPHYLLA—Rockspray Cotoneaster. 2-3 ft. A fine low evergreen shrub with spreading branches forming a dense mass. White flowers and purple anthers in May to June. Scarlet fruit.

C. MULTIFLORA. Grows to 10 ft. bush. Arching, spreading branches in late May erupt along entire length into clusters of white Hawthorn-like flowers. In fall crimson fruits fringe the branches. Broad foliage of a soft blue-green.

Crataegus—Hawthorn. Belongs to the rose family. Some have fragrant flowers, many are white, others pink or scarlet. All have thorns, attractive foliage, good autumn coloring and conspicuous autumn fruit. When cutting, wear garden gloves and beware of thorns. Of value to arranger from early spring through late fall.

C. ARNOLDIANA—Arnold Hawthorn. Small ornamental tree 15-20 ft. forming a broad, irregular crown. Large white flowers in early May, large scarlet or crimson fruit in August-September. Falls rather early.

C. CRUS-GALLI—Cockspur Hawthorn. Grows 20-30 ft. Attractive white flowers in May or June. Bright red fruits in fall and winter. Glossy foliage turns to orange and scarlet in fall. Thorns make it useful where an impenetrable hedge is desired.

C. OXYACANTHA—European Hawthorn. Best var. Paul's Double Scarlet. One of the most brilliant small flowering trees 15-25 ft. Double bright scarlet flowers in late May. Rosea is a lighter pink and plena a double white.

C. PHAENOPYRUM—Washington Hawthorn. One of best, 20-30 ft. with profuse white flowers in May-June and lustrous scarlet small fruit in large clusters in September-October, which last well into the winter. Last to bloom in spring. Good autumn coloring.

Cytisus—Broom. Will grow in poor sandy soil and hot, dry climates.

CYTISUS PRAECOX—Warminster Broom. Attractive May flowering shrub 4-5 ft. high. Mass of sulphur-yellow pea-shaped blooms in May along branches. Brush-like foliage, picturesque throughout season. Good in line arrangements.

CYTISUS SCOPARIUS—Scotch Broom. Excellent for line arrangements. Measure and then cut branches necessary length. Easily bent into curves or branches, may be tied into desired forms, placed in cold water until lines are fixed, removed and then dried before untying. Foliage lasts well. Dry seed pods for winter use.

Daphne cneorum—Rose Daphne, Garland Flower. Useful as ground cover with fragrant pink flowers in terminal clusters in early spring, and dense carpeting effect. Good edging plant. Likes well-drained, light soil. Grows to 12", trailing branches. Good in miniature or small-scale bouquets.

Desmodium penduliflorum. Shrub-like plant producing arched, slender branches, lovely in effect, covered with hundreds of purple blossoms in late fall. The mass of long drooping racemes is a magnificent sight. Plant in full sun. Cut all growth back to the ground in early spring. Excellent cut and combined with purple, yellow or bronze mums or asters.

Deutzia. Showy flowering shrub of bushy habit. Many stems rising from the root, arching upward and outward, thickly covered with foliage which almost disappears in May under masses of small, frilled, bell-like flowers. Petals shed easily when cut, but abundance of bloom make them effective and worth cutting. All deutzias need drastic thinning of old canes after flowering to form new flowering wood for next season, during early summer growth.

D. GRACILIS. Grows 2-3 ft. Graceful, fountain-like bush, symmetrical and attractive throughout year. In May covered with a profusion of delicate snowy-white flowers. Pale green leaves. Does well in light. Many hybrids.

D. KALMIAEFLORA. Slender, slightly arching branches of this low 3 ft. growing shrub is covered in late May and early June with kalmia-like pink flowers.

Eleagnus angustifolia—Russian Olive. Tall, hardy shrub to 20', sometimes becoming a small tree. Silvery-yellow flowers in early June inconspicuous but fragrant. Distinguished by its silvery-green-gray foliage. Brown shredding bark ornamental in winter. Showy yellow berries with silvery scales in early fall.

Enkianthus campanulatus. Striking orange-scarlet fall foliage, excellent for decoration. Rather erect, charming, graceful shrub of narrow outline to 10 ft. or more. Pleasing foliage in early autumn turns to striking orange and scarlet tints. Likes acid soil, full sun or partial shade. In May has dainty little pendulous clusters borne on long, slender stems. These drooping bell-shaped flowers come in subdued tones of yellow to light orange to red. Good bush for small grounds. Belongs to same family as the Rhododendron.

Euonymus. Both evergreen and deciduous types. Grown for their dense attractive foliage, good autumn coloring and highly decorative fruit. Highly useful for the arranger, especially so in the fall.

E. ALATUS. A large deciduous shrub 8-10 ft. almost as wide with small yellowish flowers in May and June. Foliage is rose-scarlet in early spring and again in the autumn. One of the most brilliant of plants. Conspicuous "wings" in the bark. Dwarf variety 5-8 ft. Slower growing and more compact.

E. ATROPURPUREUS—Burning-Bush. Grows to 25 ft. Has yellow flowers in May but grown for red autumn fruits and yellow foliage.

E. FORTUNEI. Broadleaf evergreen with many varieties. E. f. coloratus—Purpleleaf Wintercreeper. Is an excellent ground cover, leaves purplish-red in fall and all winter. E. f. minimus—Baby Wintercreeper. Very slow growing, tiny evergreen leaves. E. f. radicans—Common Wintercreeper. Used as a low shrub or climbing vine.

E. LATIFOLIUS. Broadleaf, deciduous shrub or small tree 14-20 ft. Greenish-yellow flowers in May-June. Bright red and orange fruit in September.

E. RADICANS VEGETUS. Evergreen Bittersweet. Excellent wall cover. Produces bright orange-red berries.

E. YEDOENSIS. Grows to 10-15 ft. Deciduous, leaves 4-5″ long, pinkish-purple fruit and brilliant red autumn foliage.

Forsythia. Cherished as a heralder of spring, this showy April spring-flowering shrub, with its brilliant yellow flowers, needs plenty of room. Grows 6 to 8 ft. or more. Prune to keep it shapely and in bounds. Cut branches from pruning force easily. Use with early flowering bulbs, like narcissi and crocuses. Flowers appear before leaves. Many varieties on market, select choicest for your location. Dwarf varieties are now available. Holds foliage late into fall. Some varieties turn olive, red and purplish bronze.

F. INTERMEDIA (hybrid of suspensa and viridissima). Showiest, upright, good in large borders for masses of gold-yellow color. Arching and broad in habit, grows to 8 ft. Fall foliage dark red to purplish bronze. Floriferous. Var. spectabilis is an 8 ft., strong, upright grower with golden-yellow flowers, the largest and showiest of the group. Var. primulina flowers are a pleasing pale yellow.

F. OVATA. Least attractive. Grown because hardiest and earliest to bloom. Smaller growing, amber-yellow flowers borne singly.

F. SUSPENSA OR WEEPING FORSYTHIA. Huge, good rock, wall or arbor shrub, half vine and half shrub with slender branches which root at tips. In bloom, forms a golden-yellow mound. Grows 8-15 ft., irregular. Var. sieboldii has even more slender branches with bright yellow flowers. Var. fortunei vigorous upright grower to 8 ft. with arching branches. Effective for masses of bold canary-yellow blossoms. Foliage not interesting. Var. sieboldii low, vigorous spreading shrub, valuable as robust ground-cover to place high on slope or atop retaining wall. Will stream down in veritable cascade. Var. fortunei builds up a firm, erect shrub to 8 ft. and pours out a stream of long, pendulous branches, beautiful fountain effect. Leaves 3 lobed.

F. VIRIDISSIMA. Upright in growth, 9-10 ft. high. More tender than most and later to bloom. Rather stiff habit. Conspicuous bright green stems. Holds its leaves which turn dark purple to brownish-purple in fall, late in autumn.

Fothergilla. Brilliant leaves in autumn desirable for cutting and decoration.

F. GARDENI. Grows to about half the height of the other varieties with proportionately smaller leaves. Colors brilliantly in fall.

F. MAJOR AND F. MONTICOLA. Upright rather roundish shrubs to 8 ft. Bears profusion of fragrant, small white flowers in short, broad spikes at ends of the branchlets. Good quality foliage which turns brilliant yellow to orange and scarlet in fall if not too shaded. Bloom comes with unfolding of leaves in April or May. Easily forced indoors in early spring. Related to witchhazels.

Hedera—Ivy. Cut branches will last for months, will take root in water. Versatile foliage with hundreds of variations in growth habit, and leaf shape, size, and veining. Will blend with anything you might arrange. Cut stems just above a node. Strip any leaves that come below the water line in the arrangement. Submerge cut sprays in cold water for about 2 to 3 hours to con-

Of all evergreens, none lasts as well as Japanese yew (*Taxus cuspidata*).
Its needles do not drop and the excellent green color remains for weeks.
Here it is combined with berries of *Viburnum opulus*, but any number of
fall fruits go with it equally well.

ARRANGEMENT BY MARION ROWLEY   ROCHE PHOTO

Hydrangeas are effective in large, bold arrangements. All types are good to use in a fresh state, while the late summer blooming *H. paniculata grandiflora* is long-lasting when dried.

ARRANGEMENT BY JULIA S. BERRALL   ROCHE PHOTO

dition. If you want a special line or curve tie spray in desired curve before submerging. Dry while still tied.

H. HELIX—English Ivy. Beautiful evergreen vine with glossy foliage. Good ground cover. Smaller-leaved forms are hardiest. Var. baltica said to be hardiest.

H. HELIX GRACILIS—Baltica Ivy. Hardier than H. helix.

H. HELIX BULGARIS—Bulgarian Ivy. Hardier than H. helix.

Hibiscus syriacus—Althea or Rose of Sharon. Of erect columnar growth 8-10 ft. Be careful choosing colors. Avoid the numerous magentas. Good singles and doubles in white and various pink and reddish forms. There is also a good blue "Celestial Blue." Bloom from July to frost when most other shrubs have finished. Colorful wide open disk flowers, deeper colored at center, contrast beautifully with dark green foliage. Flowers last only 2 days but buds continue to open. Cut branches with one flower open and several buds ready to bloom. Very tight buds will not open in water, but are attractive as a decoration. Remove faded blossoms as new buds open.

Hydrangea. For blue flowers use acid soil. The cut branches are excellent for large mass arrangements. Bloom mostly in July. Cut when half the panicle is open. If mostly open when cut, will not keep long. Remove any unnecessary foliage. Hold stem-ends in 2 or 3 inches boiling vinegar and count to 30 or sear stem-ends in flame for 15 seconds. Condition overnight in pH4 water. Using 1 heaping tablespoon sugar and 2 tablespoons white distilled vinegar to each quart of water. Flowers should keep a week. Submerge flower heads in cold water until crisp. Cut for drying when flowers turn crisp and papery.

H. PANICULATA. An attractive shrub or small tree to 15 ft. Var. grandiflora often called "P. G." or "Pee Gee" from 4 to 6 ft. Huge white to pink blossoms from late July to frost.

H. PETIOLARIS—Climbing Hydrangea. Bold, rich dark green foliage. White fragrant blooms throughout the summer. Woody and of slow growth. Does equally well in sun or shade.

H. QUERCIFOLIA—Oakleaf Hydrangea. Big, indented, artistic leaves somewhat ruffled, which color brilliantly in fall. Flowers similar to H. paniculata. Does well in shade.

Hypericum—St. Johnswort. Attractive low shrub with small narrow olive-green leaves, covered with showy bright yellow flowers with attractive stamens, from early summer until frost. Good in flower border or in foreground of taller shrubs. For arrangements let blooms open fully before cutting. Split stems and condition overnight. Tight buds will not open in water, but are decorative as they are.

H. SUNGOLD. Shapely dwarf oval shaped shrub 2½-3 ft. diam., 18-25″ high, densely covered with handsome foliage. Bears its golden flowers 2½-3″ across at the end of every shoot of the summer's new growth.

H. CALYCINUM. May also be used as a ground cover. Height 12-18″.

H. HIDCOTE. Twiggy shrub 18″ tall, same diameter. In cold winters freezes back to ground, but comes back in spring. Excellent for foreground in border in cold climates. Warmer climates grows higher 3-4 ft. Flowers appear late June until frost.

Ilex. Belongs to holly family, valuable for beautiful green foliage. Of value to the arranger when branches with small glossy dark green leaves are wanted the year round; may be used in place of boxwood. Treat as you do any cut woody branches.

I. CONVEXA. Informal evergreen, grows to 4 or 5 ft. Very shiny dark green boxwood-like foliage. Good substitute for boxwood. Does not resent pruning.

I. CRENATA—Japanese Holly. Grows to 10 ft. Useful evergreen because of its attractive small glossy foliage and blue-black fruits. Not completely hardy in New England.

I. CRENATA CONVEXA. Spreading pyramid shape, dense. Most attractive. Hardy in New England.

I. GLABRA—Inkberry. Hardy, loose spreading evergreen shrub 4-5 ft. high with small glossy dark green leaves, which turn purplish in winter, has a profusion of black fruit through the winter.

I. OPACA—American Holly. Decorative evergreen with tree like habit even when young. Need plants of both sex to produce berries.

I. SERRATA. Deciduous holly to 10 ft. In winter after leaves have been shed makes a cheerful showing against the snow because of persistent bright red berries which appear in August. Excellent for cutting.

I. VERTICILLATA—Common Winterberry. Deciduous. Grows 6-12 ft. White flowers appear in June and July. Bright red persistent fruit in fall.

Kalmia latifolia—Mountain Laurel. Usually grows 5 to 6 ft. Likes an acid soil, full sun or partial shade. This lovely evergreen presents a gorgeous spectacle in late May or early June, with its blush-pink clustered flowers. Foliage may be cut any time of year and is long lasting. Cut some of the young pale green foliage and some of the older, larger darker foliage for contrast. Cut flowers as they begin to open. Split stems and condition as any woody branches and flowers will last a couple of weeks.

Kerria japonica and var.—Kerrybush or Globe Flower. Excellent for cutting. Prune as you cut, taking branches half in flower. Cut stems to ground, as they will die back anyway and not put forth new upper growth. Buds will continue to open in water. Ornamental bright yellow flowers last about 5 days. Remove foliage along stems not necessary for arrangement. Best form double, golden, ball-shaped flower, not unlike button mums (K. j. pleniflora). Bushy shrub grows to 6 ft. Many bright green branches decorative through winter. In sunny location will bloom all summer, from early June-September. North of Baltimore liable to have branches killed back in severe winters.

Kolkwitzia—Beautybush. Closely related to Weigela, hardier and more attractive. Graceful, upright, shapely shrub 6-8 ft. high. Of great beauty in full bloom, late May or early June, with showy long sprays of bell-shaped shell-pink flowers, with yellow throats. Branches are arching at the ends. Attractive foliage and showy fruit. Graceful and attractive in arrangements.

Laburnum—Goldenchain Tree. Outstanding for garden effect and also for arranger. Prune carefully as you cut branches, gathering clusters when one-half open. Remove any foliage not necessary in the arrangement. Split woody stems and condition overnight.

L. VOSSI. Small tree-like shrub with green bark and foliage like exaggerated clover leaves. Flowers pure golden-yellow formed like those of Wisteria. Hanging clusters are 18-20″ long, borne profusely in late spring. Excellent cut in arrangements.

L. WATERERI. Beautiful small tree 12-20 ft. with showy pendulous racemes of golden-yellow flowers in May or early June. Well adapted to smaller home grounds.

Leucothoe catesbaei—Drooping Leucothoe. Graceful curving branches, excellent background in flower arrangements. Cut foliage any time, will last about a month. Cut flowers when ¾ of the raceme is open. Flowers will last week or more. Press foliage for winter use or treat with glycerin and water. Evergreen shrub grows to 6 ft. Long, glossy dark green leaves turn bronze in fall. White flowers borne in clusters bloom in May on graceful arching branches. Best in partial shade.

Ligustrum—Privet. Useful as hedges, in groupings and for screening. Although flowers are insignificant, foliage is useful to the arranger in need of green foliage or branches to create outline or line arrangements. Deciduous and evergreen. Excess foliage may be removed for better line effects.

L. AMURENSE—Amur Privet. Grows 6-15 ft. White flowers in June or July. Dependable hedge plant. Attractive black fruit.

L. OBTUSIFOLIUM REGELIANUM—Regel or Ibota Privet. Grow from cuttings for the true dwarf type. Compact dense form, 4-6 ft. high and across, yet spreading and branching, so makes a beautiful thick hedge. Covered with black berries in autumn.

L. SINENSE—Chinese Privet. Hardy, upright, bushy plant; has a formal appearance in hedge, even though not pruned. Evergreen unless winter is extremely severe.

L. VULGARE—Common Privet. Attractive with slender spreading branches, very useful for foliage arrangements. Green fruit or lustrous black berries when mature. Plant not fussy as to soil and will thrive in shade.

Lindera benzoin—Spicebush. Large, dense, coarse growing shrub to 15 ft. high with attractive small greenish-yellow bunched flowers which appear on naked branches before the leaves in

April; spicy fragrance. Cut branches easily forced. Bright green oval pointed leaves 4″ long turn golden-yellow in autumn. When they fall red berries are left. Excellent for arranger.

Lonicera—Honeysuckle. Valued for showy, fragrant flowers and decorative fruits. Flowers last 4 to 8 days when cut, depending on variety. Cut branches with some old wood and when about ¼ to ⅓ the flower clusters on the branch are open. Bush forms good in mixed shrub plantings or for screening.

L. JAPONICA. Has white or purplish flowers in May. Red berries in fall and winter. Some varieties are good as vine and ground covers, for trellises, pergolas, etc. Also excellent for cutting when a drooping curved branch is needed. Goldflame grows 8-10 ft. Immense showy clusters of trumpet-shaped buds and fragrant blooms. Outside petal flame-pink, inside a creamy, golden-yellow. Blooms freely from early June until frost. Dark green foliage. May be sheared to form a hedge or allowed to grow naturally as a vine. Halleana, Hall's Honeysuckle grows 20-30 ft. Favorite old-fashioned vine with fragrant buff-yellow almost white flowers throughout summer. Does well in shade or sun. Excellent for covering unsightly objects or banks.

HENRYI—Evergreen Honeysuckle. Flowers unimportant. Grown for its long, dark green leaves, which remain on vine all winter. Blue-black berries in autumn. Does well in shade. Excellent windbreak.

SEMPERVIRENS MAGNIFICA. Evergreen with cheerful large coral blossoms and beautiful blue-gray, green foliage. Well adapted to smaller space. Does not grow as big as others.

L. FRAGRANTISSIMA. Straggly habit, grows to 8 ft. Delightfully fragrant blush to creamy-white tiny flowers appear in early spring in April. Only grown because of early bloom. Cut branches easily forced into flower indoors.

L. GRACILIPES. Small growing 5-6 ft. Has broad, bright-green, rosy-edged leaves and solitary, stalked, pink to carmine drooping flowers in early May, followed in June by longish, scarlet berries.

L. KOROLKOWI. Broad shrub to about 10 ft. and of greater width. Broad oval slightly bluish-green, soft hairy leaves, small pink flowers and red berries. Var. floribunda is floriferous and lovely. Var. zabellii has deep-rose flowers in May and June. Blue-green leaves. Grows to 5 ft.

L. MAACKI. Large shrub 15 ft. or more. Flowers are yellowish and the dark red fruit which ripens in mid-summer persists on bush for a long time. Var. podocarpa most often recommended.

L. MORROWI. Broad rounded or buldging shrub to 7 ft. high and of greater width. Blooms end of May. White flowers changing to yellow and red berries lasting into August. Var. xanthocarpa has yellow berries.

L. TATARICA—Tatarian Honeysuckle. Grows to 12 ft. Most popular shrub species. Comes in white, rose and deep rose flowered forms. Blooms end of May. Red berries that ripen in early summer last into August. Rose forms charming, best combined with white. Lutea is yellow fruited variety.

Magnolia. If frost threatens when blossoms are ready to burst into flower, cut branches to open indoors. Won't hurt tree. Blossoms appear before leaves. Cut well-developed buds. Largest and most advanced will open fully, sometimes requiring a couple of days. Last about four days. M. soulangeana exotic and dramatic in appearance and lasts especially well cut. Magnolia foliage attractive and long lasting. Condition as any woody branches. Can treat foliage in glycerin and water.

M. SIEBOLDI. Large shrub or small tree 15 ft. Strikingly handsome, flowers 4″ across, white with deep pink at the base of the stamens. This variety blooms after the leaves appear, somewhat sparsely and intermittently from June until August. Foliage covers plant to ground.

M. SOULANGEANA—Saucer Magnolia. Rounded form as wide as high. Pink magnolia of city gardens and parks. Flower 4″ across, purplish outside, white inside, come in April before the leaves. Tree to 30 ft. with gorgeous shining attractive foliage.

M. STELLATA—Star Magnolia. This is the only variety that may be planted on a small lot. One of the loveliest and earliest flowering of the magnolias. About 10 ft. high, 8 ft. in diameter. Exotic, bold, modern in form. It is covered with fragrant white star-like blossoms early in spring, and so is often injured by late frosts. Gorgeous shiny dark green foliage, long and narrow, turns bronze in fall. Likes full sun. Var. rosea is pale pink.

M. VIRGINIANA—Sweet Bay. Shrubby and deciduous in north, nearly evergreen in south. Reaches 20 ft., bushier in sun, taller in shade. Waxy creamy-white cup-shaped fragrant flowers appear in late May or early June and continue through summer. Leaves white on the under-surface, gray bark. Excellent glossy, leathery oblong leaves to 6″. Foliage alone justify its planting.

Mahonia aquifolium—Oregon Holly-Grape. Evergreen to 3 ft. in height with large, spiny, metallic-looking leaves, resembling those of holly, which turn a bronzy red in autumn. In May attractive clusters of bright yellow flowers, followed by blue fruit in June and July. Very ornamental foliage for cutting. Produce new plants from underground stolons.

Malus—Flowering Crab-Apple. One of the most valuable groups of flowering trees and shrubs. Hardy, graceful and dainty. Blossoms come in a wide color range, pure white, through pale pinks to red and pinkish-purple; bloom profusely. Some fragrant. Bloom from early until late May. Fruits in green, yellow, orange, scarlet and crimson. Some fall early, others persist into winter. Select varieties with dwarf habit for small grounds. Cut and force blossoms in early spring for indoor decoration. Flowers last well. The trees are beautiful in all seasons but showiest in flower and in fruit.

M. FLORIBUNDA AND VAR.—Japanese Crab. Wide spreading, mound-shaped tree, 18-20 ft. high with spreading arching branches. Red-rose buds fading to nearly white flowers literally cover branches in May. Profuse bloomer. Fruit small and yellowish-green.

M. PURPUREA AND VAR. Very early. Comes with cherries and magnolias, just after forsythias. Reddish-purple flowers, purplish leaves and reddish-purplish fruit, so be careful in placing it to avoid clashing colors.

M. SPECTABILIS AND VAR.—Chinese Flowering Crab. Upright, vase-shaped. Grows to 25 ft. Showy semi-double to double pink flowers that fade to nearly white. Good shiny foliage. Roundish, yellow fruit ¾″ in diameter. Distinctive, graceful, small tree.

Neillia sinensis—Chinese Neillia. Closely allied to spiraea. Small, dense shrub, not over 6 ft. high, with showy terminal clusters of dainty pink to white flowers. Attractive, dark green toothed leaves. Cut flowering branches for arrangements when $\frac{1}{4}$ to $\frac{1}{2}$ branch is in bloom. For forcing into flower indoors in early spring cut when buds begin to swell. Blooms in May and June.

Oxydendrum arboreum—Sour-Wood. Year round appeal with pyramidal grace, lustrous laurel-shaped leaves which turn brilliant scarlet in fall. Creamy, white pendulous clusters of flowers in July when few other trees are in bloom. Likes acid soil, full sun or partial shade. Excellent as backdrop in the flower border.

Philadelphus—Mock-Orange. Shrubs should be pruned directly after blooming, to encourage new growth, so prune during blooming if you wish, shaping as you cut. Cut when a quarter of the blossoms along branch are open. Buds will continue to open in water. Remove at least half of foliage to display flowers more attractively. They will also last longer if this is done. Split stems and condition overnight. If you want more foliage cut some branches without flowers and condition overnight. Flowers drop but are so numerous on stems cut branches will last and look well for a week. Double flowering types last longer, singles tend to fall apart when cut.

P. CORONARIUS. Grows to 12 ft. An old-fashioned favorite with fragrant white flowers in May and June.

P. SPLENDENS. Rounded in habit. Flowers single, borne in groups of five and noted for their brilliant yellow stamens. Produced in immense quantities in mid-June.

P. VIRGINALIS. Grows 6-8 ft. Covered with large semi-double fragrant white flowers in June. Produces a few flowers throughout the summer.

Belle Etoile. Bushy shrub to 5 ft. high, 4 ft. in diameter. Fragrant star-like white flowers bloom in May and June. Centers show a light purple flush.

Frosty Morn. New dwarf mock-orange which grows to 40". White flowers in June and July.

Pieris—Andromeda. Foliage is ideal for cutting at any time of year. Long lasting. Lovely bronze in spring, lustrous dark green in summer and attractive green-bronze foliage in autumn useful in arrangements. Combine large with delicate-leaved branches for variety and interest. Cut bell-shaped flowers, like lily of the valley, in April and May, when clusters are about half open. Condition as for any woody branches. Flowers last week or longer.

P. JAPONICA. Choose this larger variety rather than P. floribunda. Will grow to 8' or more. Handsome, creamy-white flowers in April and May. Ornamental, compact, shapely. Good to frame entrance to front door. Does not like lime. Likes partial shade.

Pinus mugo pumilio—Shrubby Swiss Mountain Pine. Shrubby, with bright green leaves 2" long, 2 in a bundle, cones $2\frac{1}{2}$". Useful in arrangements, particularly through winter.

Polygonum—Silver Lace or Fleece Vine. Prune constantly to keep vine within bounds. Furnishes a steady supply of lovely long green sprays, useful for the arranger who wants something trailing to soften a bare spot.

A. AUBERTI. Fast growing. Covered with foamy sprays of white flowers in midsummer. Handsome green foliage.

A. BALDSCHUANICUM. Fast-growing, pinkish flowers.

Potentilla fruticosa and var.—Buttercup Shrub. Compact shrub grows to 4 ft. Small fern-like leaves studded with bright yellow buttercup-like flowers from early June till frost. Keep pruned to size. Yellow flowers will drop some when cut, but bright yellow color and attractive foliage are useful for arranger.

Prunus. This genus includes the ornamental flowering almond, apricot, cherry, peach and plum trees. Loaded with single or double pink or white flowers of great charm and beauty from early to late May. Upright, spreading and weeping forms. Cut after buds begin to swell in late winter or early spring for forcing indoors. If cut too early buds shrivel and drop before opening. Cut too late, plants may blossom outdoors before forced indoors, so no point to forcing. Cut 6 to 8 weeks ahead of normal flowering time. Prune judiciously. Select branches with pleasing curves. Flowered branches excellent in line arrangements. Colored foliage also attractive.

FLOWERING ALMOND

P. DAVIDIANA. Earliest flowering tree, blooms in April. From deep pink to white. Valuable, for early bloom and forced branches in late winter.

P. GLANDULOSA. Flowering Almond. Lovely dwarf shrub. White and pink, single and double forms.

P. TENELLA. Dwarf Russian Almond. Small shrub 3-5 ft. with white to pinkish flowers.

P. TRILOBA. Called both Flowering Almond and Flowering Plum. Double pink flowers borne in profusion. Blooms before peach. Shrub and tree form to 15 ft. or more.

FLOWERING APRICOT

P. MUME AND VARIETIES. Color range from white to red. Flower before peaches and are much like them.

FLOWERING CHERRIES

Well publicized because of spectacular planting in Washington, D.C. For small lot select dwarf varieties.

P. SARGENTI. Yama or Sargent Cherry. Tree 40 to 60 ft. Hardy and handsome. Flowers single, clear-pink, clustered with reddish bracts subtending the clusters. Blooms ahead of P. serrulata and its hybrids. Young foliage is brownish red and bright orange-scarlet in autumn. Small black fruit in July and August.

P. SERRULATA. Many varieties of this in catalogs. Hardy, will grow to 50 ft. Sargent Cherry is P. serrulata var. sachalinensis.

P. SIEBOLDI. Small upright tree to 20 ft. Can be grown on small place. Bears mostly semi-double, light-pink to white fragrant flowers which fade out carmine.

P. SUBHIRTELLA. Rosebud, Spring or Higan Cherry. Spreading, graceful tree to 25 ft. or more, drooping branches. Many forms, some weeping. Flowers appear before leaves in very early spring. Small, single, delicate pale pink flowers $\frac{1}{2}''$ in diameter, which practically hide the leafless branches. Form a dense round bush. P. subhirtella autumnalis flowers in spring and again in fall.

P. TOMENTOSA. Manchu Cherry. Spreading shrub 8 to 10 ft. In April covered with small light pink to whitish flowers before leaves come. Showy bright red fruits in fall.

P. YEDOENSIS—Yoshino Cherry. Grows 30 ft. Most famous because planted around Lincoln Memorial and Tidal Basin in Washington, D.C. Slightly fragrant, pale pink to nearly white flowers in short stalked small clusters. Quick growing but short-lived tree. Flower buds apt to be nipped in our climate.

FLOWERING PEACH

P. PERSICA. Double flowering most conspicuous. Stay in bloom a long time. Short-lived tree, however. Not suitable for small place. Needs to be heavily pruned; cutting for decoration accomplishes the purpose.

FLOWERING PLUM

P. CERASIFERA—Cherry Plum. Purple and bronze leaf forms. Small trees to 15 ft. Flowers inconspicuous.

P. MARITIMA—Beach Plum. Straggly shrub to 6 ft., grown in seashore gardens.

P. TRILOBA var. multiplex. Double. Usually grown as small tree. Lovely bouquet of large, soft pink blossoms in spring, packed solidly along branches.

Pyracantha—Firethorn. Evergreen or nearly so. Attractive green foliage. Grows 4-6 ft. Tiny, inconspicuous white blossoms in May. Spectacularly showy orange-red berries in autumn. Var. lalandi, hardiest form. Can be trained against a wall. Plant in sunny, protected location. Use some leafmold or peat in soil. Cut sprays with white blossoms and tiny green leaves in May and branches with orange-red berries in fall. Remove thorns at base of stems for easier handling before conditioning. Remove any leaves that hide fruit. To lessen fruit from shriveling and dropping off, spray with clear plastic.

Pyrus atrosanguinea—Carmine Crab Apple. Handsome bush like P. floribunda but flowers deeper rose not fading white.

Rhododendron. No more attractive or desirable shrub for cutting. Blooms cover a wide color range from white, pink and lavender, to lilac, reddish-purple and red. Cut when half or less of the flowers in a cluster are open. The dark green leathery, usually evergreen, foliage of both the large-leaved and small-leaved varieties offer contrast and are attractive throughout the year, last well and are interesting in cut arrangements. Cut branches just above a node where leaf or leaf-stem joins the main stem, to encourage graceful branching, just above bud on the outer side of the stem, so new growth will extend outward, but watch and do not cut next year's flower buds, unless you have quantities of material. Effective combined with iris. Roots near surface, so do not cultivate.

R. CAROLINIANUM—Carolina Rhododendron. Compact plant grows to about 6 ft. Light purplish-pink form and also a very beautiful completely white form. Some are yellowish in bud, but become white on opening. Flowers are much smaller and fewer to a truss than R. catawbiense. Small leaves size of a kalmia. Blooms middle to end of May.

R. CATAWBIENSE—Catawba Rhododendron. Round and well-formed evergreen shrub, grows 6-15 ft. tall and usually as broad. Ornamental with flowers borne conspicuously about the foliage. Trusses are large and round with good-sized flowers presenting a sea of light violet-purple to light reddish-purple color. Everything in its favor, except persistence of blue in most all its hybrids. For superior colors, buy the hybrids. Light rose, pinkish-lavender and white are available. There is a dwarf form var. compacta which remains 3 ft.

R. MAXIMUM—Rose Bay. Valuable because of late bloom. Slower growing and less vigorous than R. catawbiense; has longer, narrower leaves. The flower buds have conspicuous green bracts. Flowers are also somewhat smaller and borne in less conspicuous trusses. Free from the purple tinge, its apple-blossom pink flowers come late, in early July, and fade to almost white when fully open. Also pure white flowers.

R. MINUS—Piedmont Rhododendron. Similar to R. carolinianum, but taller, less compact, sometimes straggly. Blooms five to six weeks later, last week in June. Flower color darker and lilac-tinged, although a shell-pink form exists.

Universally known and loved, glorified in poem and song, roses are excellent for both the garden and cutting. The lovely double flowers and rich, dark glossy foliage are elegant and effective used alone.

When plants are large and vigorous cut rose stems as long as you like, about ¼″ above a leaf letting at least two well developed leaves remain on the stem (between the cut and the place where the side stem joins the main stem). This will produce bushy, attractive plants. Avoid taking too much stem and foliage the first year.

COURTESY: STAR ROSES, WEST GROVE, PA.

R. RACEMOSUM. Will endure where boxwood is hardy. Shrub grows 3-4 ft. covered with small bright pink flowers.

Rose for hedges, borders, beds, over porches and back fences. The flowers should be cut when the buds are just beginning to unfold and show their color. They will last a week or more in the house. For the beginner, the new floribundas and climbers are easy to grow and 2 or 3 shrubs will supply an abundance of cut flowers which keep well.

Fragrance is an asset, yet the color, prolific continuous bloom and disease resistance of some nonfragrant kinds make them desirable. Some favorite Hybrid Teas in the apricot, coral, peach, pink and salmon-blend group: Angels Mateu, Countess Vandal, Mrs. Sam McGredy, President Herbert Hoover, Tiffany; Yellow and yellow-blend: Golden Dawn, Peace, Sutter's Gold. Red: Christopher Stone, Crimson Glory, Etoile de Hollande, Rubaiyat. Pink: (single) Show Girl, The Doctor. White: Frau Karl Druschki, a hybrid perpetual, best white, strong grower and free flowering, although lacking fragrance.

Old-fashioned fragrant Moss Roses are favorites with many arrangers for period bouquets, where they just naturally belong. They bloom for about a month in the spring. The bushy shrub roses Cardinal de Richelieu of the Gallica class are excellent in period arrangements (although very fragile) if you need a double, rich violet color. Shrub roses which require plenty of room include favorites as: Rosa hugonis (Father Hugo's Rose) and the Golden Rose of China, some of the first to bloom. With fragile, single, pale yellow blooms borne singly on long, drooping branches they are graceful and attractive but scatter quickly both outdoors and as cut flowers. Good for short time use only. Rosa rugosa is valuable as a shrub and has shining dark green foliage, useful in arrangements.

Avoid taking much stem and foliage the first year. After the plants are large and vigorous, cut stems as long as you like. Cut about $\frac{1}{4}''$ above a five leaflet leaf, letting at least two well developed leaves remain on the stem, between the cut and the place where the side stem joins the main stem. These two remaining eyes will develop into new shoots, making a bushier plant. The top eye should be on the outside of the stem so the new growth will branch outward and not inward. Remove un-

ROSES

Uses

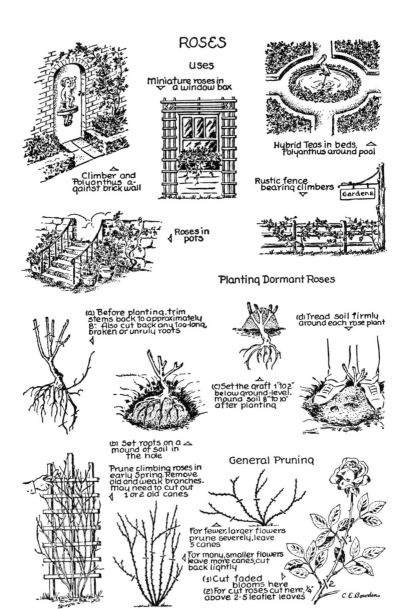

Miniature roses in a window box

Climber and Polyanthus against brick wall

Hybrid Teas in beds, Polyanthus around pool

Rustic fence bearing climbers

Gardens

Roses in pots

Planting Dormant Roses

(a) Before planting, trim stems back to approximately 8". Also cut back any too-long, broken or unruly roots

(b) Set roots on a mound of soil in the hole

(c) Set the graft 1" to 2" below ground-level. Mound soil 8" to 10" after planting

(d) Tread soil firmly around each rose plant

General Pruning

Prune climbing roses in early Spring. Remove old and weak branches. May need to cut out 1 or 2 old canes

For fewer, larger flowers prune severely, leave 5 canes

For many, smaller flowers leave more canes, cut back lightly

(1) Cut faded blooms here
(2) For cut roses cut here, ¼" above 2·5 leaflet leaves

C.E. Bowden

Roses last longer if cut when the buds are just beginning to unfold and show their color. Here they have been cut in various stages of development for a more interesting design. The flowers were conditioned overnight, before arranging, to increase their life expectancy.

ARRANGEMENT BY MRS. W. E. ROWLEY   ROCHE PHOTO

Peace, a lovely hybrid tea, is one of the better known roses. Also try some of the floribundas with showy clusters that look like miniature hybrid teas. They bloom abundantly and continuously from June until frost. The bushy-type plants are hardy and easy to grow and will supply cut flowers throughout the summer.

ARRANGEMENT BY MYRA J. BROOKS   ROCHE PHOTO

necessary foliage from the cut stem. Split vertically, so plenty of water will enter, and condition overnight. If your local water supply is not acid (pH4), add 1 heaping tablespoon of sugar and 2 tablespoons of white vinegar to each quart of water.

CLIMBING OR PILLAR ROSES. These include the large-flowered climbers like the old favorite Paul's Scarlet Climber. Blaze is another good red, White Dawn, a good white. Dr. J. H. Nicholas is a fragrant rose-pink fully double and 5-6″ across. Primrose is a hardy climber with attractive canary-yellow flowers. The Ramblers with smaller flowers in clusters are also in this group and typical varieties are Dorothy Perkins (shell-pink), White Dorothy Perkins and Princess Van Orange (orange red). The fragrant buff-pink Gloire de Dijon is a favorite climber in southern gardens. The big, well established climbers produce abundant flowers excellent for cutting.

FLORIBUNDA OR CLUSTER ROSES. Floribundas, introduced at the New York World's Fair in 1939, are excellent in the garden and for cutting. Bloom continuously and prolifically from June until frost with showy clusters of roses, which look like miniature hybrid teas. Hardy and easy to grow, these bushy-type plants should be planted about two feet apart. Garnette is an excellent red, Vogue a good coral, Fashion, Betty Prior and Cecile Brunner good pinks, Glacier and Summer Snow whites, Goldilocks is gold and Yellow Pinocchio yellow. Pinocchio is multicolor, pink with gold at the base. Ma Perkins is pink with yellow at the base. Garnette is an exceptional keeper.

HYBRID TEAS. Combine the everblooming quality of the Teas with the hardiness of the Hybrid Perpetuals. Until the introduction of the new Floribundas, by far the most important rose group and a joy to the arranger because of their long lasting quality when cut. Some good keepers include White Swan and White Briarcliff, Radiance (pink), Red Radiance, Crimson Glory, Etoile de Hollande, and Charlotte Armstrong (red), Eclipse (golden yellow) and Peace (yellow edged with pink). Plant 18″ apart in the garden.

SHRUB ROSES. Cut as you would any other flowering shrub. Single or double flowers in wide color range. Rosa hugonis, a yellow, and Harisons Yellow, a prolific bloomer and a double, are two old-timers and lovely as shrubs in the landscape around Decoration Day. The slender arched sprays with delicate pale-yellow flowers and bright-green fine foliage are graceful and attractive indoors. Red hips and reddish stems are also interesting later in the season. Wear gardening gloves when cutting.

Sciadopitys verticillata—Umbrella Pine. Gives rich, velvety green accent to planting. Grows slowly, reaching 25 ft. in 50 years. Excellent in arrangements; thin out as necessary for more delicate effects.

Spirea—Bridal Wreath. For forcing into flower in early spring, cut when buds begin to swell. Cut flowering branches for arrangements when one-fourth to one-half branch is in bloom. Flowers will last a week. Shed easily, but so prolific, it is effective and lovely for arrangers.

S. ANTHONY WATERER. Dwarf shrub. Grows 2 to $2\frac{1}{2}$ ft. high. Deep rose-red flowers in June and more or less continuously throughout the late summer until September, if pruned back after first burst of bloom. Good low hedge.

S. THUNBERGI—Thunbergs Spirea. Light, roundish bush, grows to 4 ft. First to flower. Tiny, feathery foliage turns orange to scarlet in autumn. Loosely arching branches are covered with clusters of dainty, white fragrant flowers in May which come simultaneously with leaves.

S. VANHOUTTEI—Vanhoutte Spirea. Broad, informal shrub, grows to 6 ft. Graceful branches heavily covered with snow-white blossoms in May. Excellent foliage. Makes good tall hedge.

Stewartia ovata grandiflora—Showy Stewartia of the tea family. Erect, large, stately shrub 10 ft. high and 10 ft. wide. Excellent deep-green, oval, pointed leaves. From June through August bears stunning white flowers referred to as "imitation camellia," 3" or more across, with an ample crown of purple stamens. Foliage turns orange to scarlet in fall but not so brilliant as S. ovata. Good for larger grounds.

Symphoricarpos—Snowberry, Coralberry. Of the honeysuckle family, valuable low shrub for shade. Needs severe pruning each spring as new young stems produce handsomer masses of fruit than old ones. Branches with masses of white or red berries, useful to the arranger in the fall.

s. ALBUS—Snowberry. Grows 3-4 ft. Great masses of waxy, white berries in autumn.

s. ORBICULATUS (vulgaris)—Coralberry or Indian Currant. Grows 2 ft. high. Reddish berries brilliant in masses.

Syringa—Lilac. A favorite for cutting in May. Never hesitate to cut from well established plants as flower clusters that go to seed draw on strength of shrub. Cutting flowers makes a stronger plant and better flowers for the following year. Prune when cutting for arrangements to keep plants desired height and size. Cut branches when $\frac{1}{4}$ to $\frac{1}{2}$ panicle is open. Remove all foliage from flowering branch. Cut non-flowering branches to arrange with flowers replacing them as leaves drop. Split woody stems at base. Condition overnight or until panicles are thoroughly filled with water. Flowers should last a week. Broad, informal plants; use as a tall unclipped hedge or for corner plantings. Dig lime in around the roots. To keep from legginess cut away old growth at roots.

s. PERSICA—Persian Lilac. Charming, neat, small shrub, not over 6 ft. high and 8 ft. wide, clothed in small tapering dark bluish-green leaves. Charming clusters of "lilac" flowers with an exquisite, spicy fragrance appear at the ends of the branches. Excellent for small place. Var. alba white-flowered form.

s. VULGARIS—Common Lilac and its "French Hybrids." Include both single and double varieties, as well as fragrant white, pink, blue, lilac, purple and magenta colors. Almost too large for small lot.

Tamarix—Tamarisk. Pink Cascade. Beautiful shrub with masses of cascading panicles of pink flowers. The flower trusses are carried well above rich blue-green foliage. Occur from July to September. Compact in growth, about 6 ft. high. Prune back severely each spring. Valuable in seashore gardens. "Summer Glow" has lacy loveliness. Silvery blue-green feathery foliage. Rose-pink flower spikes appear on top of the delightful foliage all summer long. Flowers and foliage are lovely for cutting. Ultimate height of shrub is 8 ft. Can prune and keep to 5 to 6 ft.

Taxus—Yew. The lovely rich evergreen foliage is useful to the arranger the year-round. Prune to keep plants within bounds. The branches may be used in fresh bouquets. At Christmas a charming little upright evergreen yew may be constructed from short clippings.

T. CUSPIDATA—Japanese Yew. Spreading form 6-8 ft. tall. Will grow larger if untrimmed. Red berries in October-November. Upright form 15-50 ft. tall. Rich green foliage and red berries in autumn. Useful in hedge, foundation planting or as single specimen.

T. CUSPIDATA nana. Dwarf form, slower growing, more compact and wide spreading.

T. MEDIA—Hicks Yew. Narrow, columnar form with upright branches 6-12 ft. Excellent as a hedge or accent plant. Also very narrow form 5 to 6 ft., excellent for accent.

Vaccinium corymbosum—Highbush Blueberry. Ornamental plant, interesting in growth, 6 ft. or more. Young branches yellowish-green or red. Dense clusters of white or pinkish flowers in May. Blue or blue-black edible berries in July and August. Brilliant scarlet autumn coloring. Cut lovely young branches with flowers in May, berried branches in July and August or brilliant foliage in fall. Attractive in all stages for the arranger.

Viburnum. Popular ornamental shrubs all having white or whitish flowers, many with conspicuous red to black fruit and colorful fall foliage. Cut branches are highly ornamental used as flowering branches or in fall with colorful fruit and foliage.

V. BURKWOODI. Bushy shrub, 6 ft. high and 5 ft. across. Waxy, blush-white, fragrant flowers in round, domed clusters are produced in early spring when leaves are unfolding. Foliage shiny green in summer, brilliant reddish in fall, red to black berries.

V. CARLCEPHALUM. Deciduous, may be pruned to any size and shape desired. Large clusters of white blossoms 6″ across, flattened or globular, mostly the latter. Very fragrant, leaves like V. carlesii.

V. CARLESI—Mayflower Viburnum. One of the most desirable shrubs. Rounded form. Lovely, fragrant waxy-white or pinkish flower clusters in April and May, opening with the leaves. Blue-black berries are not freely produced. Handsome gray-green foliage turns reddish in fall.

v. FRAGRANS. Earliest to bloom in April. Buds pinkish, flowers white. Slender, erect shrub 8 ft. Delightfully fragrant. Branches easily forced into bloom in house.

v. OPULUS—Cranberry Bush. Large flat clusters of bloom sur-rounded by margin of larger florets appear in spring. Leaves lobed like red maple, turn bright red in fall. Red fruits.

v. TOMENTOSUM. Handsome shrub 8 ft. high. Flat heads of creamy-white flowers in June. Borne on upper sides of grace-fully curved branches. Double form, the "Japanese Snowball," is equally attractive and valuable. Effective in fall with bright red berries changing to bluish-black and dull red foliage.

Vitex—Chaste Tree. Distinctive exotic looking gray-leaved shrub which must be pruned back to keep to 4-5 ft. Attractive lilac-like spikes of lovely lavender-blue flowers which bloom pro-fusely from July until fall. If branches are killed back in winter, roots usually survive, but character of plant is to remain dor-mant until very late in spring. Prune and shape tree to graceful shape when cutting for arrangements. Cut spikes when only a few buds are showing color since flowers last longer if allowed to open indoors. Flowers last about a week. As with lilacs, re-move all foliage from stems. Leaves are fragrant when crushed. If you want foliage, cut non-flowering branches and condition as you do flowering branches. Hang to dry fruits of vitex. Gather when green and firm for best results. Plant is gaunt in winter without any delicate twig pattern.

Weigela. A brilliantly flowered upright group of shrubs with white, pink and red blossoms in May, June and July. Flowers shaped like those of a foxglove are borne in immense quantities. Grow 5 to 6 ft. Prefer a moist soil, full sun. Do not like roots of large trees encroaching on them. Tendency to shatter when cut, but abundant color gives pleasing effect.

Avalanche. Thousands of pure white trumpet-like flowers in late spring and early summer, 5-6 ft.

Eva Rathke. Grows 4-6 ft. Splendid shrub with dark red trumpet-shaped flowers in May and June.

Fairy. In spring completely covered with light pink blossoms which possess great depth of color and sparkle. Early flowering. One of Lemoine's hybrids, grows to 5 ft.

Vaniceki. Cardinal shrub. Grows to 6 ft. Large, red, trumpet-shaped flowers in spring, summer and fall. An improved Eva Rathke.

w. FLORIDA (*rosea*). Old-fashioned weigela, 6-10 ft. tall. Handsome species with charming rose-pink flowers in May and June. Dark red and white varieties.

Wisteria. Vigorous twining vine with attractive flowers and foliage. Likes alkaline soil. Flowers in May. Cut Chinese Wisteria in the advanced bud stage. Whole cluster bursts into bloom before leaves appear. Japanese Wisteria starts opening at the top of the long cluster, the lower buds opening slowly as the foliage leafs out. Cut Japanese Wisteria when cluster is about ¼ open, but before open florets at top begin to fade. Split woody stems and condition overnight. Vines and tendrils are attractive fresh or dried. Hang to dry. Pods also used in dried bouquets.

w. FLORIBUNDA—Japanese Wisteria. Varieties in white, rose, violet and violet blue. Buds open progressively. Start opening at top of the drooping cluster.

w. SINENSIS—Chinese Wisteria. Has clusters of delicate blue flowers, deliciously fragrant. Also a white form. Needs a suitable large building because strong growing. Prune to keep within bounds. Pendulous cluster of flowers open simultaneously before the leaves.

QUESTIONS AND ANSWERS

Is spring or autumn the best time to plant lily bulbs?

Although many kinds of lilies can be planted in the early spring, the fall is the best season to plant all kinds of lilies. The madonna lily, however, requires immediate planting, since it sends up a cluster of green leaves before cold weather arrives. All other lilies may be planted through September, October, November and even December, provided the ground does not freeze. Planting the bulbs, however, as soon as possible results in good root development.

3

ANNUALS IDEAL FOR CUTTING

Annuals add color and sparkle to a garden and fortunately are ideal for cutting purposes. Planted in clumps in the open spaces between shrubs and herbaceous perennials for quick seasonal color effects, they also furnish useful cut flowers during the period when perennials are generally not blooming. Interplanted among early-flowering spring bulbs and other perennials they give the garden color when the foliage of the permanent plants is unsightly. (See pages 217 ff. for annuals grouped according to color.)

If space permits, a cutting garden planted in rows will supply quantities of cut flowers to decorate your home as well as those of friends and neighbors and flowers can be cut as needed, without worry about garden looks. The greater part of the cutting garden should consist of annuals, since they flower over a longer period of time and the more you cut, the better and more profusely they bloom, ideal for the arranger. Easily grown, relatively free of insect pests and diseases, many with good long stems for cutting, and good keepers, they are the best source of summer material for variety in color, form, and height.

Any well-prepared retentive soil one to two feet deep will give good results and under normal weather conditions a weekly watering should be sufficient.

SEEDLINGS FOR EARLY FLOWERS

The seeds of hardy annuals may be sown directly in the garden where they are to bloom any time from February until June,

ANNUALS

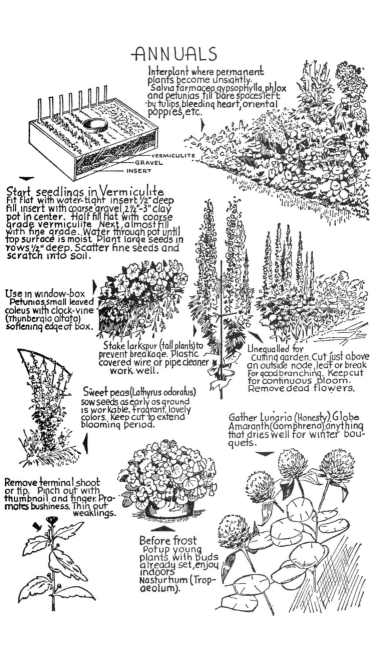

Interplant where permanent plants become unsightly. Salvia farinacea gypsophylla, phlox and petunias fill bare spaces left by tulips, bleeding heart, oriental poppies, etc.

VERMICULITE
GRAVEL
INSERT

Start seedlings in Vermiculite
Fit flat with water-tight insert ½" deep Fill insert with coarse gravel. 2½"-3" clay pot in center. Half fill flat with coarse grade vermiculite. Next, almost fill with fine grade. Water through pot until top surface is moist. Plant large seeds in rows ½" deep. Scatter fine seeds and scratch into soil.

Use in window-box
Petunias, small leaved coleus with clock-vine (thunbergia altata) softening edge of box.

Stake larkspur (tall plants) to prevent breakage. Plastic covered wire or pipe cleaner work well.

Unequalled for cutting garden. Cut just above an outside node, leaf or break. For good branching. Keep cut for continuous bloom. Remove dead flowers.

Sweet peas (Lathyrus odoratus) sow seeds as early as ground is workable, fragrant, lovely colors. Keep cut to extend blooming period.

Gather Lunaria (Honesty), Globe Amaranth (Gomphrena) anything that dries well for winter bouquets.

Remove terminal shoot or tip. Pinch out with thumbnail and finger. Promotes bushiness. Thin out weaklings.

Before frost
Pot up young plants with buds already set, enjoy indoors Nasturtium (Tropaeolum).

depending upon when you have your last frost. Some seeds, like the sweet pea and bachelor button that like cool weather to germinate are sown in late fall, to germinate as soon as the season opens in the spring. Seeds of the half-hardy and tender annuals need more protection during their early stages of growth and must be started in a protected area. Biennials may be started early indoors and then planted out and treated as annuals. To hasten the season and have earlier flowering annuals, seeds may be started early in a protected spot like a hotbed, coldframe, greenhouse or under artificial light or flats placed in a glassed-in porch or a sunny window. The cellar window may be good. (See Farmer's Bulletin 1743, Hotbeds and Coldframes, U.S. Department of Agriculture). Seedlings may be started in a mellow soil with proper moisture conditions for germination, but more recently the U.S. Department of Agriculture has developed two other methods, one with shredded sphagnum (See Leaflet 243, Sphagnum Moss for Seed Germination) and another using expanded vermiculite. To start seedlings in vermiculite fit a $\frac{1}{2}''$ deep watertight aluminum foil insert into the flat. Then, fill the insert with coarse gravel, first placing a $2\frac{1}{2}''$ or 3″ clay pot in the center to use for watering. Now, half fill the flat with a coarse grade of vermiculite. Next, almost fill it with a fine grade of the same material. Water the pot to subirrigate the vermiculite and eventually wet the surface to settle it. Seeds planted in vermiculite generally germinate more readily than in soil and the percentage of germination is higher. There is also no trouble with weeds or damping-off fungus.

Large seeds like nasturtium, zinnia and the sunflower are planted in rows $\frac{1}{2}''$ to $\frac{3}{4}''$ deep, while the finer, smaller seeds of the petunia and snapdragon are generally scattered on the surface and lightly scratched into the soil with a coarse comb. The finer and smaller the seeds, the shallower the depth of planting. Carefully read directions on all seed packets.

Since vermiculite does not contain enough nutrients for good plant growth, fertilize using one tablespoon of any good complete fertilizer to each gallon of water. Apply just as soon as the seedlings start to come up, and at weekly intervals until they are transplanted. Seedlings started in vermiculite develop a heavy root system which rarely injures in transplanting. Harden the seedlings off to some extent by withholding all fertilizer for a few weeks before transplanting outdoors and allowing the flats to dry out slightly for easier handling. Plant out when danger of frost is over.

Start seeds in flats from four to eight weeks before the last frost, guided by past years' experiences. For a continuous supply of cut flowers throughout the season several sowings should be made at two week intervals. Seeds of many annuals may be sown in rows in the vegetable or cut flower garden and transplanted from there to their permanent locations.

For those who do not have the time or care to grow annuals from seed, seedlings may be purchased from growers, garden centers or your florist in the spring. Be sure you are familiar with the named varieties of the plants you wish to buy, as that is the only way you can be sure of getting what you want as to color, size and habit of growth.

ANNUALS FOR CUTTING

Each year new introductions are listed in the seed catalogs. Look them over and if you are a beginner, talk with garden club members or experienced gardeners to get advice. There are many improved varieties which are increasingly tolerant of conditions they formerly could not take, due to the work of enterprising hybridists. Choose varieties best suited to your local conditions and you will be successful. Keep in mind that unless you remove the faded flowers you will not enjoy the prolific continuous bloom you should, for with annuals the more you cut, the more you will have. Do not let seed pods develop unless you want them for dried arrangements. Cut back straggling growth to keep the plants trim and in a healthy condition.

GOOD ANNUALS FOR ARRANGEMENTS

Ageratum houstonianum—Floss Flower. Dense, fluffy heads of blue flowers from midsummer until frost. Violet, pink and white varieties less popular. From 3-12″ high. Cut when half of the flowers in each head are open, remaining buds showing good color. If cut too early buds will not open, cut too late short-lived. Condition overnight in warm water to start with. Last about a week cut. Filler type flower "Midget Blue" 3-4″, excel-

lent for edging. "Blue Perfection," excellent cutting flower, 9-12"
high. Plant seeds in frames or flats indoors for early flowering,
outdoors after frost for late flowering. May propagate by cuttings. Space seedlings 10-12" apart. Good as an edging and in
window boxes. Self-sow, but do not always come true from seeds.
Full sun.

Althaea rosea—Hollyhock. Biennial, also new strain sold as annual, which flowers same year from seeds sown in February.
Single, semi-double and double flowers; plain, fringed, some
ruffled in shades of pink, rose, yellow, copper, red, scarlet,
violet, maroon and purple. Bloom July-August, 6-8 ft. tall. Group
together outdoors in bold masses at back of border, 18" apart.
Require rich, well-drained soil, full sun. Cut late in afternoon
or early morning, with three or four flowers open on stem. Well
developed buds will open in water. Remove all but smallest
leaves near the tip of the stalk to better show the flowers, which
will last two or three days. Buds, if not too tight, open on stem
over period of a week. Split stems 4-6" and sear ends in flame.
Condition overnight in warm water to start with until more
blossoms open. Double varieties last longer than single. Both
are ideal for large, exotic arrangements. For low designs cut
long stems into sections of one, three and five flowers each. Very
weak solution of potassium nitrate (obtain at drug store) benefits
keeping quality, pinch to one quart water.

Anagallis—Pimpernel. Charming plant covered with five-petaled
star-shaped flowers, about 1" across in lilac, scarlet, blue, brick-
red and white, 4"-10". Effective as edging, in rock garden or
used in porch or window boxes. Sow seeds where to be grown in
full sun. Long blooming season. Good filler flower in arrangements.

Anchusa capensis—Summer Forget-me-not. "Blue Bird" attractive, free-flowering plant with many long stems, each topped with
a cluster of brilliant blue forget-me-nots with white eye in graceful sprays, blooming from early summer until late fall, if kept
cut. Bushy plants 18" tall. Likes moist location and full sun. Good
filler flower in arrangements where blue is wanted. Cut when
about half in flower. Remove unnecessary foliage and condition
overnight in warm water to start. Will last four to five days.

Antirrhinum majus—Snapdragon. Perennial but spike flowered plant usually grown as annual. Excellent for cutting. Come dwarf, intermediate and tall, 8″-36″, in pink, rose, red, bronze, yellow and white. Sow seeds in February or March for midsummer bloom. Sown in June and wintered in cold frame, will give early summer flowers. Miniature to large-sized flowers, some have a ruffled edge, some double. Cut to within 4″ of base of plant and new flowering stalks will come up making a bushy plant. Cut spikes when half in flower. Condition overnight in hot water (80-100° F.) to start with, water adjusted to pH4 (1 heaping table-spoon sugar, 2 tablepsoons white distilled vinegar to 1 qt. water). For curving stems, to relieve stiffness of all upright, place slant-wise while conditioning. With scissors carefully snip off blooms from lower stems as they fade. Spikes will last week or more. Useful for height and lovely color range.

Arctotis grandis—Blue-eyed African Daisy. Silver-white, daisy-like flowers $2\frac{1}{2}$″ across with blue eye, grow 12″-18″. Silvery, wooly foliage. Flowers close at night. Bloom all summer till frost. Grow well in full sun, sandy soil. Very satisfactory cut for daytime use. Conspicuous blue eye bordered by white petals unusual.

Calendula officinalis—Pot-Marigold. Excellent for cutting, for they last a long time, 1-2 weeks. Medium height, 12″-48″ with rich yellow, gold, apricot and orange flowers in many varieties, some with darker contrasting eye; single, semi-double and double. Seeds germinate quickly. Space 8″ ·10″ apart. Bloom late into fall as they like cold weather. Grow in full sun. Plant seeds indoors in flats for early flowering; outdoors after frost in June for later flowering. Cut when flowers are $\frac{3}{4}$ open. Buds develop slowly and not too successfully in water. Recut stems under water just before conditioning. Zinc sulphate (buy in drugstore), 1 tsp. crystals to 1 qt. water, will retard decay of stems.

Calliştephus chinensis—China Aster. Excellent long lasting (to two weeks) cut flower. In a wide range of colors, from light to dark blue, light pink to scarlet, rose, lavender, crimson, royal purple and white; single daisy-like flowers or semi-double and dou-ble; peony-shaped, some fluffy, others globular, small and giant sized; 12″-24″ in height. Cut when $\frac{3}{4}$ to fully open. Recut stems under a sugar solution (1 teaspoon to 1 qt. water). Condition over-

Annual pinks (*Dianthus*) are not difficult to raise but they do prefer cool, rather than hot, dry summers and need sun to bloom. Although less fragrant than the perennial kinds and with broader leaves, they are excellent for cutting.

Although popular in England, the hardy annual chrysanthemum is not grown much in this country. Given a well-drained soil and full sun it will provide a wealth of cutting material in brilliant colors from July until frost. Pinch for good branching.

Arrangement by Catherine H. Smith   Roche Photo

night. Remove leaves as they wilt before flowers, and substitute appropriate foliage. Revive any prematurely wilted asters by placing stems in 80-100° F. water. With proper selection and successive crops you may have asters in bloom from July to frost. For early flowers start seeds indoors, sow outdoors for later bloom.

Calonyction aculeatum—Moonflower. Rapid growing vine with large white flowers which open after sunset, close in early morning. Soak seeds in water or cut notch in them. Plant indoors in March to get bloom before September. Only half hardy, so do not sow outdoors until May. For cutting, select stem with few open flowers and many well-developed buds. Split stem, condition overnight. Carefully wrap largest buds about to open in tissue paper to keep them from opening too soon. Before arranging, unwrap, and petals will open and spread. Flowers last one or two days but buds continue to come. Remove dead blooms.

Campanula ramosissima—Canterbury Bell. Good for cutting. Not as showy as the biennial, but blooms quickly in less than six months from seed. In lavender, blue, rose, pink and white. Grows to 30″. For earliest flowers start seeds indoors.

Campanula medium—Canterbury Bell or Bell Flowers. Biennial, good for cutting as flowers will last one to two weeks. Pyramidal plant 2-3 ft. tall covered in June with large bell-like and cup-and-saucer-shaped blooms, with edges softly rolled back, attractively fluted. Flowers single and double in white, rose, violet-blue and light to dark blue colors. Sow seeds in summer for bloom following season. Cut when stalks are $\frac{1}{4}$ to $\frac{1}{2}$ open for lasting quality, but for better color, cut when nearly fully open. Split and sear stem ends in flame as stems have a milky juice. Condition in 100° F. water, to start with, overnight. To revive premature wilting, recut and sear stems and recondition using hot water. Remove flowers as they fade for neat appearance.

Celosia—Cockscomb. Prized for cutting both fresh or dried. Showy flower heads come in yellow, orange, bronze, red with scarlet highlights, purple or white. Dwarf and tall, growing 10″ to 3 ft. Blooms from midsummer until frost, depending upon plantings. Foliage varies from light to dark bronzy-green.

C. CRISTATA. Comb or crested type, resembles a cock's comb.

c. PLUMOSA. Feather or plumed type, more graceful and popular as cut flowers. Well branched.

c. CHILDSI—Chinese Woolflower. Has large, wooly, round flower heads, extremely showy. Much branched. Valued for cutting.

c. SPICATA. Narrow, silvery-white spike, delicately tipped with rose.

Start all varieties indoors for early bloom. Like rich, moist soil and sun. C. cristata likes light soil. Cut plume or feather type when at least ¾ developed. Undeveloped flowers will not keep. Remove lower leaves, and any not necessary in arrangement. Cut comb or crested type when size and color you want. Cool weather intensifies hues. A good crested variety is "Princess Feather." Grows tall and straight. For curves in stems, place slantwise in container when conditioning. Condition overnight or until flowers and foliage become turgid. For drying cut flowers at their most perfect stage, strip off the foliage.

Centaurea—Bachelors-Button, Cornflower. Excellent cut flower in blue, white, pink, purple and yellow; also showy in garden. Keep faded flowers cut for more and longer blooming.

c. CYANUS—Common Bachelors-Button or Cornflower. In fall or early spring sow where they are to flower as they like cool weather. Seed themselves, but tend to run out. Grow 2-2½ ft. (may need some staking). Kept cut, will produce large, double blooms on long stems throughout summer. Bright blue, light pink, red and white colors. Dwarf varieties one ft. tall. Cut flowers when fully or nearly open. Even half open buds will not open in water. Condition overnight. Flowers turn paler in color but still beautiful. Should last week.

c. AMERICANA—Basket-Flower. Display of thistle-like lilac or lavender blooms, shell-pink and clear white; in July and August. Largest of centaureas. Excellent in cut arrangements. Cut at various stages: in tight bud, half open and fully opened. Fully opened flowers are fragile, so handle with care. Tight buds remain fresh and may be used a second time, when open and half open flowers go after a week. Split stems and place in warm water, to start, conditioning overnight.

c. MOSCHATA—Sweet Sultan. Hybrid imperialis. Long-stemmed,

For this type of design it is important to condition the flowers overnight filling the stems, foliage and blooms to capacity with water. This will increase their lasting quality, adding hours to the life of the arrangement.

ARRANGEMENT BY MYRA J. BROOKS   ROCHE PHOTO

Bells-of-Ireland (*Molucella laevis*), popular in old gardens, have recently become in vogue again because of their cut value, in both fresh and dry arrangements, either by themselves or combined with other annuals. Easily grown from seed, they will self-sow in favorable spots.

COURTESY: NORTHRUP, KING AND CO.

sweet-scented fluffy, double flowers, exquisitely fringed and graceful; excellent for cutting. Bloom freely for many weeks. Like cool weather.

Cheiranthus—Wallflower. Sweet-scented flowers in oriental colorings of yellow, orange, red, mahogany, russet and brown. Blooms in May. Grows 12"-15"; flowers single and double. Blooms within five months of seed. Sow indoors in February. Cool weather plant. Likes moisture. Treasured cut for delightful fragrance.

Chrysanthemum. Summer mums provide a wealth of beautiful cutting material as well as mass color in the garden. Grow 18"-36" tall. Sow seeds in cold frame or where they are to flower. Space 15"-24" apart. Likes full sun. Good colors: white, yellow and red; single, semi-double and double. Bloom from July until frost; best in cool weather. Need staking. Annual varieties usually have soft stems, so recut under water. Condition overnight in cold water using three or four level tablespoons of sugar to one qt. water (three for a few, four if many). Last well, two weeks. Mums last longer when leaves are left on stem. However, in deep containers strip any leaves below water line because they deteriorate rapidly in water. As foliage wilts, remove it and substitute other suitable foliage. Mum flowers will outlast foliage.

Clarkia. Superior for cutting and for massing in garden. Sow where plants are to flower. Pretty, dainty single or double flowers resemble those of flowering almond. Does best where weather is not too hot. Grows 1-3 ft. Lovely colors: salmon, pink, mauve, rose, carmine, purple, red and white; long season of bloom from July until frost. Will grow in partial shade. Cut stems just as buds are ready to unfold into flower with three or four of the lower blossoms fully open. Split stems, condition overnight. Last about a week as buds continue to open.

Cleome spinosa—Spider Flower. Grows to $3\frac{1}{2}$-4 ft. with large, unusual pink, red, white and yellow flower heads 6" to 7" across. Self-sows freely. Giant Pink Queen, a favorite, blooms freely from July till frost. Likes full sun. Cut for arrangements when clusters are $\frac{1}{2}$ in flower. Will wilt when cut, but revives rapidly. Split stems, condition overnight in warm water, to start. Lasts four or five days.

Cobaea scandens—Cup and Saucer Vine. Rapid grower, climbing to 25 ft., with bell-shaped purple flowers. Place seeds edgewise when being sown and start indoors. Purple flowers on trailing sprays excellent for softening edges of container. Select curving branches with a few open flowers and many well-developed buds. Condition in water overnight.

Coleus. Brilliant, rich-colored, tender foliage plant, usually propagated by cuttings, but seedlings offer interesting variations in leaf colors and markings. Grows 24"-30" high. Likes heat and full sun for vivid coloring. Semi-shade produces larger leaves and more subtle colors. Last almost indefinitely cut and after two or three weeks in water will root. Cut frequently to keep plants under control and shapely. Split cut stems and condition overnight.

Coreopsis—Calliopsis. Useful cut flower with long season of bloom, from June till frost. Excellent for those who need brown, with brown, mahogany, orange, yellow and red flowered varieties. Cut frequently to encourage blooming, cutting fully open flowers with tight centers. Use one tablespoon of salt to each one quart water and condition overnight in cold water. Place stems deep in the water. Long lasting, from one to two weeks. Plant grows 18"-24". Likes full sun. Will self-sow.

Cosmos. Useful cut flower in white, lavender, pink, red and yellow, with fine foliage. May create airy, delicate effect or mass toward bottom for heavier results. Start indoors and only transplant strongest seedlings. Stake, since they grow from $2\frac{1}{2}$ ft. to 5 ft. Many new early-flowering varieties on market. Bloom late June till frost. Disbudding will result in larger flowers. For cutting choose blooms with widespread petals, but very tight centers. Buds will not develop after cutting and blossoms with powdery, well-developed centers with mature pollen will not last well. Cut and discard all matured flowers to encourage blooming and better branching. Place stems in cold water to condition overnight, with water reaching almost to flower heads. One night in water will not bother foliage. Flowers will last a week. Pollen contains moisture which may cut through a table polish, so be careful in placement.

Cynoglossum amabile—Chinese Forget-me-not. One of the few, truly blue flowers; highly valuable to the arranger. Graceful, loose sprays of large forget-me-not-like flowers are freely produced throughout the summer, most profusely in July. Grows 15″ to 30″. Comes in pink and white, also a dwarf variety. Will self-sow. Can take hot, dry conditions. Likes sun. Cut for arrangements when about $\frac{1}{2}$ in flower. Condition in hot water.

Dahlia. Tuberous, tender perennial. Many, particularly the dwarf singles, are grown from seed and treated as annuals. Seeds should be sown indoors in early spring or may be sown in the open, when danger of frost is gone for late bloom. Single dwarf varieties come fairly true in soft pink, deep rose, salmon, buff, yellow, orange, scarlet and crimson; single and double; excellent for cutting. Cut just after flowers have fully opened. Remove any foliage below the water level. Place in cold water and leave overnight in a dark, cool place. Add one pinch potassium nitrate (from drug store) to each quart water. Revive prematurely wilted dahlias by recutting and placing in warm water.

Datura metel—Angels-Trumpet. Excellent in bud, blossom and fruit for the arranger, but takes up considerable space, 2′-5′ x 2′-5′. Excellent large, bold effect where space will take it. Sow seeds indoors; profusion of large, white, trumpet-like flowers borne in midsummer. Coarse, long, heavy leaves and trunk-like stems. May self-sow. Cut blooms in advance of bud stage, when petals show color, ready to unfold. Cut in late afternoon, buds open by morning. Do not handle delicate buds or flowers, handle by stem only. Condition in cold water overnight. Flowers last about five days; close at night. Dry both blooms and seed pods for arrangements.

Delphinium ajacis—Annual larkspur. Attractive spikes make excellent cutting flowers, growing 1′-5′ with a variety of colors including blue, lavender, pink and white, blooming from June to September. Sow in very early spring or in fall, like a biennial. Likes lime soil, cool weather, full sun; can take some shade. Sows self, but reverts to purple and pink shades and single flowers. Cut for arrangement when spikes are $\frac{1}{4}$ to $\frac{1}{2}$ open. Buds will unfold in water. Spikes last better than a week as buds continue to open. Remove faded flowers. Condition overnight in pH4 water. For drying cut when flowers are $\frac{3}{4}$ open; be certain blooms at base are fully open and in good condition.

Dianthus. Brilliantly colored, sweet-scented, old-fashioned flower, excellent for border edging and delightful for cutting. The dwarfs are 6″, others grow to 12″; free blooming producing clusters of single or double white, pink, rose, scarlet, crimson and bicolored (with contrasting edges) flowers on upright stems, some petals finely fringed. Sow seeds indoors or in an outdoor seed bed. Dianthus likes a well-limed soil. Cut when clusters are ½ in flower. Condition overnight. Keep well in arrangements. Good filler flower or may be grouped to make large, round circular form.

DIANTHUS BARBATUS—Sweet William. Old-fashioned biennial, pink. Newport Pink is a lovely salmon-pink, Homeland a fine crimson with a white eye, Scarlet Beauty a bright scarlet and Midget a 4″ dwarf of mixed color. Start in frame in late summer for bloom next year. Cut when clusters are ½ in flower. Buds open well in water. Flowers last one to two weeks, so watch stems and recut if they decay.

DIANTHUS CHINENSIS—Garden Pink. Biennial or perennial form which flowers first year from seed.

Dimorphotheca aurantiaca—African Daisy, Cape-Marigold. Daisy-like ray flowers 2″-3″ across; white, sulphur yellow, golden yellow, orange, salmon, rose and apricot. Narrow leaves are toothed to 3″ long. Plant grows 12″-18″. Long blooming season. Good edging and cutting plant. Sow indoors early. Likes dry, hot situation. Excellent for fine masses of color.

Dolichos lablab—Hyacinth Bean. Attractive, rapid growing vine, with broad 6″ leaves and clusters of white or purple flowers; grows to 10 ft. Good screen on fence or trellis. Sow seeds outdoors in spring, in full sun. Purple flowers have decorative purple pods, white ones green pods; both useful in dried arrangements.

Echinocystis lobata—Wild Cucumber. Quick growing vine of the gourd family. Grows to 20 ft. Many clusters of white, lacy flowers borne in July. Papery, puffy seed pods covered with long spines in autumn useful in arrangements. Self-seeds. Sow seeds outdoors in April, to cover unsightly areas. Cut for arrangements if trailing sprays are needed.

Eschscholtzia—California Poppy. Sow seeds in September or

March, in sunny location, sandy soil with good drainage where they are to grow. Yellow, orange, salmon-pink or white single flowers in early summer. Grows 9″ to 15″ tall. Free blooming over a long season. Flowers close toward late afternoon without detracting from beauty or keeping qualities, open next day. Cut buds when petals are length of open flower. Condition overnight. Will last about five days.

Euphorbia. Grown for showy, colored leaves on 2-3 ft. plants.

E. MARGINATA—Snow-on-the-Mountain. Grown for its attractive light gray-green leaves, margined with white. Use flame or boiling water treatment to check flow of milky juice in stems. Foliage will last a week. Self-sows freely. Flowers with white petal-like appendages inconspicuous. Plant seeds in March in full sun. Tolerates dry, sunny location.

E. HETEROPHYLLA—Annual Poinsettia, Mexican Fire Plant. Three feet, with large leaves, upper ones marked or blotched in red. Excellent for foliage in flower arrangement. Plant seeds in April in full sun. Cut when brilliant color is showing on upper leaves, when flower cluster shows seven or eight buds and one or two completely opened flowers. Stems are hollow; contain small amount of milky juice, but searing not necessary. Split stems and condition overnight in cold water.

Gaillardia. Endures heat and drought admirably. The doubles particularly make excellent cut flowers. Grows 12″ to 24″ tall. Yellow-orange, mahogany-red and claret ray flowers 2″ across with 3″ hairy leaves. Sow indoors for early blooms, in open for late bloom. Flower until frost. Cut when blossoms are fully open, centers still tight. Will last a week or more.

Godetia amoena and grandiflora—Satin Flower. Of slender, graceful growth, 12″ to 36″ high. Flowers in lavender-red, red, rose, salmon, coral, pale pink and white. Used for masses of color in border and for cutting. Sow seeds outdoors in April in light sandy soil, full sun or partial shade. Does not like heat. Cut when flowers are ¾ to fully open. Split stems. Condition overnight. Will last two to five days. Filler flower.

Gomphrena globosa—Globe Amaranth. An everlasting, growing to 18″, dwarf form nana 8″. Four inch leaves; flowers formed in clover-like heads of white, purple, rose, red and orange. Seeds may be sown indoors in March or outdoors after danger of frost. Long season of bloom. Dried for winter use. Excellent as a fresh cut flower. Cut when ¾ to fully open, with yellow stamens showing. Remove any unnecessary foliage. Split stems, condition overnight in warm water, to start with. Last one week. For drying, gather open flowers when they have acquired their globe-like shape. Strip off foliage. Hang to dry.

Gourds. See page 147.

Gypsophila—Babys-Breath. Old-fashioned favorite, from 12″-30″ high. Upright, branching stems, lance-shaped leaves and many small, airy white, blush or rose-pink flowers. Sow seeds in open where they are to grow. Successive sowings at monthly intervals, for long flowering, as plants bloom themselves out. Lightens heavy masses of color, excellent in old-fashioned bouquets mixed with other flowers. Cut sprays when ½ in flower. Condition stems in cold water overnight. Dry for winter arrangements.

Helianthus—Sunflower. Yellow to copper, orange and brown, red and rose-pink; in heights from 4′ to 12′. Coarse and of great height, but excellent as hedge or for cutting. Plant seeds where plants are to grow in full sun, when danger of frost is past. Bloom in August. Double forms more interesting than single. Cut when petals are turned back but centers tight. If more than one blossom tops the stem take where clusters are at least ½ open. Remove any unnecessary leaves. Stems need support to carry massive flower heads. Strengthen by inserting heavy wire through center, up stem, into the calyx. Interesting dried. Let flowers go to seed and dry on plant, then gather. Attractive even after seeds have fallen or have been removed.

H. ARGOPHYLLUS—Silverleaf Sunflower. Has 3″ brown-disk flower heads and large silvery leaves to 10″. Cherished by flower arrangers as dried material.

Helichrysum bracteatum—Strawflower. Everlasting, produces solitary 2½″ heads of white, yellow, orange or red; to 36″ tall; nanum is dwarf variety. Start seeds indoors in March or later where they are to grow. Like full sun. Harvest for drying just as they open; hang upside down in a shady, well-aired place.

A good, simple arrangement of the miniature type, daisy-like sunflower (*Helianthus annuus*). Easily grown, decorative, and available in colorful shades of yellow, gold or bronze, it is now readily available in many sizes.

Bedding or dwarf dahlias are generally handled as annuals. They are excellent and long-lasting flowers for cutting if cut just before or as blossoms are fully open. Sear stem ends and condition overnight in cold water. The compact plants are covered with flowers, useful for cutting, from midsummer until frost.

COURTESY: NORTHRUP, KING AND CO.

Heliotropium—Heliotrope. A tender perennial grown as an annual. Valuable for use in old-fashioned bouquets, good for color and scent. Both violet and white. Plant indoors in March or propagate by cuttings. Likes light, rich soil in sunny location with plenty of moisture. Cut when ½ to ¾ cluster is open. If possible, include portion of woody stem. Split stems and condition overnight in hot water, 100° F. to start. Keep foliage well above water line. If necessary to recut for other lengths, use hot water treatment for new cuts or sear stem ends.

Helipterum—Everlasting. Pink, white, yellowish-green and yellow disk flower heads 1½″ across, smaller and daintier than strawflowers. Attractive gray-white foliage; 1½ ft. plant. Plant seeds outdoors where they are to grow. Need full sun. Harvest flowers as soon as opened for use in winter bouquets.

Iberis—Globe Candytuft. Used chiefly for edgings or near front of border; fragrant forms are desirable as cut flowers. Grow 6″-12″ tall, in white and lavender. Cut when ½ out and condition overnight in cold water. Sow seeds where they are to grow. Blooms appear in two months and continue until frost if old flowers are kept cut.

Impatiens balsamina—Garden Balsam, Patience. Flowers borne in clusters close to the stem.

I. BALSAMINA—Garden Balsam. Old-fashioned annual with light green, juicy stem, lance-shaped leaves and many single or double showy white, blush, rose or rose-purple flowers, borne close to the main stem along the top ⅓ of its length. Seeds self freely. A gem for cutting. Cut when ½ or slightly less flowers are fully open along stem. Buds continue to open in water. Remove lower flowers as they fade. Some dwarf, double varieties have central blossom atop a rosette of leaves. Cut this type as soon as tip blossom is fully opened. Split stems. Remove enough foliage to show flowers to best advantage; will last longer too. Condition overnight. Place tall stems slantwise in container to get graceful curves. Seed pods are decorative. Remove leaves and use with fresh or dried material. For fresh arrangements, if seed pods are green, condition overnight in cold water.

I. SULTANI—Patience. Tender perennial, grown as annual. Juicy stems with glossy, pale green leaves, large white, pink, rose, brick-red or salmon single flowers borne profusely on bushy, much branched plants. Thrives in sun or partial shade.

Ipomoea purpurea—Morning-Glory. Fast growing vine with blue, pink or white flowers which open early in morning and close before noon. Soak seeds in water before sowing outdoors in May. Heavenly Blue, popular variety with pale blue flowers. Will grow in poor soil. Dwarf varieties produce sturdiest flowers for cutting. Select branches with a few open flowers and many well-developed buds. Split stems. Condition in water overnight. Wrap large buds in tissue paper to keep from unfolding. Unwrap before arranging next day. Flowers last one to two days, buds continue to open.

Lantana. Bushy shrub to 2½ ft. high with rough, handsome, dark-green foliage which sets off the many small, cream, yellow, orange, red-orange or lavender flowers, produced in profusion the entire season; very showy. Also trailing variety. Plant seeds indoors in January. Like sun or very light shade and rich loam. Increase by cuttings. Remove faded flowers to induce better blooming. Cut when outer three or four flower rows in each cluster are fully open. Include a portion of woody stem. Split stems, condition in hot water 80-100° F. Buds open in water. Flowers continue opening up to six days.

Lathyrus odoratus—Sweet Pea. Likes cool, moist weather and rich soil. Needs support. Indispensable as a cut flower because of attractive form, delicious fragrance and extremely wide range of lovely colors. Flowers must be kept cut to prolong blooming season. Sow seeds outside in late fall or early spring. Gather annual sweet peas by cutting slender stems when only the tip of the flowering stem remains in bud. Will last about one week cut. Condition overnight in warm water, to start, using one slightly rounded tablespoon sugar to one quart water. Avoid wetting flower petals.

Lavatera trimestris—Tree-Mallow. Majestic, bushy plants with maple-like leaves and large, single cup-shaped white, pink or rose blossoms, similar to those of the hollyhock in appearance. Grows 3-4 ft. tall. Long season of bloom. Cut when one or two flowers in each cluster are open. Buds develop in water. Split

Not grown nearly as much as in bygone years, the sweet pea (*Lathyrus ordoratus*) must have cool, moist soil and cool weather for best results, flowering best during the spring and early summer. Although the blooming period is short they do bring unequalled joy while in flower because of their delicate beauty and fragrance.

One of the most profuse flowering of all annuals, the versatile petunia is widely grown. Excellent in arrangements, the singles keep better than the doubles when cut. Of easy culture almost anywhere petunias are quite adaptable but they must have sun to bloom. Keep dead flowers picked off for better flower production.

COURTESY: BURPEE SEEDS

stems. Condition overnight. Buds on stem continue to open for a week.

Leptosyne stillmani—Leptosyne. Excellent for cutting, with large, yellow single flowers on long stems. Plant grows 18″-24″. Seeds sown indoors for early flowering. Flowers in six to eight weeks from sowing.

Limonium—Statice, Sea-Lavender. Airy spikes of yellow, rose, white, blue and lavender flowers. Plant seeds indoors in March. Likes sandy loam, full sun. Long season of bloom. Popular dried for winter arrangements.

Linaria—Toadflax. Narrow-whorled leaves and purple blossoms with orange throats; plants grow to 12″-30″. Also white and deep purple variety, with yellow throats and flowers in colors from pink to blue; resemble miniature snapdragons. Flowering season extends over a long period.

Lippia citriodora—Lemon-Verbena. Usually grown from cuttings. Popular because of fragrant, attractive foliage with odor of lemon. White flowers in spikes. Shrub to 10 ft. high. Cut flower spikes when ¼ to ½ open. Split woody stems and condition overnight in hot water 80-100° F., to start with. Defoliate to some degree to show off white spikes. Foliage also an asset.

Lobelia siphilitica. Plant literally covered with bright jewel-like flowers. Also white variety. Well-established plants produce many long-stemmed flowers for cutting. Sow seeds indoors in early spring. Prefer a sunny location. Cut when ¼ to ½ flowering spike is open. Remove faded flowers as upper buds unfold. Buds open well in water. Split stems, strip lower leaves, condition overnight or until spikes open more completely. Should last a week.

Lobularia—Sweet Alyssum. One of best edging plants; come in white and violet. Seeds may be sown outdoors in early spring. Long blooming season. Shear back occasionally for continuous bloom. Excellent for cutting. Cut stems when flowers are ½ in bloom. Buds open in water. Condition overnight. Will last about a week. The delightfully fragrant blossoms are good filler flowers· in arrangements.

Lonas inodora—African Daisy, Dahlberg Daisy. Plants form mats 6″ to 8″ across, 6″-12″ high covered with tiny, yellow flowers. Sometimes grown as yellow sweet alyssum. Sow seeds where they grow in sunny location. Long season of bloom. For arrangements cut stems when half of flowers are in bloom.

Lunaria annua—Honesty, Penny or Satin-Flower. A biennial with white or purple flowers in May-July. Grows to 2½ ft. Grown mainly for its silvery seed pods for winter bouquets. Grows best in partial shade and light humus soil.

For fresh arrangements cut long stems with clusters half open. Condition overnight in warm water, to start with. Flowers should last about a week.

For drying, cut when seed pods are past the soft-green stage and starting to dry and turn tan. Tie in small bunches and hang. Will take four weeks or more to dry. When dry, carefully remove the tannish-green paper covering from each side of the parchment-like silvery disk. Hold a pod between your thumb and forefinger, pinch gently and push off both sides at the same time.

Lupinus—Lupine. Excellent for cutting. Handsome palm-like leaves and spikes of showy flowers in many colors including yellow, rose, red, blue and white. Plant seeds indoors in March or outdoors in May. Prefer poor, sandy soil neutral or slightly alkaline, likes full sun and cool weather. Cut when flowering spike is half or slightly less open. Stems will curve only slightly when placed slantwise, while conditioning.

Lychnis viscaria—German Catchfly. Perennial, treated as an annual. May be used as Gypsophila (Babys-Breath). Excellent for cutting when used in sufficient quantity. Showy white, pink, red or purple flowers, many fragrant. Cut when ¼ to ½ flowering stem is open. Condition overnight in warm water, to start with. Flowers should last four days.

Machaeranthera tanacetifolia—Tahoka Daisy. Biennial, grown as annual. Fern-like leaves and 2″ ray flowers in lovely violet, blue or yellow. Grows 12″-15″ tall. Long-stemmed, daisy-like flowers are good for cutting. Have long blooming season.

Mathiola—Stock. Among oldest and most valuable of garden flowers for color and fragrance, outdoors and for cutting. Needs cool weather to form buds. White, yellow, lavender, purple, blue, pink, rose and red; a wide range of soft and distinctive shades. Sow seeds indoors six to eight weeks before outdoor planting time. Cut flowering spikes when $\frac{1}{4}$ to $\frac{1}{2}$ open, but before flowers at base begin to fade. Split woody stems. Condition overnight in very cold water, to begin with, adjusted to pH4 (one heaping tablespoon sugar and two tablespoons of white distilled vinegar to one quart water). Flowers last a week and a half. Doubles last better than singles.

Momordica balsamina—Balsam-Apple. Slender vine which climbs by tendrils to 20 ft. and makes pleasing trellis or screening plants. Shiny sharp-lobed, toothed leaves; yellow flowers and ovoid orange fruit 3″ long. Quickly grown from seed. Cultivated for ornamental fruits which split open on maturity. Flowers and fruits are showy in cut arrangements.

Myosotis sylvatica listed commercially as M. alpestris. Forget-me-not. Perennial grown as annual. Seeds sown early indoors in January and February. Prefer moist soil and partial shade. The "grateful" plant of our grandmothers' day is most valuable for cutting, used as a filler, or in miniature bouquets. Flowers true blue, also white, pink; tall and dwarf varieties, 6″ to 24″. Excellent for edging pool or stream. Once established will seed self. Flowers three months from seed. Blooms until frost if faded flowers are kept removed. Cutting necessary for continuous blooming. Cut for arrangement when half stem is in flower. Condition stems in 80°-100° F. water, to start with. If material does not respond, recut and dip stem ends in boiling water for $1\frac{1}{2}$ minutes, protecting upper leaves and flowers from steam. Then condition overnight. For low arrangements, with an ample supply lift small plants about $\frac{1}{4}$ to $\frac{1}{3}$ in flower. Wash soil from roots. Condition roots overnight in cold water. Buds will open and plant will stay fresh a week.

Nemesia strumosa—Nemesia. Includes many large-flowering hybrids and dwarf-free blooming, showy plants. Good for edging and border. Pretty tubular flowers in white, yellow, orange, pink, crimson, rose and blue are borne in terminal racemes. Likes cool weather and will bloom all summer where nights are cool. Grows 12″-18″ tall. Tender plant, so start seeds indoors. Excellent filler type flower in a wide range of colors.

Nemophila menziesii—Baby Blue-Eyes. Profusion of lovely, cup-shaped, sky-blue flowers with white centers. Good prostrate edging plant; grows to 20″. Sow seeds where they are to be grown. Will bloom over long period, through late spring and summer. Likes sun. Another good filler type flower for the arranger.

Nicotiana—Flowering Tobacco. Tender perennial, grown in North as an annual. Tufted leaves form a decorative rosette. Terminal panicles of tubular flowers on long, graceful stems are white, rose, lavender or maroon with a delicious night fragrance. Large and dwarf varieties grow 18″-60″ tall. Start seeds early indoors or out in mid-April where they are to grow. Semi-shade extends blooming period and produces slightly larger flowers, also more vivid colors. Seeds self. Cut when one or two flowers in cluster are fully open. Well-developed buds will open in water. Condition overnight with stems in warm water, to start with. Flowers last two or three days but clusters will continue to open up to a week in water.

Nierembergia caerulea—Cup-Flower. Tender perennial treated as annual. Sow seeds early indoors. Purple Robe popular variety. Produces deep lavender-blue cup-shaped flowers, with bright yellow eyes, borne freely at the tips of many slender stems. Narrow simple leaves give whole plant a dense, compact appearance. Grows to 12″ tall. Excellent for window boxes or as edging around a terrace. Good filler flower for arranger.

Nigella damascena—Love-in-a-Mist, Fennel-Flower. Grow for cutting. Interesting old-fashioned, single or double flowers in shades of blue and white surrounded by feathery bracts, which add to their attractiveness. Flowers nestle among the fine feathery foliage; plants are slender and grow 18″-24″ high. Sow seeds in open garden in sun. Blooming season short, so plant seeds in succession, about a month apart, for continuous color and cutting. Self sows, plants do not transplant well. Cut stems when central flower and one or two more are open. Condition overnight in warm water, using one slightly rounded tablespoon sugar to each one quart warm water. Flowers will last one week or more. Globular, balloon-like seed pods just beneath flat flower are attractive when green, or as they turn tan and brown in late autumn. Cut in various stages of coloring. Effective in arrangements. If cut green for fresh arrangements, condition overnight in water. Dry for winter bouquets.

Papaver—Poppy. Annual poppies are a colorful group with showy flowers that bloom freely on long flexible stems. Offer a wider range of soft pleasing colors than do the Orientals, including white, yellow, orange, scarlet, pink, salmon, apricot, and terra cotta. Some are edged or suffused with a second tint, some have golden anthers and white centers; come in single and double forms and grow from 1-3 ft. tall. Sow seeds where they are to grow in late fall or very early spring in full sun and sandy loam. Will self sow.

Properly handled the flowers should last four days cut. Pick in the advanced bud stage, when the flower is ready to unfold. Sear stem ends in flame, at correct length for use in arrangement. Condition in deep cold water overnight. In morning, carefully drop inside each bloom at base of petals, a little melted candle wax, same color as petals, to delay shattering.

Penstemon gloxinioides—Beard-Tongue. Perennial grown as annual in North. Sow seeds indoors in February or March, transplant to open garden in late May in full sun with ample moisture. Exceptional cut flower with flower spikes closely set with gloxinia-like blooms, in brilliant colors from red to white, and even blue flowers. Plant grows to 36". Cut when $\frac{1}{4}$ flowering stock has opened. Condition overnight in cold water. Will get beautiful, curving stems from plant at times. May develop more curves by placing stems slantwise in container while conditioning.

Petunia. Very satisfactory cut flower. With the many new hybrids on the market there is a type for every use. Prefers full sun but will grow in partial shade. Beginner should buy seedlings, as seeds are tricky to start. Six distinct groupings:

BEDDING TYPE: Grows from 1-2 ft. Snowstorm, good compact white in this group. Blooms from early summer until late fall. In blue, crimson, cerise, salmon, rose and white.

BALCONY TYPE: Sometimes called large-flowered bedding petunia. Has large 2"-3" flowers, with trailing branches $1\frac{1}{2}$ or 2 ft.

DWARF TYPE: Mound-like plant a foot or so in height, producing an abundance of moderate sized flowers. An excellent pot plant for indoor use.

MINIATURE TYPE: Grows only about 6″ tall, forming mounds of 6″-8″.

ALL DOUBLES: Some rampant growers, forming plants up to 3 ft. across, others quite dwarf. Needs some staking, good for porch or terrace boxes or large flower pots. Very effective as cut flowers.

GIANT FLOWERING: Include two distinct types. Those with ruffled petals, giving the effect of doubles, flowers up to 6″ across, and the Giant Fringed.

Cut flowers when nearly or fully open and cut from plants just above outside buds or break so new growth will branch outward and produce a shapely plant. Do plenty of cutting for continued bloom. Flowers and foliage may collapse directly after cutting, but will revive when placed overnight in water, using one slightly rounded tablespoon of sugar to each quart of water. Strip leaves below water level as petunia foliage decays rapidly in water. Flowers keep up to one week.

Phlox drummondi—Annual Phlox. The quick growth, long season of bloom and interesting color range of the phlox make it popular as a garden and cutting flower. The tall varieties, with their colorful flower heads are excellent for cutting. Seeds are best started indoors early as they are slow to germinate. May be sown outdoors in April for late bloom. Phlox are classified under the following six types:

TETRA: Tallest and most vigorous of all phlox. Individual flowers to 1½″ across. Tetra red and Tetra salmon are the two colors available now.

BEAUTY: An improved strain of dwarf Phlox. Mound-like plants, 6″-8″. high, with flowers nearly double the size of ordinary varieties.

DWARF COMPACT: Fine for pots, 6″-8″ tall, with large flowers in good colors.

TALL, LARGE FLOWERED AND GIANT FLOWERED: Grow to 15″ in many fixed colors including pastels.

STARRED OR FRINGED: Deeply lacinated, painted petals in a wide choice of colors and color combinations. Much prized for flower arrangements. This is an old type, popular in Europe. A new strain, the Twinkles, is being enthusiastically acclaimed in this country.

GLOBE: A new strain of dwarf plants of perfectly rounded habit.

For arrangements, cut phlox when clusters are $\frac{1}{4}$ to $\frac{1}{2}$ open. If too open flowers will drop quickly; should last about twelve days. Split stems and condition overnight in cold water. Cutting encourages a second flowering later in the season.

Quamoclit pennata—Cypress-Vine. Quick growing climber, with attractive scarlet and white trumpet-shaped flowers $1''$-$1\frac{1}{2}''$ across. Handsome, fine, fern-like, rich green foliage. Sow seeds where they are to grow. Likes full sun. See Ipomaea (Morning-Glory) for cutting procedure. Valuable to arranger as trailing form with scarlet and white flowers.

Reseda odorata—Mignonette. Old-fashioned, sweet-scented garden annual. Valuable for cut foliage in mixed bouquets. Plant seeds where they grow, in part shade or start early indoors in pots as seedlings resent being moved. Like moisture and lime. Heavy spikes of small red, whitish or yellow flowers, delightfully fragrant but not showy. Both dwarf and large varieties. Cut flowers when $\frac{1}{4}$ to $\frac{1}{2}$ the spike is open. Condition overnight in 80°-100° F. water, to start with. For drying, cut when most of the flowers are fully open, but before those at base start to fade. Excellent in winter bouquets.

Ricinus communis—Castor Bean. Large plant grows 6'-10' spreading to half its height. Prized by arrangers for tropical effect of seed heads and foliage. The side branches particularly take graceful curves, which lend themselves well to line arrangements. Large, dramatic dark red leaves are divided into five to eleven lobes. Inconspicuous cream flowers on dark red stems are borne in fine heads or panicles, followed by showy, prickly, bronzy-red seed pods. Gibsoni is a smaller form. Deeply cut leaves may be selected in various sizes and colors at various stages from green, greenish-red, greenish-bronze to bronze. Spiny seed pods are first green, then vivid-orange to bronzy-crimson. At certain stages in growth a perfect arrangement may be cut in one piece from Castor Bean plant.

Cut flowers when half spike is open. Cut fruits when formed, at stage most appealing for your purpose. Fruits do not dry well, loose color and substance. Cut foliage when size and color you wish. Split stems and condition overnight in warm water, to start with. Foliage lasts three to four weeks. Submerge flowers and fruits in cold water for one to two hours, until crisp and firm. Lift out and keep stems in water. Flowers and fruits last about ten days.

Rudbeckia—Coneflower. Excellent long-stemmed flowers for cutting, flourish almost anywhere. Sow seeds in frame or open ground. Blooms from late July until frost.

R. BICOLOR. Annual form of Rudbeckia. Two foot plant with rough stems and leaves and yellow ray flowers, often with a black disk at the base. Some varieties double, from pale yellow to dark mahogany, some blossoms 5″ across.

R. HIRTA. Common Wild Black-eyed Susan. Handsome biennial with golden rays and dark brown cones. May be grown as an annual. Blooms freely over a long period. Cut when flowers are open but centers still tight. Condition overnight in cold water. Foliage may wilt before flowers. Flowers will last one to two weeks. Snip off dead leaves and substitute other suitable foliage.

Salpiglossis sinuata—Painted-Tongue. Graceful in mixed bouquets. A slender 2 ft. plant with toothed, oblong leaves and large flaring flowers, veined with a contrasting color, lavender-blues are netted with silver or dark blue; crimson and rose veined with gold. There are available self-colors for those who do not like the veining contrast. Plant seeds indoors in March or plant outdoors in mid-April where they are to grow, in full sun. These plants will bloom later. If brought into bloom before hot weather, they will flower until frost.

Cut flowers as soon as fully open. Condition overnight with stems in cold water almost up to flower heads. Should last about a week cut.

Salvia splendens—Salvia, Sage. The bad taste used in over planting the blazing Scarlet Sage and using it indiscriminately should not keep one from using the lovely plants in this group.

S. FARINACEA—Blue Salvia. Grows to 2 ft. Tender perennial grown as an annual in the North. Pretty gray-green lanceolate leaves on shrubby stems with long racemes of violet-blue tubular flowers. Excellent spike material for cutting.

S. PATENS—Gentian Sage. Perennial treated as an annual. Grows 30″ tall with toothed arrow-shaped leaves and intense gentian blue 2″ flowers.

S. SPLENDENS—Scarlet Sage. Reddest of the annuals. Grows to 3 ft. Plant seeds indoors in February or March. Set out in garden in May in sun or very light shade.

Blue Salvia is excellent for the arranger either fresh or dried. Cut when lower half of flowering spike has opened. Condition overnight in warm water, to start with. Place some stems slantwise in the container to produce curved stems.

Cut Gentian and Scarlet Sage when $\frac{1}{2}$ to $\frac{3}{4}$ of spike is open. Split stems and condition overnight in warm water, to start with. Cut Scarlet Sage for drying when petals drop and red bracts along the stem feel papery in texture.

Sanvitalia procumbens—Creeping Zinnia. A little 6″ trailer with stems well clothed with ovate leaves. Bear waxy, bright little flower heads with deep yellow rays, surrounding a dark purple disk. Double variety (flore pleno). Blooms all summer. Sow seeds where they are to grow in full sun. Excellent for small yellow arrangements.

Scabiosa atropurpurea—Pincushion Flower. Important annual for cutting. Taller types invaluable for arrangements. Blooms from midsummer until frost, if flowers are not allowed to go to seed. Slender plant with lyre-shaped basal leaves, finely cut; double cushion-like flower heads in blue, lavenders, red, rose mahogany and white. There are dwarf, medium and tall growing strains. Sow seeds in frame in April, as they are slow developing but of easy culture.

Cut when flowers are almost fully open. Buds must be well-developed to open in water but are interesting unopened with color darker than the flowers. Split stems and condition overnight. When petals fall, immature seed pod remains, of an unusual green color which can be used effectively by the arranger. Late in season collect seed pods for winter arrangements.

Sidalcea—Prairie Mallow. Perennial treated as annual. Grows 2 to 3 ft. Sow seeds very early indoors. Erect, slender spikes covered with purple, crimson, rose, blush-pink or white mallow-like blooms, interesting in border and excellent for cutting during June and July.

Tagetes—Marigold. Offer a wealth of color all summer and fall. Include almost all conceivable tints and tones of orange and yellow and a goodly range of reds in many combinations. All lovely for cutting, with great diversity in flower forms, colors and habits of growth. Range in height from 6″ to 4′, in flower size from 1″ to 6″ across; next to the zinnia is the most easily grown of all popular annuals. Warm weather plant, so no time is saved if seeds sown outdoors too early. Place in full sun. Stake tall plants. Cut when petals are reflexed but centers are tight, or when the very double flowers are ¾ open. Not necessary to put marigolds in water immediately, but recut under water before conditioning overnight in cold water using one teaspoon of zinc sulphate crystals (drugstore) to each quart of water. Marigolds will last one to two weeks.

Thunbergia alata—Clock-Vine. Charming little vine, which grows 3 to 6 ft. in the North. Has twining stems covered with triangular, winged leaves; interesting little flowers of white, buff and orange-yellow with dark centers. Because of the orange flowers with the black eye it is often called Black-eyed Susan. Good ground cover, excellent in urns or window boxes. Start seeds early indoors. Will do well in full sun or partial shade. Very useful where a trailing form is needed. Cut and handle as you would any annual vine.

Tithonia hybrids—Mexican Sunflower. Start seeds indoors in small pots or plant bands. Large, coarse, showy 3′-6′ plant with large, coarse lobed leaves which practically cover strong stems and branches in late summer and fall with an abundance of brilliant 3″ broad, flat, velvety, red-orange ray flowers surrounding a showy disk. Looks like handsome single dahlia. Excellent for cutting.

Cut just after flowers have fully opened, but before pollen has developed in center of blooms. Condition overnight, starting

Marigolds (*Tagetes*) are grown for their showy flowers and undemanding, reliable performance in the garden. They furnish quantities of flowers throughout the summer months for both garden and house. The prevailing colors of yellow, gold and orange bring sunshine indoors. Their stiff stems and good keeping qualities make them a valuable cut flower. Remove the bottom leaves to avoid contaminating the water.

Courtesy: Burpee Seeds

A universal spring-time favorite, the appealing pansy comes in rich velvety colors of blue, gold, red and white. Not easy to propagate so buy young plants. The site should be cool and moist and never more than half shaded. Summer heat usually kills them.

with warm water. Cut buds in various stages for added interest. Foliage lasts well cut, flowers about a week. Do not wet flower petals or foliage.

Torenia fournieri—Wishbone Flower. Excellent edging plant 12″ high. Start seeds indoors early. Will self sow. Blooms in late summer and fall. Likes shade and cool weather. Its two lipped tubular flowers are pale violet and yellow, with the velvety lower lip of the blossom a rich purple marked with yellow. The shiny leaves and stems turn rosy, then plum colored in autumn. Pot and bring indoors before frost for winter bloom. If you have enough small plants lift entire plant when half in flower. Trim away excess foliage. Wash soil from roots. Condition overnight with roots in cold water. Plants will last a week handled this way. For cut flowers, choose those almost fully open and condition the same way.

Trachymene caerulea—Blue Lace-Flower. Very popular for cutting. Much like Queen Anne's Lace or Wild Carrot. Plant grows to 2 ft. with lobed compound leaves and long-stemmed pale blue or lavender-blue flowers in showy umbels. Sow seeds outdoors where they are to grow or start indoors in pots. Cut when $\frac{1}{4}$ to $\frac{1}{2}$ flower cluster is still in bud. Condition overnight in cold water, reaching almost to flower heads. Place some stems slantwise in containers to produce curves. Flowers should last a week.

Tropaeolum—Nasturtium. An old-time favorite, their popularity is increasing again because of recently improved varieties, some sweet scented. All valuable for cutting. Sow seeds where they are to grow in a soil not too rich and in full sun. Dwarf kinds are excellent for borders and the climbing kinds may be used as screens or in window and terrace boxes. The leaves are round and padlike on slender, succulent stems, producing cream, yellow, gold, salmon, scarlet and crimson single and double flowers. Before frost bring the dwarfs indoors for winter color.

Cut flowers as soon as they have fully opened, with large buds just ready to unfold. Split stems and condition overnight in cold water. After arranged, flowers will turn toward the light and stems will stretch into position, so arrangement is better and more permanent the second day. Use foliage alone, in mixed bouquets or with own flowers, as it has much character. Condition foliage for twenty-four hours, starting with warm water. Prematurely wilted foliage will revive with this treatment. The green seed pods are effective in small arrangements.

Ursinia. Desirable for fragrance. Daisy-like flowers in yellow or orange with purplish markings on large, graceful stems. Grows 12″-24″ tall. Start seeds indoors. Likes full sun in garden. Useful in arrangements.

Verbena. V. hortensis is the common garden Verbena—many improved varieties of this form. Notable for broad, flat heads of bright white, pink, rose, red, blue-lavender or purple flowers and spreading, recumbent stems with ovate green leaves. Blooms freely throughout the summer, right up to hard freezing. Bring plants indoors for winter color. Cuttings may be rooted readily or start seeds indoors in February. Likes full sun and rich but well-drained soil.

Cut flowers when two or three outside rows of buds are open, when most other buds are showing their true color. Split stems. Condition overnight, starting with warm water, using one teaspoon of sugar for each quart of water. Flowers will last about a week.

Vinca rosea—Madagascar Periwinkle. Glossy-leaved ground cover. Wonderful for arrangers. The foliage alone, with its glossy, green leaves is invaluable. A tender perennial grown as an annual. Likes sun and good soil. Flowers are rose colored or white (alba), set off like jewels on glossy, green-leaved, erect 18″ plant. Excellent where low or medium height mass of foliage is needed.

Cut when two or three flowers on each stem are fully open. All buds showing color will open in water. Split stems and condition overnight in cold water. Remove excess upper foliage to show flowers off to better advantage and help them last longer. Remove faded blooms. Flowers last about four days, but buds continue to open for a week or longer.

Viola tricolor hortensis—Pansy. Many wonderful modern named varieties have been derived from this plant, though biennial and perennial pansies are commonly grown as annuals in the North. One of the first spring flowers, bright and gay in a wide assortment of colors, they make wonderful edging flowers and are excellent for cutting. Gather when fully open with as much stem and foliage as possible, since leaves are an asset, as with mums, in helping the flowers last longer. Condition overnight in cold water. Flowers should last about five days. If you have enough plants, lift an entire plant when half in flower. Wash soil from roots, condition overnight with roots in cold water. Plant will last a week or more.

Zinnia elegans—Zinnia. From the smallest to the great "giant" sizes all are excellent for cutting and arrangements, either by themselves or in combination with other flowers. Sow indoors for early blooms or outdoors for later. Easily grown and will flower within two months from date of sowing. Advisable to start a second crop about mid-June for late summer flowers, as May sown plants may bloom themselves out by September. Available in about every color but blue, and diversified forms: some with curved petals, others like the "Cactus Flowered" with very irregular, narrow, twisted petals (a joy to the arranger), still others like the lovely Z. linearis, one of the smallest-flowered of all, which forms a solid mass of foliage and flowers growing to 10″ in height. Certainly there are zinnias that suit your needs both outdoors and in.

Cut for arrangements when flower is completely open but center is still tight. Buds do not open well in water. Remove all unnecessary leaves, all you can spare. Plunge the stems immediately into cold water for overnight conditioning. Flowers should last one to two weeks.

QUESTIONS AND ANSWERS

My cannas, which were planted directly in the garden, bloomed late last year. Should they be started indoors now?

Although cannas can be planted in the garden after all danger of frost is past, where the season is short they come into bloom too close to frost time to be of any value. In such cases, start the divisions in flats of soil indoors four to six weeks before they can be safely planted in the garden. Keep in the sun and grow at 60-70° F. As plants develop transfer to individual pots.

What might be the cause of a reddish discoloration on the undersurfaces of bean leaves?

It is probably the work of red spiders, small mites which feed on the undersides of the leaves. Spray with rotenone at 10 to 14 day intervals.

4

PERENNIALS, BACKBONE OF
THE FLOWER BORDER

Plants which live more than two years are known as perennials.
The term is generally applied to those herbaceous plants which
die when winter comes but whose roots continue to live and
send up new stems and flowers year after year. This distinguishes
them from the group of woody trees and shrubs which also live
more than two years. Some perennials live indefinitely, while
others tend to die out after three or four years unless the roots
are taken up, divided and replanted every two or three years.
Our grandmothers grew many hardy perennials, among them the
familiar phlox, peony, delphinium and bleeding heart. They were
the backbone of the flower border because of their hardiness,
permanency and variety in color, height, foliage and bloom. Differing from the annuals which blossom over a long period of
time, very few perennials bloom all season. As some plants come
into bloom, others stop blooming. With forethought and planning one may be assured of continuous change from early spring
until late fall, constantly giving the gardener something to look
forward to with pleasant anticipation.

GROUPING PERENNIALS

With a hedge or shrub background to frame and hold together
the flower border, you are ready to think about perennials, the
backbone and more permanent part of the flower border. In planning for a succession of bloom and good color consider spring,

early summer, late summer and fall blooming varieties. The length of the blooming period is also important. Hardy asters, the earlier mums, delphiniums, iris, peony and phlox have a long blooming period, an important consideration where space is limited. Plants like the old-fashioned bleeding heart, candytuft, columbine, flax, meadow-rue and Oriental poppy bloom over a comparatively short period, so are not advisable for the small garden.

Limit the perennials to several choice favorites massed in groups of three, five or seven, so the showing will be large enough to be effective, rather than planting a skimpy display of many different kinds. Choose varieties with similar basic requirements as to soil, moisture and sun for healthy, prolific blooming. Select two or three kinds that have the same blooming period and group them together; the number used will depend upon the space. Repeat this grouping two or three times throughout the border to maintain a pleasing continuity.

The two or three kinds used may form a harmonious blending of related colors or create a bold color contrast. Which type of arrangement do you prefer in your home? Personal taste and your indoor color scheme will determine your choice. A harmonious blending of related colors is nicely achieved by grouping together in mass effect many varieties of one kind of flower. For example, phlox in many different tones combine well. The colors come in various degrees of intensity and lightness and darkness, so interesting variety may be obtained. Or you may want to use different kinds of perennials of one color. For example, yellow varieties of the spike thermopsis with the disk-shaped coreopsis will bloom together in June and July.

Many people enjoy the vitality of striking color contrasts such as the scarlet Oriental poppy with blue delphinium, a combination often seen in the spring of the year. Held in check, using larger masses of the less intense delphiniums, the vivid contrast is stimulating and exciting.

Others like to choose a dominant color and use it throughout the garden during each flowering season. Other colors are introduced in lesser degree for contrast but they do not compete, rather they accentuate the dominant color. Perhaps, this is the easiest and safest system for the beginner. Nature's seasonal colors are yellow and white for spring, rose for early summer,

PERENNIALS · · ·

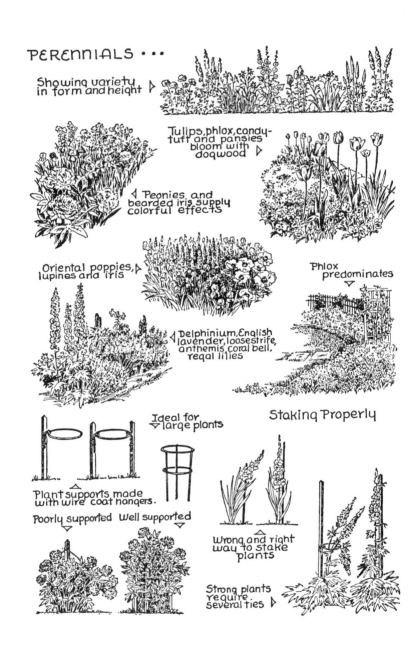

Showing variety in form and height ▷

Tulips, phlox, candytuft and pansies bloom with dogwood ▷

◁ Peonies and bearded iris supply colorful effects

Oriental poppies, lupines and iris ▷

Phlox predominates ▽

◁ Delphinium, English lavender, loosestrife, anthemis, coral bell, regal lilies

Ideal for ▽ large plants

Staking Properly

Plant supports made with wire coat hangers.

Poorly supported ▽   Well supported ▽

Wrong and right way to stake plants

Strong plants require several ties ▷

blue and gold for midsummer, pink for late summer and blue, purple and gold for autumn. There is an abundance of color from which to choose and to satisfy all tastes. See pages 217 ff. for perennials grouped according to color and season of bloom.

Place the tallest species in the background, especially those which provide a good display of foliage. Some of the tall sorts should extend into or toward the front, especially in the wide parts of the border to provide interest and relieve any possible monotony. Dwarf edging plants of compact growth are used in the foreground with plants of intermediate height distributed throughout the rest of the border.

PROPAGATION OF PERENNIALS

Some perennials may be grown successfully from seed, yet others, especially the wonderful new hybrids, the name varieties, do not come true from seed and should be increased or propagated by stem and root cuttings or by division. Under *Perennials For Cutting* we recommend the best method. A good fertile, well-drained soil at least a foot deep is important for good results. Some perennials like the English daisy will produce flowers the first year, while others like monkshood, gas-plant and the globe-flower must be two or three years old from seed before they bloom. Many people prefer to buy well-established plants from a local grower or florist. Perhaps a neighbor or friend is dividing some of her perennials and if they are good varieties will share them with you or you may make an exchange with her from your garden if the plants are well-established. Some perennials like the shasta daisy and most chrysanthemums may be divided after the first year, yet others like iris, columbine and phlox should not be disturbed until the third year. Plants like bleeding heart, the gas-plant, lupines and peonies should not be disturbed for years, as it takes them some time to become established and recover from transplanting.

Perennials are excellent for cutting. If space permits, you may want a separate cutting garden. This often borders the vegetable garden or is screened by shrubs; it is not a part of the garden picture. The flowers are planted in rows, one or two plants of a kind, or in any quantity desired for the sole purpose of furnishing the owner with just what she wants to cut for indoor arrangements. Delphiniums, peonies, most of the daisy-flowered kinds, iris, campanulas, dianthus, gaillardia, rudbeckia, platycodon, hemerocallis, salvia (the lovely blue), pyrethrum, scabiosa and veronica are all choice perennials for indoor arrangements. However, your taste, likes and dislikes will determine what you plant. A garden should be fun, so grow what you like and enjoy cutting for indoor use.

After the earliest spring-flowering bulbs have gone, spring color depends to a large degree upon the perennials. Early iris, peonies and columbine, in combination with canterbury bells, delphinium and foxglove, keep the garden bright with color until the annuals come into bloom.

PERENNIALS FOR CUTTING

Achillea milfoil—Yarrow. Yellow, white, pink, crimson or purple. Blooms from June to September. Silvery grayish-green, aromatic, finely cut foliage which adds considerably to the beauty of the plant. Likes sun. Cut shoots back directly after they are through flowering. Lift, divide and replant at least every third year.

For arrangements, cut when half of the flowers in the cluster are open. Condition overnight in cold water using two tablespoons salt to each quart of water. Will last up to two weeks cut. A favorite plant for drying. To dry, cut when flowers are fully open.

Aconitum—Monkshood. Tall plants, 2-7 ft. with attractive foliage and handsome branching spikes of amethyst blue, dark blue, bicolored blue and white, violet or mauve flowers which come in late summer and autumn. Cut arrangements when $\frac{1}{3}$ to $\frac{1}{2}$ spike is in flower. Condition overnight. Cut flowers will last a week. Likes shade or part shade, rich soil, cool climate and moisture. Propagate by division but do not disturb unless necessary. Beebalm, phlox and mistflower, all tolerant of shade, are good garden companions.

Alyssum saxatile—Basket-of-Gold. Clusters of golden-yellow flowers in May and June. Double form desirable. Leaves grayish. Plant grows to 16″. Likes sunny, well-drained location. Propagate double form by cuttings or division. Good for small scale arrangements. Plant in sunny spot for border edging with spring bulbs or use in rockery. Cut when half in flower. Place stems in cold water overnight. Will last four or five days cut.

Anemone—Windflower. Propagate by division. Plants grow from one to three feet tall and in white, pink, rose, red, and violet, blooming from early spring until frost, depending upon the varieties. Plants tolerate partial shade, some like lime. Valuable because of length of blooming period and vivid colors. Cut when petals are open but while centers are still tight, or when buds show plenty of color and are about to burst into bloom. Place stems in cold water overnight. If not crowded stems will take on interesting curves. Flowers should last a week or more.

Aquilegia—Columbine. Leave undisturbed for five or six years. Likes light humus soil and partial shade, grows from $1\frac{1}{2}$ to $3\frac{1}{2}$ ft. Excellent hybrids. Flowers come in rich colors of red, lavender-blue, blue, pink, lemon or golden-yellow with long spurs, from May through August depending upon the variety. Propagate by division in early spring. For arrangements, cut when $\frac{2}{3}$ flowers on stem are open. Buds sufficiently advanced to show color and about to bloom will open in water. Place stems deep in cool water about 45°-50° F. to start with, and condition overnight. Flowers should last about a week.

Artemisia—Wormwood. Plant A. lactiflora for showy, fragrant, white cut flowers in August and September. Plants grow four to five ft. tall. Not reliably hardy in northern sections. Has finely, divided aromatic foliage also attractive for cutting. Likes light, well-drained soil and full sun.

A. STELLERIANA—Dusty Miller. Hardy, grows 2-3 ft. Small, yellow flower heads insignificant but var. Silver King highly prized for silvery-white foliage, effective foil for blue-flowered plants. Cut when one-half spike is open. Split stems and condition at least twenty-four hours in deep, cold water, removing unnecessary leaves. Flowers should last a week. Revive prematurely wilted foliage by recutting stems and placing in 80°-100° F. water until revived. Leaves of different varieties vary from gray, gray-green, silvery-gray or white to light and dark green. Useful to arranger dried, when it will last indefinitely.

Aster—Michaelmas Daisy. Group includes both spring and summer flowering, as well as late summer and fall blooming varieties; both dwarf and tall kinds, growing from 6″-24″ high. A wide color range includes white, heliotrope-blue, lavender-blue, blue, rose-pink, reddish-rose, violet-purple, and purple and the flowers measure from 1½″-3″ across. With a wise selection of varieties,

Tough crown may be
separated with axe

Use outer stems
for new plants

Clump of HARDY ASTER
needs attention

asters will bloom in the garden from May into October. A. novae-angliae is the New England aster, A. novi-belgi, the New York aster. Asters like a medium, rich soil and a sunny exposure. Do not grow named varieties from seed as they do not come true. A source of excellent material for the arranger. Cut hardy asters when ¾ of the flowers in each cluster are open. Recut stems under water using one teaspoon of sugar for each quart of water, and condition overnight. Foliage will wilt before the flowers, which should keep a week. Remove dead foliage as it wilts and when necessary, substitute other appropriate greens.

Astilbe (often called Spirea). Select some of the better hybrids listed under A. arendsi. Flowers are borne in erect spikes from June to September, depending upon the variety; in white, pink, purplish or red. Plants grow two to three ft. tall. Cut when spikes are half open for fresh arrangements. Split stems and condition overnight. Flowers will last a week. Valuable dried in arrangements. Gather when flowers are all open or just a very few buds remain at top of spike. Retains color and form when dried. Astilbe likes rich humus soil, plenty of water and partial shade.

Every third year, in early spring when plant is through flowering, divide.

Baptisia australis—False Indigo. A good spike form, flowers deep indigo blue, bloom in June and July with attractive foliage. Plant grows three to six ft. tall. Likes good drainage and sun. Propagate from seeds which should be soaked in warm water for two hours before sowing in spring. Do not transplant unless necessary. Cut when $\frac{1}{3}$ flowers are open on stem. Condition overnight in cold water and spikes should last about a week. Inflated seed pods in summer and autumn, first green and later gun-metal in color, are attractive. The foliage treated with glycerin and water turns an attractive dark-blue.

Bellis perennis—English Daisy. Large-flowered, double types usually treated as biennials; White, pink and red flowers which bloom in April and May and will continue to flower during most of summer in cool climate if dead blooms are kept cut. Excellent for cutting if short stems are useable. Cut when flowers are $\frac{3}{4}$ open. Split stems and condition overnight. Flowers will last a week.

Boltonia. Of the composite family, like the aster and daisy. An excellent cut flower. B. asteroides flowers from July through September. Grows 6'-7' tall, with white or pale violet flowers $\frac{3}{4}''$ across. B. latisquama flowers at the same time. Grows 4 to 6 feet, with handsome pale, pink-lavender flowers, 1" across. They will last best if flowers are cut when three-quarters open.

Campanula—Bellflower, Canterbury Bells. Cup and saucer plant of our grandmothers' day. From dwarfs to 3 ft. high. Tolerant of semi-shade, prefers full sun. Varieties will bloom from June to October in a wealth of white and blue blooms, bell or cup and saucer-shaped. Divide every third or fourth year. For arrangements, cut when stalks are $\frac{1}{4}$ to $\frac{1}{2}$ open to last two weeks, but for best color and beauty cut when nearly fully open; so cut they will last one week. Stems contain a milky juice, so condition in 100° F. water, to start with, or sear ends in flame for fifteen seconds, then condition starting with hot water. Remove faded flowers as new ones open.

Centaurea—Knapweed. Attractive thistle-like flowers. Plant grows $1\frac{1}{2}$ to 2 ft. tall with white, violet-blue, rose, or yellow flowers from June to September. Likes sun and good ordinary soil. Divide and replant every third year. Leaves gray or silver-white underneath when young. Excellent as cut flower.

Centranthus ruber (Valeriana coccinea of nurseries)—Jupiters-Beard. Grows 2 to 3 ft. Has white, rose or brilliant-red fragrant flowers borne in panicles or umbels in May to August, sometimes blooms again in September to October. Cut flower clusters when ¼ to ½ open. Split stems and condition in cold water overnight. Flowers will last about a week. Attractive, rich-green foliage good material for arranger. Plant likes good drainage, lime and full sun. Trim after flowering and divide every third year.

Chrysanthemums. All like sun and medium-heavy, well-drained soil. Propagate by division or cuttings in spring. Mums listed in catalogues as singles, anemone-flowered, decorative, pompon, button, spoon, spider etc., so there is a wide variety from which to choose as to form, color, size and blooming period. Literally hundreds of named varieties on the market.

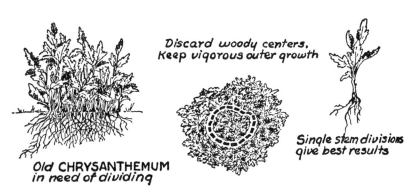

Discard woody centers. Keep vigorous outer growth

Single stem divisions give best results

Old CHRYSANTHEMUM in need of dividing

Among most lasting of cut flowers. Perennial mums often have hard woody stems. Split stems two or three inches. Condition in hot water (100° F.) using three or four tablespoons of sugar to each quart of water. Use 3 tablespoons for a few, 4 for many. Flowers should last up to three weeks. Mums last longer when foliage or leaves are left on stems, so remove few as possible, just those below water line that might decay.

C. ARCTICUM, C. COREANUM, C. MORIFOLIUM, C. NIPPONICUM (a sub-shrub), all are listed in catalogues as Hardy Chrysanthemums

Of all the garden flowers few offer greater variety of form and color than the chrysanthemum. They remain the foundation of late summer and autumn arrangement work.

Arrangement by Mary Alice Roche   Roche Photo

An old onion patterned canister jar was the inspiration for this arrangement of feathered white chrysanthemums arranged with white grapes and white onions.

ARRANGEMENT BY VERA T. BAYLES   JOHN C. BAYLES PHOTO

under various names such as Arctic Marguerites or Northland Daisies, Korean Chrysanthemums, Ameliamums, Azaleamums or Cushion mums. Varieties like the Northland, Korean, Minnesota and New Hampshire are the hardiest.

C. COCCINEUM—Painted Daisy (also known as Pyrethrum). Grows 2'. Characterized by fern-like, divided foliage; single or double blooms in crimson, pink, lilac or white in May and June. Divide every third year. Excellent for cutting.

C. LEUCANTHEMUM—Ox-eye Daisy. Plant only the double forms which bloom in May to July (sometimes in September). Plant grows to 2'. Divide every second year.

C. MAXIMUM VAR.—Shasta Daisy. Flowers to 4" across, blooms in June to July. Plants grow to 2 ft. Likes rich soil, ample watering in summer, full sun. Divide every second year.

C. ULIGINOSUM—Giant Daisy. Good at back of border. White flowers 2"-2½" across, blooms in August to October. Plants grow to 6 ft. Likes leaf mold in soil. Divide every third year.

Coreopsis. Two popular species. C. grandiflora has narrower more finely divided leaves, upper leaves 3 to 5 parted. Grows 2½ ft. tall. C. lanceolata has leaves entire, grows 2 ft. tall. Both have similar floral appearance with showy, golden-yellow flowers 2½" across in profusion during June and July. Double forms available. Will sprawl and spread by self-sown seeds. Likes a medium-heavy, well-drained soil and full sun. Take cuttings in August to maintain named varieties. Excellent for cutting. Cut fully-opened flowers with centers still tight. Condition overnight at room temperature in cold water, almost to flower heads. Use one tablespoon salt to each quart water. Cut flowers frequently to encourage plants to continue bloom. Flowers will last a week or more cut.

Delphinium—Perennial Larkspur. Named varieties must be propagated in spring by cuttings taken from greenhouse-forced potted plants. Like lime, rich, fairly heavy, well-drained soil; cool climate. Divide every third or fourth year. Many hybrids on market. Their lovely towering spires are equally desirable in the garden or in an arrangement. Attractive used with roses in late spring and early summer. Cut when about ½ the flowers on

Divide by hand or use
Knife or spade

Large DELPHINIUM
will make many plants

Make divisions with
two or more stems

a stem are open. Condition overnight in cold water in a room with a temperature of around 50° F. Do not crowd, as flowers bruise easily and become entangled. Place some stems slantwise in conditioning container for curves. Remove individual flowers as they fade. Spikes will last a week as buds continue opening.

D. CHEILANTHUM—Garland Larkspur. Flowers in June and July and once more in September if cut back in early July. Specie from which the Belladonna (to 4 ft. with pale, blue flowers) and Bellamosum (to 5 ft. with deep blue flowers) races have been developed. Less spectacular than the tall hybrids, but with considerable garden value, more truly perennial under adverse climate conditions. Moerheimi is white: These types usually long-lived.

D. CULTORUM. Treated as biennials in warmer climates. Garden forms of hybrid origin often 6' tall or more, flowers 2" across and frequently double. Bloom June to July. Usually short-lived.

D. GRANDIFLORUM—(listed by nurseries as D. chinense). Grows to 3 ft. tall with branching habit, divided leaves, clear gentian-blue flowers. Blooms from June to September. Var. album, white. Short-lived in warm regions. Druysi var. "Pink Sensation," a red delphinium satisfactory only in cold regions.

Dianthus—Garden Pinks. Great variation in hybrids in flowers, foliage and fragrance. Perpetuate named varieties by cuttings or division. Remove flowers as they fade to prevent seeding and lengthen blooming period. Dianthus likes a medium-heavy, well-drained soil and full sun. Cut plants back in September, removing all long growth to help plant winter safely. Divide every second or third year. Cut flowers when ¾ open and recut under cold water, conditioning overnight in water right up to the flower heads. Only remove foliage at base of stem which will come below water line in arrangement. Flowers should last week or more. Excellent particularly in small scale arrangements.

D. CAESIUS PLENUS—Cheddar Pink. Low growing, not over 10", with fragrant rose-pink to red double flowers in May to June. Handsome, glaucous foliage attractive at all times. Forms low mats.

D. DELTOIDES PLENUS—Maiden Pink. Another mat forming kind with almost turflike growth, small, bright double pink flowers freely produced on stems 8" to 15" high in June to July.

D. LATIFOLIUS—Button Pink. These grow to 16" with single or double flowers an inch across with a good range in color from white through pink to crimson-scarlet in June to August. Produced in clusters similar to Sweet William. Divide every second year.

D. PLUMARIS—Cottage, Scotch or Grass Pink. Excellent for cutting. Grows to 18". Leaves bluish-grayish-green. Fragrant flowers white, pink, red or purple; bloom in May to August. Cuttings taken in June or July will stand the winter better than older plants. "Old Spice" is a quite hardy variety.

Dicentra spectabilis—Bleeding Heart. The old-fashioned bleeding heart with delightful rosy-red, or pink and white flower pendants hanging from gracefully arching branches in late spring, May to June. The beautiful early season foliage, during dry weather, becomes shabby in late summer, so needs a companion plant like blue sage or snapdragon to hide its late-season unattractive foliage. A loose, humus soil with good drainage and partial shade are important. Do not disturb once established. Cuttings may be taken as flowers start to fade; root in sand and peat moss. Keep cuttings only moderately moist. Carefully cut sprays when ½ flowers on spray are open. Bruised stems deteriorate quickly. Condition overnight in cold water. Flowers should last five days. Do not take much foliage from young plants, as it is needed to produce strong growth next year. Use other suitable foliage if necessary. Picturesque in arrangements where delightful curved sprays are needed.

Dictamnus albus—Burning-bush, Gas Plant. Grows to 3 ft. Much garden value as an accent when in bloom in June-July. Foliage is excellent all season. White and rose and purple varieties. Likes lime, rich rather heavy soil and full sun. Hardy and long-lived. Once established do not disturb. Cut flowering spikes when ⅓ open. Buds will open in water. Condition overnight in cold water. Spikes will last a week as buds continue to open. Seed pods are attractive in form and color both green or dried, so use them in arrangements, too.

Echinacea purpurea—Purple Cone Flower. Listed by nurserymen as Rudbeckia purpurea. Hardy, likes full sun, fairly rich, deep soil. Grows to 5 ft. Purplish-red, rose or white flower heads 6″ to 7″ across in July-September. Propagate by division in spring. Do not disturb for five or six years. Cuttings must be short, young shoots, cut below soil level, taken in spring. Plant new improved varieties. Will last one to two weeks in cut arrangements. Cut when flowers are completely open but centers still tight. Remove foliage as it wilts.

Echinops—Globe Thistle. Grows 3 to 7 ft. Coarse looking but just right for some arrangements with its globular pale steel to dark blue colored heads in July-August. Coarse but attractive grayish-green leaves with white underneath. Likes full sun, fairly heavy, somewhat alkaline soil. Propagate by seed, root cuttings or division in early spring. Cut when ¼ of globe is covered with open flowers. Buds open in water. Split stems. Condition overnight in cold water. Will last about a week.

Eremurus—Desert-Candle, Foxtail Lily. Spectacular spikes. Stalks 4 to 10 ft. long, carry hundreds of flowers almost size and color of apple blossoms. Flowers come in white, pink and yellow to peach. Varieties bloom from May-July. Plant in September or early spring in sandy loam in sun, good drainage important. Leave undisturbed as long as possible. Seedlings take 4 to 5 years to flower. Good for large scale arrangement. Cut when about ½ flowers on stalk are open.

Euphorbia—Spurge. Two species valuable in perennial borders and also for cutting.

E. COROLLATA—Flowering Spurge. Grows 1 to 3 ft., with umbels of flowers with white appendages that look like petals blooming, resembling gypsophila in appearance, in July-August. Tendency to self-seed and become a weed. May be used cut as a substitute for gypsophila. Cut when ½ stem is in flower. Place in hot water 80°-100° F. to check flow of milky juice. Searing stems is not necessary.

E. EPITHYMOIDES (polychroma)—Yellow or Cushion Spurge. Makes handsome mound one ft. high with umbels of bright yellow, showy flowers and bracts, end of April to May. Likes a well-drained, sandy soil, full sun. May leave undisturbed for many years. Cut when clusters are half open. Sear each stem end in flame counting slowly to fifteen. Then, place in warm water to condition overnight. May be successful placing in hot water at once, not searing. Flowers will last about a week.

Filipendula—Meadowsweet, Dropwort. Formerly included with Spirea. Characterized by its large, feathery panicles of small blooms in bright, deep pink, purplish-pink or white with red stamens. Different varieties grow from 1' to 6'; bloom from June-August. Grows best in good medium soil, full sun, can take some shade. Divide every fourth year.

F. RUBRA, var. venusta. Effective at back of border. Grows to 6 ft. with bright-deep, pink flowers in June-August.

F. PURPUREA (sold as Spirea or F. palmata). Grows to 4 ft. Flowers which bloom in June-July are purplish-pink. Var. elegans very graceful and attractive with white flowers and red stamens.

Some double white forms are excellent both for border and cutting. Cut when ¼ to ½ branch is in bloom. Split stems and condition overnight in warm water, to start with.

Gaillardia aristata (G. grandiflora)—Blanket Flower. Its red and yellow flowers provide color over a long period, blooming from June until frost, if you keep them from seeding by cutting faded flowers. Grayish foliage. Plants grow to 2½ ft. and like full sun, medium-heavy, well-drained loam. Cut back to ground level in September to help plants through winter. Protect lightly with pine branches. Propagate from stem or root cuttings or by division. Divide every third year. Cut blossoms for arrangements when fully open, but with centers still tight. Split stems, remove lower leaves and condition overnight in water using one slightly rounded tablespoon sugar to each quart of water. Fruits are attractive and last well both before and after maturing.

Geum—Avens. Showy blooms and good foliage throughout the growing season, but some varieties may not come through a severe winter in climates more severe than Long Island, New York. In such localities treat as annual, start seeds early indoors. Plants like a medium-heavy, humus soil and slight shade. Protect with pine branches in winter. Divide every second year in spring.

G. CHILOENSE. Most garden varieties are forms of this native of Chile. Frequently listed by nurseries as G. coccineum. Possibly hybrids from both. Named varieties come in colors of red, bright scarlet with yellow stamens, orange-scarlet, rich golden-yellow and coppery orange, $1\frac{1}{2}''$ to $3''$ across in both semi-double and double forms and bloom from June-September. Cut for arrangements when flowers are $\frac{3}{4}$ open. Tight buds will not open in water. Condition overnight in warm water to start with. Flowers should last almost a week.

Gypsophila paniculata—Babys-Breath. Sometimes called Chalkplant because it likes lime, a pH7 or pH5 soil. Variety Bristol Fairy, a double-flowered form, has myriads of small flowers in July and August, in large, loose panicles. May be propagated by cuttings rooted in sand. The double-flowered form of Grepens, var. bodgeri is a pale pink and grows to $1\frac{1}{2}$ ft. tall; attractive. Plants like full sun, a deep, light soil, well-drained. Should not be disturbed once established. Cut sprays when $\frac{1}{2}$ in flower. Condition in cold water overnight. Will last about one week. Excellent dried for winter bouquets. Double forms are best for this purpose.

Helenium autumnale—Sneezeweed. Floriferous group of plants, to 4 ft. tall, blooms in late summer and early fall, related to Sunflowers. Valuable cut. In mahogany, gold and yellow from July-September. All like full sun. Divide every third or fourth year. Cut when petals are open but centers tight. If several blossoms on a stem, cut when clusters are at least $\frac{1}{2}$ open. Remove any unnecessary leaves. Condition overnight starting with water 80°-100° F. Flowers should last a week or more.

Helianthus—Perennial Sunflower. Coarse and too large for a small place. If room permits some varieties have attractive, exotic foliage effects, all bear yellow flowers. Plants like full sun and good drainage. Divide every third year in early spring. For cut arrangements handle like Helenium autumnale.

H. DECAPETALUS FLORE PLENO. Golden-yellow double flowers to 3½" across in July-September. Grows to 4 ft. Excellent for cut flowers.

H. SALICIFOLIUS. Flowers rather small, yellow with purple centers in September-October. Grows to 8 ft., willow-like leaves 12" to 16" long, give plant exotic appearance.

Heliopsis scabre—Ox Eye, Orange Sunflower. Select improved forms. They grow to 3 ft. and bloom in July-September. Coarse plants with large semi-double or double orange-yellow flowers, useful in arrangements. Likes full sun, medium-light soil and lime. Divide every third year. Cut and handle as Helenium autumnale.

Helleborus niger—Christmas or Lenten Rose. Lovely, white flowers 2" across or more from December to March, where weather permits. Grows about 12" tall with evergreen foliage. Cut blossoms keep indefinitely although color fades. Foliage is not good for cutting and it should not be cut anyway, unless plants are very well-established. Substitute a green which can be spared like pachysandra.

H. ORIENTALIS—Blooms March-April; in white to shades of purple or reddish-brown. Both types like partial shade, lime and fairly heavy, well-drained soil. Leave undisturbed as long as possible. Seedlings take four to five years to flower. Split stems of Christmas rose and condition overnight in deep, cold water. This exotic flower is a joy to the arranger at Easter.

Hemerocallis—Day-lily. Many wonderful hybrids on market. Joy of the gardener for they adapt readily to most any condition. Although a bloom lasts only a day, some longer, an individual stalk carries so many blossoms which open in succession that a single stalk may be in flower for weeks. All stalks do not develop at the same time, so a single plant with its graceful, effective foliage may be colorful and lovely for months. Once

Break into several
small sections

Overgrown DAYLILY
before separating

Divisions now ready
for planting

planted, they are satisfactory for many years, although some of the strong-growing kinds may need replanting every three or four years. For cutting, select stems with several well-developed buds, so stems continue to open. Condition overnight in cold water. Arrange informally, so you can easily remove faded blossoms. Subdued light and a cool spot will help blossoms last. Refrigerate sprays to retard opening and they will open at night for an evening party. Creams, yellows, red-oranges, browns, pinks, reds and purples (some nearly black), monochromes, bi-colors and polychromes.

Heuchera sanguinea—Coral-Bells. A tufted plant, with rounded leaves, lightly lobed or toothed with ciliate margins. Has an airy grace with slender 1 to 2 ft. tall stems topped by loose clusters of small, bright-red, pink or white bell-shaped flowers in June-August. Likes sun or partial shade and medium-heavy garden soil. Divide every third year in early spring. Cut when half the spray is in flower. Buds do not open in water. Condition overnight in cold water and for curved stems place slantwise in conditioning container. Excellent delicate, dainty and oriental effects possible.

Hosta (Funkia)—Plantain-Lily. Easy to transplant, but may be left undisturbed for a long time. Divide in early spring. Likes rich soil and partial shade. For cutting, cut when two or three basal flowers are open. Split stems. Condition overnight in cold water almost up to flower heads. Place some stems crosswise in container while conditioning to develop curves. Spikes will last a week with buds continually opening.

Leaves are highly decorative and ornamental in arrangements. To dry, hang hosta leaves several weeks in a dark room. Will take on delightful forms and colors.

H. CAERULEA. Three ft. flower stalks, leaves deep green, flowers lavender-blue, blooms in July-August.

H. FORTUNEI. Two ft. flower stalks, leaves bluish-green, flowers pale lilac, blooms in June-July. Var. gigantea has larger leaves.

H. LANCIFOLIA albo-marginata. Two ft. flower stalks, leaves white margined, narrow and tapering at both ends. Frequently used as an edging plant. Lilac flowers bloom in August-September.

H. SIEBOLDIANA. Large seersucker-like leaves of glaucous, blue-green. Pale lilac flowers in May-June.

H. UNDULATA. $2\frac{1}{2}$ ft. flower stalks, leaves with wavy margin, striped and splashed lengthwise with cream or white. Lavender flowers in July-August. Frequently used for edging.

Kniphofia—(usually offered as Tritoma)—Red Hot Poker-Plant, Torch-Lily. New hybrids can withstand below zero temperatures. Have broad, grass-like leaves up to 3 ft. long. From tuft of foliage stout flower stalks arise with closely packed flowers near the tip. Dense, showy spikes come in colors of coral-red, yellow, cream or white and depending upon the variety will bloom from May to September. Likes full sun and light, sandy soil with good drainage. Leave undisturbed as long as you can. Propagate named varieties in spring by division. Cut when $\frac{1}{4}$ to $\frac{1}{3}$ flowers on spike are open. Split stems and condition overnight in cold water. Place some stems slantwise in conditioning container to bend them into graceful curves, or work stems gently with warm hands to curve. Spikes with green shaded buds, before opening, are excellent in arrangements, if green is wanted. Large flower stalks take up a lot of water, so keep container filled.

Lathyrus. Handsome perennial of the pea group, excellent in shady borders, also good for cutting.

L. LUTEUS. Has yellow to orange flowers in June-August and grows to $2\frac{1}{2}$ ft. tall.

L. VERNUS (Spring Vetchling). Has white, blue-violet or rose-pink flowers in March to May. Both varieties like partial shade and a rich, loose, humus soil. Leave undisturbed for several years. Propagate by division in August or September. Cut when clusters are about ½ in flower. Recut under water at length to be used in final arrangement. Condition overnight using one slightly rounded tablespoon of sugar to each quart of water. Flowers will last a week.

Lavandula officinalis (L. spica) Lavender. Fragrant leaves and fragrant lavender flowers in July and August; of shrubby growth to 2½ ft. tall. Likes full sun and light well-drained soil. Although not hardy in the north, cuttings may be made and rooted in sand, then wintered indoors. Or pot up outdoor plants in fall and winter in a cool room with a sunny window. Cut when ½ flowers on spike are open. Split stems and condition overnight using warm water, to start with. Flowers will last a week or more. For drying, cut flowers when ¾ to fully open. Spread on sheets of newspaper to dry. The flowers will drop from the stems. Stand in can or jar until wanted.

Liatris—Blazing Star. In late summer and early fall, August-September, plants produce dense spikes of purple-rose or white flowers. Like full sun. Propagate named varieties by division in early spring. Leave undisturbed five or six years. One of the best is L. scariosa and vars. Cut spikes when ½ flowers are open.

Limonium (Statice of gardens)—Sea-Lavender. Propagate from seeds sown in spring. Leave plant undisturbed. Likes full sun and sandy loam soil, give some protection in winter (cover with pine branches). Will grow to 1½ ft. Blooms June-September. Purplish-blue flowers with white calyx. For fresh bouquets cut when clusters are half in flower and condition overnight in cold water. Will last a week or more. For dried arrangements cut when ¾ open and hang to dry.

L. LATIFOLIUM. Most commonly grown. Var. album, white; roseum, rose and var. elegantissimum has larger flowers.

Linum—Perennial Flax. Bright blue or yellow flowers in June and July. L. flavum (Golden Flax) grows 12″ to 20″, has bright yellow flowers; also a dwarf variety. L. narbonnense grows to 2 ft. and has blue flowers 1¾" across. Flax likes full sun and a light well-drained soil. Divide every third or fourth year. L. flavum may be raised from cuttings. For cutting, choose stems with a few open flowers. Split woody stems and condition about 24 hours in warm water, to start with. Flowers will last five or six days.

Lobelia. Two species valuable in garden and for cutting.

L. CARDINALIS—Cardinal Flower. Cardinal red flowers produced in spikes the end of July-September. Plants grow to 4 ft. Excellent for shady position, naturalized near stream. In border leave for three years or treat as biennial. Cut for arrangements when ¼ flowering stem is in bloom. Split stems and sear ends in flame while slowly counting to fifteen. Place in warm water, to start with, and condition overnight. Should last about a week.

L. SIPHILITICA—Blue Lobelia. Blue or white flowers in July-September. Plants grow to 3 ft. Hardy and longer-lived than L. cardinalis. Produces many long-stemmed flowers excellent for cutting. Cut when ¼ to ½ flowers on spike are open. Buds will open in water. Split stems, remove lower leaves, condition overnight in deep, cold water. Flowers should keep a week or more. Remove faded flowers as upper buds unfold.

Lupinus polyphyllus—Lupine. Upper ⅔ of flower stalk densely packed with pea-like blooms in almost every imaginable color; self and bicolors; including blue, purple, pink, rose, red, yellow, orange or white. Flowers bloom end of June-August. Grows 3-5 ft. tall. Like full sun and light, sandy, somewhat acid soil. Cut plants back after flowering. Many named English varieties are long-lived and should be left undisturbed once established. Cut when flowering spike is ½ open. Do not cut any more foliage from plant than necessary. Split stems and condition overnight in cold water. Stems will curve only slightly placed slantwise in conditioning container. Flowers will last about a week. Cut buds are apt to drop or shrivel on stem. This may be helped somewhat by spraying flowers with a fine mist of cold water, when you put them aside to condition.

Lychnis. Two hardy kinds good for cutting. Grow in full sun and medium-heavy, well-drained soil. Propagate from cuttings or by division in spring.

L. CHALCEDONICA—Maltese Cross. Scarlet, sometimes white flowers in June-August. Plants 1½-3 ft. tall. Cut when just less than ½ flowers in each cluster are open. Split stems and condition overnight in warm water using one slightly rounded tablespoon sugar to each quart water. Will last about a week, buds continuing to open.

L. CORONARIA—Dusty Miller, Mullein Pink. Rose-purple flowers sometimes white, in June-August. Leaves and stems densely white, wooly. Plants 2 ft. tall. Live only three to five years, but reseed self. Cut when two or three flowers are well open on each stem. Recut as stem ends dry quickly, conditioning overnight, in warm water, to start with. Flowers will last around five days. Leaves decorative and useful if whitish, wooly texture is wanted.

Macleaya cordata—Plume-Poppy. Feathery, pinkish-white flowers in July-August. Plants 6 to 8 ft. Likes sun and a fairly rich, deep soil. Do not disturb plants for five or six years. Propagate by removing suckers with spade in spring. Cut panicles when just less than half open. Split stems, sear ends, to stop flow of yellow juice. Condition in cold water overnight. Will last four days. Remove most of large leaves to show flower heads to advantage. To dry for winter cut panicles when ¾ to fully open. Sear stems, remove leaves and condition flowers overnight for best results. Then hang to dry.

Mertensia virginica—Virginia-Bluebells. Blue flowers fade to pink. Blossom in April-May. Plant dies to ground in summer. This 15″ to 20″ plant prefers partial shade and medium-heavy soil, does not like lime. Propagation best from seed sown in September or cuttings in spring. Leave established plants undisturbed. Attractive with daffodils. Cut when three or four of the nodding blossoms in each cluster are fully open. Split stems and place in 80°-100° F. water, let condition overnight. May need second application of hot water in morning. Flowers last to five days.

Oenothera—Evening Primrose. O. fruticosa and its variety youngi commonly grown in East. A strong, stocky, large-leaved plant with firm, shiny foliage, these free-flowering plants produce numerous bright yellow flowers on stems about 24″ tall from

Many garden shrubs such as mockorange (*Philadelphus*) are excellent in arrangements and should be used more often. Here, single peonies go very well with the single mockorange flowers, creating a unifying bond which would be lost if either of the materials used were double.

Arrangement by Julia S. Berrall   Roche Photo

This is a beautiful arrangement with the double ranunculus predominating in the center.

Arrangement by Mrs. Anson Howe Smith   Zitzo Photo

June to August. Like full sun, medium-heavy, well-drained soil. Propagate from seed or cuttings in spring. Leave plants undisturbed if possible. Foliage and flowers both attractive for cutting if supply is plentiful.

Paeonia—Peony. Popular for years. P. albiflora varieties are the most important and best known; the last of the peonies to bloom and at their best in June. Hardy, with gorgeous flowers, they bloom in some sections around Decoration Day. P. officinalis varieties are among the first to bloom in the spring.

Showy blooms in wide color range and decorative foliage from early spring to fall make them a joy to arrangers. Cut when flowers are less than ½ open and the green covering (sepals) on the buds are separated enough to display the true coloring of the flower. Cut single and Japanese types when blooms are ½ open. Never cut stems way to the ground, leave at least two sets of leaves for the health of the plant. Split stem ends a couple of inches and place in cold water overnight and until buds are as open as you want them. Stored in a cool room or cellar, at 45°-50° F. blooms may be held two or three weeks. Flowers in arrangements should last a week or more. When exhibiting peonies in a class where fragrance is considered, cover blossoms loosely with thin waxpaper or cellophane while conditioning.

Papaver orientale—Oriental Poppy. Contrary to general belief, properly handled flowers will last up to four or five days. Gather in advanced bud stage when petals are ready to unfold. Tight buds will not open. Sear stem ends at length to be used in arrangement in a flame, while slowly counting to fifteen. Condition in deep, cold water overnight. As buds open, drop a little melted wax, same color as petals, inside each blossom at base of petals to delay shattering. Plants grow from 1½ to 3½ ft. tall. Have scarlet, cherry-red, pink or white flowers in May-July. Propagate named varieties from root cuttings in August. Like full sun, medium-heavy, well-drained soil. Die to ground after flowering and start growth again in fall. Leave plants undisturbed.

Penstemon—Beard-Tongue. Beautiful hybrids in many colors grow from 1 to 3 ft. Bloom June-August. Like full sun, fairly rich, well-drained soil and named varieties are propagated from cuttings or by division. Divide every three or four years. Two handsome, long-flowering and easy to grow kinds are: P. digitalis, with pale pink or white flowers and P. diffusus, with flowers gentian-blue. Cut when $\frac{1}{4}$ flowers on stalk have opened. Split stems and condition in water overnight. Develop curved stems by placing slantwise in conditioning container. Will last a week cut.

Phlox. With proper selection it is possible to have some kind of phlox in bloom from early spring until fall. Use P. subulata, the Moss-Pink which blooms in April and May, followed by P. divaricata, Blue Phlox, which blooms in May and June, next P. arendsii with P. carolina flowering in June-August, and in July the long-blooming Garden Phloxes come into the picture and remain until September.

Divide PHLOX every 2 to 4 years

Large clumps may be broken with pitchfork

Allow two or three stems per section

P. CAROLINA. Hardy and persistent. Grows $2\frac{1}{2}$ to $3\frac{1}{2}$ ft. with narrow, shiny leaves. Flowers in June-August.

P. DIVARICATA—Blue Phlox or Wild Sweet William. Likes partial shade. Grows 10″ to 14″. Blooms in May-June. Its hybrids with P. paniculata called arendsii come between parents in blooming period and height.

P. PANICULATA—Garden Phlox. Grows 2-3 ft. tall. Blooms in a wide range of color in July-September. Overhead sprinkling may cause mildew.

P. STOLONIFERA. Prefers alkaline soil and partial shade. Grows to 10″. Flowers in May and June violet-blue or purple. Spreads by runners.

Cut phlox when clusters are $\frac{1}{4}$ to $\frac{1}{2}$ open. Split stems and condition overnight in cold water. Flowers will last week or longer. Cutting encourages a second flowering later in season. Showy and colorful in pink, rose, red, lavender, blue and white, phlox is useful to the arranger all through the flowering season.

Physalis alkekengi—Chinese Lantern. Conspicuous, bright-red inflated calyx of the fruit is used in fall and winter decorations. Plants like lime, full sun, lean stony, well-drained soil and spread by underground runners, so locate where will not interfere with other plants. Divide every third year. Gather when fruits are of a papery texture and a vivid orange. Cut along the veins from tip to base, so pods will curl into interesting shapes. Split a few pods into three or more sections for variety. Remove all foliage. Dry upright, so pods will hang gracefully. When dry, spray with clear plastic if you wish to preserve pods indefinitely. Green pods may be used in fresh or dried arrangements, condition overnight in either case. Green pods have a tendency to shrivel and drop during drying.

Physostegia virginiana—False Dragonhead. Handsome plant for the sunny border or wild garden. Bright pink, rosy-crimson or purplish-crimson flowers borne in terminal spikes or branching racemes from July to October, depending upon variety. Grow from 15″ to 4 ft. tall. Like full sun, fairly rich soil. Divide every second year. Cut spikes for arrangements when flowers on stem are $\frac{1}{2}$ open.

Platycodon grandiflorum—Chinese Balloon or Bell Flower. Broad, blue or white bell-shaped flowers, some semi-double, bloom all summer. Do well in sandy gardens along the seashore. Like full sun. Leave undisturbed once established. Propagate named varieties by division or from cuttings in spring. Cut when two or three flowers on each stem are completely open. The large inflated buds will then open in water. The small tight ones will not. Hold each stem end in flame to check escape of milky juice, or place ends in boiling water for one minute. Then condition in warm water overnight using one slightly rounded tablespoon sugar to each quart water. Should last cut about one week.

Polemonium caeruleum—Jacobs-ladder. Blue sometimes white flowers, one inch across. Blooms in May-June, often again in August-September. Grows two feet tall. Propagate by division or cuttings. Divide plants every third year. Excellent combined with narcissi.

Polygonum—Fleece Flower. Plants spread by underground runners. Should be divided every second year. Like full sun and deep, fairly rich soil.

Cut branches when half in flower. Split stems. Remove some of the leaves and flowers will keep better. Condition overnight in warm water, to start with.

Primula—Primrose. Does best in partial shade, medium-heavy loam enriched with leaf mold and peat moss. Divide plants every second year immediately after flowering.

P. POLYANTHA—The Polyanthus Primrose. Comes in a wide color range blooming in April-June. Grow 10″-12″ tall. Characterized by flowers to $1\frac{1}{2}$″ across in umbels on leafless scapes 9″ to 12″ high. Very beautiful.

P. VULGARIS. English Primrose of literature, similar to Polyanthus, except their flowers seem to be produced on single stems, often nestling among the foliage and cover a wider range of color including blues. First to bloom.

Cut primula when clusters are $\frac{1}{2}$ to $\frac{3}{4}$ open. Be careful not to bruise stems. Condition overnight in warm water, to start with. Flowers should last a week.

Pulmonaria angustifolia—Lungwort. Flowers red, turning blue, Var. azurea has gentian-blue flowers. Blooms April-May; one foot tall. Arrange with narcissi in early spring.

Ranunculus—Buttercup. Double forms are most useful. Bloom in May and June. All like full sun and fairly heavy moist soil. Propagate by division in September. Divide plants every second or third year. Cut when flowers are starting to unfold but centers still tight. Will wilt when first cut but revives quickly when placed in 80°-100° F. water to condition. Use some other kind of foliage as own is insignificant.

Rudbeckia—Coneflower. Excellent cut flower. Plants like full sun, fairly rich, medium-heavy, well-drained soil. Divide plants every second or third year.

Cut when flowers are open but centers are still tight. Condition overnight in cold water. Long lasting cut, from one to two weeks.

Salvia—Sage. Showy in the garden or cut. Flowers borne in spikes, racemes or panicles are very attractive during the summer and autumn months. Require full sun, fairly light well-drained soil. Divide in spring or sow seeds or root cuttings in August.

S. pitcheri (often sold as S. azurea grandiflora) one of best with clear blue flowers in branched spikes during August and September. Plants grow to 4 ft.

Cut for arrangements when half flowers on stem are in bloom. Condition overnight in warm water, to start with.

Scabiosa causasica. Excellent for cutting with large showy blue or white flowers borne on long stems in June-September. Plants grow from $1\frac{1}{2}$ to $2\frac{1}{2}$ ft. Like full sun, medium-heavy well-drained soil. Leave undisturbed as long as possible. Propagate named varieties by division in early spring.

Cut when almost fully open. Buds which are darker than flowers are interesting and will open some in water, but must be well-developed to open fully. Remove unnecessary foliage. Condition overnight with cold water reaching almost to flower heads. When petals fall, interesting green immature seed pods remain. Late in season collect seed pods to dry and use for winter bouquets.

Thalictrum—Meadow-Rue. Has elegant, finely divided columbine or maidenhair-like foliage, most useful with other cut flowers. Rosy-lilac, purple, white or yellow flowers borne in feathery clusters or panicles. Plants do best in fairly rich, well-drained soil. Leave undisturbed for six years or longer. Grow to four ft. tall.

Cut when first buds in cluster are beginning to open. Condition overnight in cold water. Buds will open. The dark green or blue-gray foliage, depending upon the variety, will last two weeks, the flowers a week or more. Excellent as foliage with columbine as much columbine foliage should not be cut from plant. Always condition foliage overnight before using.

Thermopsis caroliniana. Yellow, graceful lupine-like flowers borne in long, terminal spikes in June and July. From 2 to 4 ft. tall. Like full sun and dry, well-drained soil. Spread by underground runners. Remove runners with spade, otherwise do not disturb.

Cut when ⅓ to ½ spike is in flower. Split stems and condition in cold water overnight. Place some stems slantwise in conditioning container and hollow stems will curve slightly. Should last about a week and a half cut.

Tradescantia—Spiderwort. Narrow, purple-veined leaves. Flowers in pure white faintly tinted with violet, enhanced by rich violet-blue, feathery center; also in wonderful blues, cattleya-mauve and brilliant purple; bloom from May until October, depending upon the variety. Grow to 2 ft., like full sun and fairly rich soil. Divide every third or fourth year. Good dwarf varieties on market. Exotic and oriental.

Trollius—Globe Flower. A swamp plant but will thrive in border. Globe-shaped flowers in yellow or orange in May-August, depending upon variety. Plants grow to 2 ft. Do best in full sun and fairly rich humus soil. Raise from seeds.

For most interesting effects cut at different stages, from tight buds to flowers ¾ open. Well-developed buds will open fully in water. Condition overnight in cold water.

Verbascum—Mullein. Tall, stately plants which flower in July-September. Leaves wooly. Yellow, violet, brown or whitish flowers borne in branched spikes. Grow from three to six ft., like full sun and well-drained soil. Short-lived but can make root cuttings.

Cut spikes when flowers are ½ open. Condition overnight with stems in cold water.

Veronica—Speedwell. Flowers tiny but effective because are freely produced on many-flowered spikes, predominantly blue,

The common mullein or velvet plant (*Verbascum thapsus*) is widely naturalized as a weed in N. A. It has long yellow flower spikes and downy leaves, both useful, especially in dried arrangements. Or take up the whole rosette of leaves that form the young plant and use as focal areas.

ARRANGEMENT BY WINIFRED TEELE   GENEREUX PHOTO

A charming spring bouquet using lilac, blue hyacinth, pheasant's eye narcissus and small double narcissus in a Delft crocus pot.

Arrangement by Edna Pennell

Courtesy: Colonial Williamsburg

from June-September, depending upon varieties. Propagate by division in early spring or from cuttings in early summer. Divide plants every third year. Do best in full sun, in any good, well-drained soil. Cut when spikes are half in flower. Buds will open. Condition in warm water overnight. Place some stems crosswise in conditioning container to make curves. Flowers will last four to six days cut.

Viola—Tufted Pansy, Violet, Pansy. Among most beloved flowers. All succeed best in cool climates and like rich, humus soil. Bloom from May to October, depending upon varieties planted. Propagate by division or from cuttings.

Pick when fully opened. Buds do not open in water. Submerge blooms in a large container of cold water for one hour. Will float to top, gently push them down with palm of hand so all flowers become soaking wet. When crisp, remove and gently shake off excess water, place stems in cold water to condition overnight. Flowers will last up to a week. You may want to group and tie together a generous bunch to use as a focal area if you have nothing else important enough.

Violets, both white and blue, may be forced into bloom in the house ahead of their outdoor blooming time. In March, dig up a plant or two from the garden, not disturbing the roots or soil around the roots. Place the plants in an attractive container and set them in a cool, sunny spot in the house. When the plants have stopped blooming, return them to their spot in the garden.

QUESTIONS AND ANSWERS

What annual seeds can I sow outdoors this fall in order to get earlier bloom in the garden next year?

Most annuals which self-sow are hardy and can be sown outdoors in the fall, depending on the section of the country. One precaution is to sow where seeds will not wash away with winter rains and melting snows. Another precaution is not to plant too early in the fall, since the seed might germinate before the ground freezes solidly. For the most part, the following annuals are hardy in most sections of the country, and if sown in the fall will flower weeks ahead of those planted in the spring. Of them, put in sweet peas just before the ground freezes, and cover with compost, straw, marsh hay or other mulch, to be removed in the early spring. Annuals for fall planting: annual poppy, balsam, bachelors-button, calendula, calliopsis, candytuft, cleome, cosmos, California poppy, four-o'clock, gaillardia, larkspur, nigella, petunia, portulaca, sweet pea, nicotiana, snapdragon and sweet alyssum.

5

FLOWERING BULBS, CORMS, RHIZOMES AND TUBERS

SPRING FLOWERING BULBS

Bulbs add interest and beauty to any garden and provide a month or more of early color before perennials, annuals and all but the earliest of shrubs come into bloom. With proper plant companions and in the right setting they are excellent in naturalized plantings. Useful in the small mixed border or in front of a foundation planting around the house, they supply color accents in the early spring. Against a hedge or shrub background a border of tulips edged with pansies creates a colorful spring scene. The smaller bulbs, species and hybrid species of the daffodil and tulip are well suited for rock garden use. Many of the bulbous plants may also be grown as winter house plants for decorating the home. Invaluable as cut flowers in early spring, the arranger combines them with forced flowering and evergreen branches to extend their cheerful, bright colors, using them sparingly, leaving plenty uncut in the garden for outdoor color.

Do not cut the foliage of flowering bulbs as it must be left, kept healthy and growing after the flowers have been cut, to produce good blooms the next year. It is during the period when the foliage is maturing that the bulb stores up nourishment and when next year's flowers are formed. Properly grown, the bulbs have stored within them all the necessary ingredients to produce roots, leaves and flowers. Nothing you do between the time of

FLOWERING BULGS

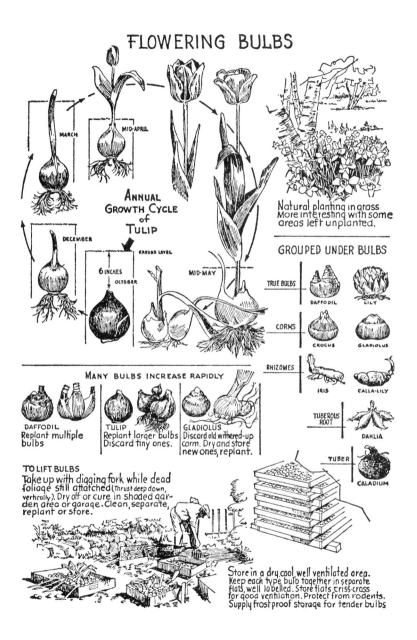

ANNUAL GROWTH CYCLE of TULIP

MARCH

MID-APRIL

DECEMBER

GROUND LEVEL

6 INCHES

OCTOBER

MID-MAY

Natural planting in grass. More interesting with some areas left unplanted.

GROUPED UNDER BULBS

TRUE BULBS	DAFFODIL	LILY
CORMS	CROCUS	GLADIOLUS
RHIZOMES	IRIS	CALLA-LILY
TUBEROUS ROOT		DAHLIA
TUBER		CALADIUM

MANY BULBS INCREASE RAPIDLY

DAFFODIL
Replant multiple bulbs

TULIP
Replant larger bulbs. Discard tiny ones.

GLADIOLUS
Discard old withered-up corm. Dry and store new ones, replant.

TO LIFT BULBS
Take up with digging fork while dead foliage still attached (Thrust deep down, vertically). Dry off or cure in shaded garden area or garage. Clean, separate, replant or store.

Store in a dry, cool, well ventilated area. Keep each type bulb together in separate flats, well labelled. Store flats criss-cross for good ventilation. Protect from rodents. Supply frost proof storage for tender bulbs

planting the bulbs until their blooming will increase the number of flowers they produce; but good soil and good growing conditions will improve the size and quality of the flowers.

PLANTING AND CULTURAL REQUIREMENTS

Dormant bulbs are available at flower shops, seed stores, garden centers and other retail outlets in September and later. Buy good bulbs from a reliable dealer. Open the bags as soon as they arrive and either plant or store in a cool, dry, airy place until planting time. Beware of damp cellars in storing bulbs.

DEPTH: Prepare a good well-drained garden soil deep enough for the roots. The depth will vary with the type bulb, but as a rule, plant large bulbs, those two inches or more at their greatest diameter, two to three times their diameter in depth and for distance apart, one and a half to two times their planting depth. Plant small bulbs, those less than two inches in diameter, three to four times their diameter in depth and for distance apart, two to three times their depth. Measure depth from top of bulbs to top of soil.

PLANTING: Place the bulbs on top of the ground, each variety in its proper location, so you can visualize the finished design. Then, dig the hole with a trowel for each grouping, placing the bulbs at the bottom and filling soil over them. Most bulbs do best in full sun. Many bloom before the deciduous trees and shrubs have leafed out to shade them. There is a difference between high and low shade. High shade will frequently let in sufficient light and sun. Although the hardy bulbs can take cold temperatures those planted on the sunny side of the house and protected from northern winds and driving early spring rains will bloom sooner and early bloom is what you want.

Crocus. One of the best known and earliest of the spring bulbs to bloom. The yellow varieties are popular planted with blue Scillas for contrast. Do not plant in the lawn as the lawn mower will cut the foliage. Plant at the edge of the border, around trees or fronting shrubbery, on the edge of a woodland or where grass does not need to be cut.

For arrangements, cut in advanced bud stage when color is freely showing. Condition overnight in cold water. In the morning, when open, a little melted candle wax, the color of the flowers, dropped inside the base of the cup will retard dropping of petals. In arranging, allow plenty of room to display the full beauty of the open blossom, which should last four to six days cut. You may lift the flowering bulbs with a generous supply of soil and plant in a low container for an indoor arrangement and then replant outdoors when through flowering.

CULTURAL REQUIREMENTS

Plant corms in clumps for effective display, one or preferably two dozen, four inches deep to the top of the bulb and three to four inches apart. Prefer soil a little on the sandy side and full sun. Their earliness depends largely upon their position, so select a sheltered location when practical, south of the house and protected from north winds.

VARIETIES

The spring-blooming varieties are well known but there are also many varieties that bloom in autumn, in September and October. Most of these are more suitable for the rock garden, but some may be planted under shrubbery or in the front of the flower border. Some spring-flowering species are: C. aureus—an orange-yellow, C. aureus sulphureus concolor—a fine, pale yellow, rich in color, C. sieberi—a good free flowering, lilac-blue with a golden throat, C. susianus (Cloth-of-Gold) early and a golden yellow with outside bronze and C. tomasinianus which is pale lavender-blue, very lovely and free flowering. The best known species for autumn are C. sativus, speciosus and zonatus.

Hyacinth. Attractive for its fragrance, planted informally in small irregular groups at the front of a mixed border, against green shrubs or around a pool. Hyacinths also make attractive cut flowers. Will last three to six days. Cut when nearly fully open and place in cold water overnight. A Twistem tied around the stem will hold it together and makes arranging easier. If hyacinths wilt prematurely, dip stem ends in boiling water for one minute, then put in cold water and condition overnight. To hold fragrance loosely enclose flower heads in thin wax paper while conditioning.

CULTURAL REQUIREMENTS

With the exception of the French Roman Hyacinths they are reliably hardy. Hyacinths prefer a rather light, well-drained soil, with peat moss to hold moisture; full sun. Plant in late September or early October four inches to six inches deep from the top of the bulb, depending on its size. Plant six inches to eight inches apart. Water as moisture is needed to help the bulb get a root system started before freezing. Hyacinth bulbs deteriorate year after year and the flowers get smaller with each succeeding year so discard bulbs after several years.

VARIETIES

There are many varieties in good, clear colors. Good whites include L'Innocence and Edelweiss. Delft Blue and Myosotis are good light blues and Ivanhoe and King of the Blues excellent dark blue varieties. Gertrude, Lady Derby, Marconi and Princess Margaret excellent pinks. Cyclops and La Victoire are good reds. City of Haarlem is a favorite yellow.

Muscari—Grape Hyacinth. Long-lasting and self-sows. Useful in rock gardens or to plant under early blooming shrubs and trees where they make interesting contrasts. M. botryoides is the good blue commonly seen. The species M. armeniacum is choice and a deeper blue, also fragrant, an excellent companion for daffodils.

In arrangements, for long stems, gently pull, do not cut, little spires from plant, being careful not to uproot it. Pull when $\frac{1}{3}$ stem is in flower. Place stems in cold water overnight. To get interesting curves place stems in ice water at the start. Flower stalks will last three to six days. The Grape Hyacinth will thrive in almost any well-drained soil in light shade or sun. Sometimes they form clumps of foliage in the fall.

Narcissus—Daffodil. The English name Daffodil is now accepted as the common name for all species and varieties of the genus Narcissus. The term Jonquil is correctly used for one very fragrant small group, N. jonquilla and its varieties and hybrids. The narcissus or daffodil is characterized by its long, narrow, rush-like foliage and bright yellow color. The larger kinds are good for

The birch branches, with their unfolding of the pale green foliage and delicately hanging catkins, combine nicely with the spring-flowering bulbs to make a pleasing design. In conditioning the branches split the stem ends vertically two to three inches with a sharp knife so they will take up water more readily.

ARRANGEMENT BY RUTH MERRY   GENEREUX PHOTO

Spring-flowering branches are invaluable to the arranger for use with daffodils. Bulb foliage should not be cut but left to ripen and nourish next year's crop. This foliage is not missed with the use of suitable flowering branches and broad leaved evergreens.

ARRANGEMENT BY MARIE COOK   GENEREUX PHOTO

borders or planting under shrubs. Those with small cups are especially valuable for naturalizing on the edge of the woods or in meadows. They like high shade. The small wild species and types are excellent in rock gardens.

Invaluable to the arranger for use with spring-flowering branches and to add color to evergreens since they come when cut flowers are scarce. Cut blossoms when they are newly opened unless you want to hold over for Flower Show purposes. Then cut buds as they are just opening and hold in a refrigerator at around 48° F. or store in a cool, dark room. Some varieties, cut when buds are just opening, will hold two weeks. Remove fallen pollen from throat of show flowers with a soft brush. Wet brush to remove dust spots or moisture blemishes. Do not cut foliage which is necessary to nourish next year's crop if you value your bulbs. Split stems and hold cut ends in hot water for a minute to check flow of sticky juice. Condition overnight with stems in cold water, 3″ or 4″ above split in stem. Open flowers normally last four or five days.

CULTURAL REQUIREMENTS

Daffodils like a rather light, sandy soil with some humus. Plant in early fall. Generally 4 to 5 inches of soil is sufficient depth to cover the bulbs. Plant 6″ apart each way. Daffodils improve and multiply if properly handled. If planted in a cultivated area, they should be lifted every three or four years because as they multiply and become overcrowded they develop mostly foliage. Never cut the foliage and always let it ripen thoroughly. Take the bulbs up in early July after the foliage is thoroughly ripened when the multiple bulbs, which have formed, will come apart easily with a little gentle pressure. Don't injure the root plate by carelessly pulling them apart. Plant outdoors at once or store in a cool, airy place until fall. Will bloom the following spring. Daffodils planted in the grass in a naturalistic setting, held tightly in place by the sod, seldom need to be taken up.

CLASSIFICATION AND VARIETIES

The trumpet is the part of the daffodil that stands out at right angles to the perianth, the six generally overlapping petals at the base of the flower head. The term trumpet is used if it is as

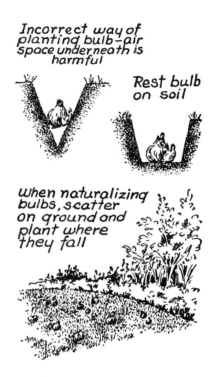

Incorrect way of planting bulb–air space underneath is harmful

Rest bulb on soil

When naturalizing bulbs, scatter on ground and plant where they fall

long or longer than the petals of the perianth. When shorter than the petals of the perianth it is called the "cup," when very small the "eye." With some species and varieties flowers are borne more than one on a stem and called "bunch-flowered," Paper Whites are a good example. We have listed varieties under their classification.

TRUMPETS include yellow, white and bicolor types. Dominator, Grape Fruit, King Alfred and Unsurpassable are yellow trumpets. White is represented by Broughshane, Beersheba and Mount Hood. Bicolor includes Trousseau with white perianth and soft yellow trumpet turning rich buff, rosy-cream as flowers age; President Lebrun with white perianth, and creamy-yellow trumpet.

LARGE CUPPED includes yellow and white perianths, both with colored cups, and all whites. Sun Chariot is yellow with an orange-red cup and Aranjuez is yellow, with a deep orange-red cup. Duke Windsor is white with an apricot-orange ruffled cup turning pale yellow as flower ages; Brunswick a white with an icy-white cup at the base, gradually shading to lemon at the brim; Dick Wellband is a white with a flame-orange cup; Jules Verne is a good example of an all white trumpet.

SMALL CUPPED includes yellow and white perianths, both with colored cups, and all whites. Chungking is a yellow with deep vivid-red cup. Crenver a white with a yellow eye edged red. Kansas is a white with lemon-yellow cup edged with cinnamon. Chinese White is a good all white small cupped.

DOUBLE VARIETIES: Numerous and lovely represented by Daphne, Golden Castle, a deep golden yellow; Golden Ducat, another yellow and Mary Copeland with creamy-white petals, center interspersed lemon or brilliant orange-red.

TRIANDRUS and hybrids: This group is later blooming. Thalia a good example is called the Orchid-flowered daffodil, produces pure white flowers.

CYCLAMINEUS and hybrids: This group is early. February Gold a lovely golden-yellow and Beryl with graceful drooping flowers, slightly reflexed, pale-primrose perianth and yellow cup edged brick red, ably represent this group.

JONQUILLA and hybrids: The single sweet scented Jonquilla with its dainty heads of small rich golden-yellow and fragrant, flowers valued for cutting. Golden Perfection is one of the largest varieties in this group, a clear yellow.

TAZETTA and hybrids: Includes the Poetaz Narcissi, Bunch-Flowered group. Good varieties include Geranium with white petals and bright orange-scarlet cup, effective late flowering variety. Scarlet Gem has primrose-yellow perianth and orange-scarlet cup; St. Agnes a large white perianth with brilliant deep red eye.

POETICUS NARCISSI or Poets have a white perianth and eye edged red or orange. Actaea is the largest in this group, with an eye margined with dark red. Sweetly scented, Queen of Narcissi has a yellow eye edged bright red.

There are many miniatures and species excellent for the small rock garden. In choosing varieties select from the earliest, middle and latest blooming kinds for a long blooming period from April into June in New England. There is sufficient variety to cover a wide form and size range.

Tulips. Offer a wide range in form, size and blooming period as well as color for the mixed border. Excellent for both color in the garden and for cutting, they bloom with spring-flowering trees, shrubs and vines, mostly in May and June along with perennials like columbine, iris, peonies and phlox.

Plant several varieties of tulips in colors which harmonize with each other and with the perennial border, in small clumps or long narrow drifts among other plants, so their ripening foliage will be easily covered by neighboring companions. If grouped in large masses, plan to have pot grown, shallow-rooted annuals like ageratum, asters and snapdragons ready to fill in the bare spaces. Always use tulips in large enough groups to be effective, planting in drifts of harmonious colors, combining lavenders, blue-violets and purples accented with smaller groups of warm pinks or soft yellows. Repeat the groupings in the border for balance and unity at least twice. In semi-shaded areas a touch of strong color is good, using related yellows and orange with white for contrast.

For arrangements, cut tulips in advanced bud stage. They open quickly. Should last about a week conditioned properly. Wrap 12 or so in a piece of wet newspaper, placing the bundle in a tall container of cold water reaching almost to the flower heads. Leave overnight. The paper should reach into the water so it will remain wet up to the very top. Buds may touch as this helps prevent them from opening and petals are less likely to drop conditioned in this manner. Drop melted candle wax, same color as tulip, into the cup where petals are joined, to hold petals at stage you want flower, also to encourage petals from dropping. Since tulips always turn toward the light after they have been cut and arranged if you must have an exact placement you may run a florist's wire through each stem until it reaches the base of the flower to hold it in position. Use weak-stemmed tulips in low arrangements.

CULTURAL REQUIREMENTS

Plant bulbs in late fall in medium, light loam at a depth of 6"
measured from the top of the bulb. Chances are your tulips will
be better the first spring after planting than they ever will be
again. Yet the bulbs should give you good flowers for several
years.

Generally speaking, for best results tulips should be lifted
every season, in late June, even before the foliage has thoroughly
ripened, otherwise they are difficult to find. Dig them up while
there are still withering leaves attached. Shake off any excess
soil. Put in a shady place until the foliage is thoroughly dried,
dry off bulbs and remove any old scales. The tulip bulbs will
simply fall apart as you remove the scales that encase them. The
bulbs split into several but only the larger ones are worth planting. Discard the tiny ones. Replant outdoors or store in a cool,
airy place until fall.

CLASSIFICATION AND VARIETIES

Early Sorts. Cover a three to four week blooming period.

SPECIES AND SPECIES HYBRIDS: Bloom ahead or with daffodils.
Short-stemmed and bright in color. Long-lasting and do not "run
out" quickly, so excellent for naturalizing. Vary in height from
6"-15". Space 5"-6" apart. Kaufmanniana, a soft creamy-white
with center slightly marked with carmine-red, blooms in April
and has long been a favorite in this group.

SINGLE EARLY: Flower next, in May. Good to grow indoors. Many
fragrant. Grow from 10"-16". Can take exposed positions. Stiff
stems, brilliant coloring. Excellent planted informally, in masses
of one variety. De Wet is a splendid, sweetly scented orange.

DOUBLE EARLIES: Similar to single. Flowers longer lasting both in
garden and cut. Equally desirable for indoor forcing. Murillo,
a very delicate rose flushed white is one of the loveliest.

TRIUMPHS AND MENDELS: Cross between Early Singles and Darwins. Ten days earlier than Darwins. Taller and larger flowered
than Early Singles, from 20"-24". Good for forcing. Stiffer, more
upright stems and longer lasting flowers than Single Early. Tri-

umphs include Bruno Walter, a deep brownish-orange, outside faintly flushed purple; Elmus a warm cherry red, deeply edged pure white with pure white base and Pax a very good white. Good Mendels are Her Grace, a lovely white, widely edged deep pink and Orange Wonder, orange-red with slightly waved petals.

PEONY-FLOWERED OR LATE DOUBLES: Really double Triumphs. Bloom with earlier Darwins. Rainy weather will bow them down. Two excellent varieties are Eros, a clear old rose color, one of the best doubles, and Mount Tacoma, which resembles a large double white Chinese Peony and lasts a long time in water when cut.

Late Flowering. The most spectacular of the tulip show includes the May-flowering Cottage, Darwin and Breeder groups.

COTTAGE: Easier to handle in arrangements than the Breeders or Darwins. Many tones and tints of yellow and orange but no purples, lavenders or bronzes. Flowers have long, pointed petals in clear, brilliant colors. Long flexible stems. Excellent cottage varieties include Advance, an orange-scarlet overlaid with a dusky shade; Carrara, pure white with yellow anthers; Golden Harvest, a golden-yellow; Mrs. John T. Sheepers, a superior yellow and Rosy Wings, salmon-pink changing to delicate yet lively pink.

DARWIN: Color range from pure white through deep shades to near black, often with strongly contrasting centers. Huge flowers are globular. Stems long and slender. Excellent in formal plantings. Some of the better Darwins include Ace of Spades, deep blackish maroon; Aristocrat, soft purplish violet-rose, with lighter edge; Blue Aimable, lilac-mauve shaded purple with bright blue base, excellent with yellow carpeting plants; Charles Needham, a brilliant red; Eclipse, crimson-maroon with steel-blue base; Glacier, a pure white; Golden Age, a deep buttercup yellow, faintly suffused with soft orange; Pride of Zwanenburg, a vivid salmon-pink; Smiling Queen, a choice pink with flush of delicate rose-pink on outer petals; General Eisenhower, a scarlet and Holland's Glory, another scarlet.

BREEDER: Usually bicolored in rich Rembrandt tones of bronze, brown, purple and terra cotta, often with a decided "bloom."

Substantial cup-shaped flowers. Stems very upright, stout and stiff.

Among the Breeders we like Indian Chief, a reddish-mahogany flushed with purple; Louis XIV, a rich purple flushed golden-bronze at margin of petals with an inside bronze shading to bronzy-purple and lilac and Tantalus, pale silvery yellow, shaded dull violet, base dark yellow with black anthers.

LILY-FLOWERED: Similar to Cottage with long, pointed recurving petals; becoming increasingly popular both for garden use and liked by arrangers for cutting. Includes the lovely varieties Golden Duchess, a deep golden yellow; Mariette, a salmon-pink and White Triumphator, a very fine pure white.

PARROTS: Really strays with characteristics distinctive from other classes. Sports from well-known garden varieties with laciniated, more or less twisted petals, often with green markings. The stems assume informal curves. Liked by arrangers used either alone or with other plant material for exotic effects. Include such popular varieties as the glossy maroon-black, Black Parrot; Blue Parrot, bluish-heliotrope, flushed steel-blue; Fantasy, soft rose with faint stripes and featherings of apple-green on its outer petals and Ivory Parrot, an ivory white, with large yellow base.

SUMMER FLOWERING BULBS

In this group we are including the caladium, canna, gladiolus, iris, leucojum, lily, lycoris and tuberous begonia, since all furnish valuable cutting material for the arranger.

Alstroemeria. A tuberous rooted plant with showy purple, red or yellow flaring tubular blossoms borne in terminal umbels on leafy stems during spring and summer. Grows 3' tall. May be planted out in garden in spring and lifted after blooming, bulbs stored through the winter or grown in greenhouse as pot plant for spring bloom; lift and shake out annually. A. aurantiaca known as Peruvian-lily often grown outdoors. A. pelergrina and var. alba are good for pot culture. Free drainage is essential, plant does not like direct sunshine, divide roots each fall as they multiply rapidly. Keep pots in house or sink in garden as desired. After through blooming keep on dry side until March. Support stems with a stake as necessary.

Caladium. Grown for magnificent foliage in an endless variety of lovely colors. Although a tender tuber and grown as a house plant in the winter, in recent years it has been grown outdoors in the north during the summer months with marked success. Colorful as any flowering plant it is excellent where color is needed in partially shaded places. The arrow-shaped leaves are thin and delicate but large, forming masses of color. The flowers are unimportant.

Treasured by arrangers, the leaves should be chosen when of the right size and with sturdy stems. Split the stems and condition overnight in cold water. If the leaves seem soft, submerge them in cold water for about $\frac{1}{2}$ hour or until crisp, before conditioning. After conditioning, to prevent curling, spray underside of leaves with a clear plastic. Cut foliage should last a couple of weeks or more.

CULTURAL REQUIREMENTS

When danger of frost is past, plant dormant tubers in a good, well-drained garden soil to which a sprinkling of bone meal has been added. Plant 2″ to 3″ deep from top of tuber, placing in a semi-shaded bed. Keep well watered. In the fall as they start to become dormant reduce watering, bring the tubers in before frost and let them dry thoroughly. Store until spring when they may be planted out again.

VARIETIES

Some varieties are suited for summer outdoor culture while others should be used for winter house plants. Following are some varieties good for the flower border and for cutting.

CANDIDUM is a favorite variety, compact, snowy white mottled in green. The fancy variegated sorts are at their best as the stronger summer sunlight brings out their colors to full intensity. We also recommend Macahyda, a large pink and white, Attala of medium height, blotched light pink with crimson veins on a deep green background, Jessie M. Thayer a robust flushed pink and white with red veins, Mrs. W. B. Haldeman a good grower with red and cream markings on a green background and John Peed with medium, round leaves, red center and veins. Excellent reds are Madame Truall with large leaves, deep purplish-red with redder ribs, edges bronze-green and Rising Sun. A good white is Marie Moir a hardy, white with green veins, greenish-white margin and blood-red spots. Our Red is a transparent, fine reddish-rose sort. E. O. Orpet is an excellent dwarf, red with dark green. General W. B. Haldeman is a good grower with red and cream markings on a green background. Rio Janeiro is a transparent pink with narrow green margin, dotted pink. Silver Cloud has pure white leaves with red veins. Triumphe De Exposition has a red center, scarlet ribs and a green background, Mrs. Sophie Nehrling has a white center, red veins and sinus, mottled green.

Canna, Cannaceae. A Victorian plant coming back into favor because of the many new fine hybrids compact in growth, with pastel shades and good new dwarf varieties. In buying Canna roots or rhizomes choose named varieties with bronze or green leaves of a height to suit your needs. They grow from $2\frac{1}{2}$ to 8 ft. in height. Use in the flower border or plant in tubs for terrace decoration. Also excellent for cutting used in large scale arrangements. Cut when first two flowers are open. Buds develop after cutting. Submerge flowers and stems until all parts are crisp. Split stems and condition in cold water overnight. The reddish-green, green or bronze foliage is long lasting and excellent for large scale arrangements. Split stems of foliage, submerge in cold water for half hour, then condition in cold water overnight. Will last a couple of weeks. Flowers last two or three days but buds continue to open.

CULTURAL REQUIREMENTS

Start rhizomes indoors, horizontally, about a month before planting outdoors or plant outdoors after danger of frost is past. Plant abut 4″ deep in rich soil, $1\frac{1}{2}$ to 2 ft. apart, with plenty of moisture and full sun. When frost darkens foliage in fall, cut to within 6″ of root, dig rhizomes, dry off, store upside down in a cool (50°-60° F.) place. Divide rhizomes in March, leaving several

124

eyes on each. Start in flats of soil and peatmoss again in early spring.

VARIETIES

It is possible to buy either dormant roots or growing plants in pots. There is a Grand Opera Series with extra large flowers in pastel shades on the market with such varieties as Aida, La Boheme, La Traviata, Mme. Butterfly, Rigoletto, etc. Green-leaved varieties include Gaiety with orange-yellow margins, President a red and R. Wallace a canary-yellow. Bronze-leaved varieties include America, a dark red, Apricot, Eureka a white, Mrs. Alfred Conard a salmon-pink, Tyrol a pink and Wyoming a yellow-bronze.

Iris. There are upwards of 200 iris species and many garden varieties. One of the most important plants for the perennial garden and for cutting because of their beauty, adaptability and long-blooming period from April until mid-July, even September and October. The main blooming season however, is in late May and early June, after the tulips and before the peonies and roses. Differing widely in both plant and flower form, varying in height from 4″ to 42″, the iris exhibits a striking range of color including white, blue, brown, red, orange, yellow, green as well as various tones and blends.

For arrangements cut bearded iris when the first bud is ready to unfold. It will be fully open by morning. Buds lower on the stem will open somewhat smaller and paler indoors but they are still beautiful. Fully-opened blooms damage easily in wind, rain or from insects, so advantageous to cut in bud stage. Iris blossoms cannot take a sudden change in temperature, so never place cut iris in cold storage. The clever arranger can do many interesting and varied arrangements with iris and iris foliage, oriental and exotic in feeling. Iris seed pods are useful in arrangements too.

CULTURAL REQUIREMENTS

Sometimes, if left undisturbed iris will bloom over a long period of time, but more often they should be divided at the end of four or five years directly after flowering. Plant in full sun.

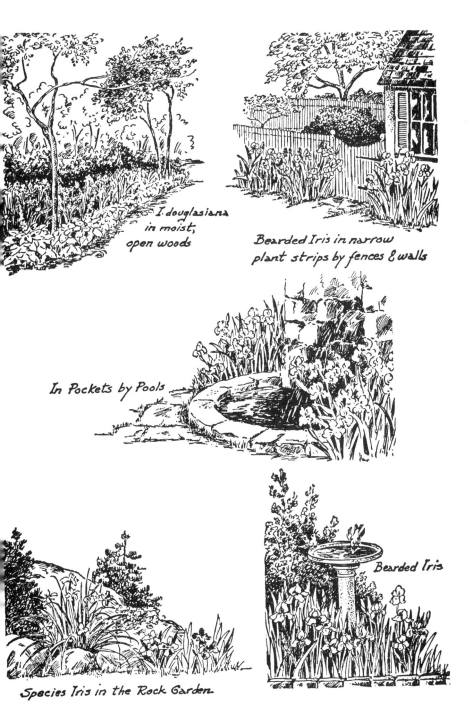

I. douglasiana in moist, open woods

Bearded Iris in narrow plant strips by fences & walls

In Pockets by Pools

Species Iris in the Rock Garden

Bearded Iris

Shallow planting is advised, so sun and air can reach the rhizomes. Plant 8″ to 18″ apart in early spring. Not fussy as to soil but it should be thoroughly dug and pulverized 18″ to 24″ deep and well-drained. Avoid nitrogen, but lime and potash is advisable, bonemeal is excellent. Use four or five pounds bonemeal to 100 sq. ft. Perhaps sufficient until division is necessary. Remove dead blossoms. In fall cut leaves close to roots.

There are two main divisions, those which grow from rhizomes and those which grow from bulbs, the latter are mostly early spring-flowering and include the Dutch, English and Spanish Iris. The more important and larger group of rhizomatous kinds are divided into the Bearded, Beardless, Crested and Pardanthopsis and these four groups are again subdivided. For our purpose we are mainly interested in the Bearded, which is divided into three groups: the Dwarfs, the Intermediates and the Tall Bearded.

Bearded Iris:

DWARFS: Earliest and first to bloom; 3″-12″ tall; flowers in white, blue, lavender, purple and yellow in early May. Transplant just after they have bloomed. Excellent in miniature bouquets.

INTERMEDIATES: Come about two weeks after the Dwarfs, 12″-18″ tall and in a wide range of color and form. Cross between Dwarfs and Tall Bearded with in between blooming period and height. Some Intermediates have a tendency to flower again in September and October.

TALL BEARDED: Bloom toward end of May, make up bulk of garden iris. Grow from 18″-42″ tall, indescribable beauty and color range.

Beardless Iris:

JAPANESE IRIS (I. kaempferi): Blooms in July. Likes a sunny location, but will thrive in shade, likes somewhat acid soil pH5.5 to 6.5. Best forms spectacular, 3½ ft. tall, flowers almost a foot across, with the petals 3, 6 or 9 held almost horizontally, so one should look down into them. Flowers in white, lavender, deep purple, blue, lavender-pink and every shade between.

SIBERIAN IRIS (I. sibirica): Tall, slender, wiry stems, with profusion of flat, open flowers rising above slender grass-like foliage. Blooms with the last of the late Bearded Iris, in early June. Grow 2'-4' tall. Come in white and various shades of blue. Divide when clumps become too large.

Ismene—Peruvian Daffodil. Spider Lily. Exotic, slightly fragrant large white flowers, a showy summer bloomer. Hybrids in yellow too. Handsome glossy green, flat foliage decorative in arrangements. Propagation by offsets. Bulbs will bloom year after year. Tender bulb but can grow outdoors in garden or pots after danger of frost and bring in house for decoration. Handle as you do gladiolus, digging up bulbs in fall.

Leucojum—Snowflake. Follow the Snowdrops in blooming. Similar but larger and taller. The Spring Snowflake (L. vernum) has drooping bell-like flowers, tipped with green. Grows to 12". The Summer Snowflake (L. aestivum) blooms in May and grows from 12"-18" tall. Plant about 3" deep. Useful for border planting and rock gardens. Also may be cut. Cut when $\frac{1}{2}$ flowers are open. Excellent for use in small scaled arrangement.

Lily. True aristocrat of the garden with graceful beauty, varied form and color; lilies are excellent for cutting. Their showy forms and sculptured quality make them an excellent "center of interest" flower.

For the garden, group lilies in clumps for most effective displays. Since some lilies have very few leaves on the lower part of their stems it is well to place them among plants with luxuriant foliage to enhance their appearance. Openings may be left in the shrub borders for plantings of lilies or in a wide border taller plants with good foliage, like Aconitum (Monkshood) and Echinops (Globe Thistle) may be planted to the rear with shorter growing plants, like Veronica, Salvia farinacea, Gypsophylla or ferns, placed in front. Thalictrum (Meadow-rue) which grows from 3 to 4 ft. and has dark green or blue-gray foliage, depending upon the variety, which resembles the foliage of Columbine, makes an attractive companion around a planting of lilies. Select dwarf varieties of Thalictrum to use with the smaller growing lily types.

When cutting lilies for arrangements, select clusters with two flowers on each stem, open. Cut lilies should last about a week. Buds will continue to unfold. In recurved types cut after petals begin to turn back. Split the stems and condition overnight. Arrangers differ on whether to remove the ripe anthers from the stamens. Some feel this detracts from the natural beauty of the flower. Others prefer to keep furniture and the inside of the flower trumpet clean and free from the smear of falling pollen. Your preference must decide what you will do. Never cut over $\frac{1}{2}$ of the leaves with the flower stem. Enough leaves must be left to nourish the bulb properly for the balance of the season, so the plant will be able to flower the following year.

CULTURAL REQUIREMENTS

Plant bulbs in early fall because that gives ample opportunity for them to become established before spring growth starts. The proper planting depth will vary with the species and size bulb. As a general rule set them three times their depth. Use a well-drained, good garden soil in an open but protected area, light shade is preferred to full sun. Allow at least 12 inches between tall growing kinds and 6″ to 8″ for the smaller ones. Provide a mulch of leaves or pine needles after the ground freezes.

Although all lilies can be grown from seed some named hybrids and varieties do not come true. To grow some takes six or seven years for the first bloom to appear. There is a group however, that can be grown easily from seed and expected to flower in two or three years after sown. Sow in flats indoors in early January or sow outdoors as soon as the ground can be worked in the spring. Plant in a slightly shaded spot if possible until two or three leaves appear. Use a soil $\frac{1}{3}$ sand, $\frac{1}{3}$ leaf mold and $\frac{1}{3}$ good garden loam. Cover seeds with 1″ of soil outdoors. A sprinkling of sand over this will prevent the soil from drying out quickly. Indoors a light covering of sand is all that is necessary over the seeds. L. formosanum, L. henryi, L. longiflorum,

L. regale and L. tenuifolium are some that will bloom in two or three years from seed. Unless you are a real gardener buy the bulbs.

Fifteen Popular Lily Species

Consult your catalogs to see the hundreds of new improved hybrids which have been developed from these species.

L. AURATUM: The Goldband Lily of Japan is both heavily fragrant and showy with yellow bands and reddish markings on waxy-white petals, grows 3′ to 6′ tall, blooms in July and August. Set bulbs 9″ to 12″ deep, depending upon size of bulb.

L. CANADENSE: The dainty Meadow Lily ranges in color from light yellow to orange-red with purplish spots on the inner side of each drooping trumpet. Grows 2′ to 4′ high and blooms in June and July. Set 8″ deep.

L. CANDIDUM: The Madonna Lily is cherished for its pure white fragrant blooms. Flowers with delphiniums and roses in June and early July. Grows 3′ to 4′ tall. Established bulbs produce 6 or more blooms on a stem. Sends forth a growth of foliage in the fall so plant in late summer, setting bulbs 4″ deep.

L. DAURICUM: Candlestick or Orange-man's Lily will flourish with little care. Mostly showy yellow, orange and red blooms held erect on 1 to 2 feet tall stems. Likes full sun. Set bulbs 4″ to 6″ deep. Numerous excellent varieties.

L. ELEGANS (thunbergianum): A dwarf species in which the orange-red flowers with purple-black spots are held erect.

L. FORMOSANUM: This fragrant, large white nodding trumpet-shaped lily is often marked on outer side with purple. Blooms are borne in clusters on sturdy stems. Free flowering, easy to grow. Some that bloom in late summer and early fall grow to 6 ft. Early summer-flowering kinds seldom grow more than 2 ft. May raise from seed getting bulbs of blooming size second year. Set mature bulbs 8″ deep.

L. HANSONI. Gay orange-yellow drooping flowers with reflex petals and purplish-brown spots. Blooms late in May or June. Grows 2 to 5 ft. Set bulbs 6″ to 8″ deep.

L. HENRYI. Tall, robust species with lemon to golden-orange re-flexed blossoms, borne in late July and August on slender arch-ing stems 4 to 6 ft. Set the bulbs 8 to 10″ deep.

L. LONGIFLORUM EXIMIUM, L. HARRISI—Easter Lily. Though usu-ally considered a greenhouse plant, this lily will survive many northern winters, especially the Croft type.

L. MARTAGON—Turks-Cap Lily. Drooping flowers with recurved petals in tiers or whorls along spikes that grow to 6 ft. tall and bloom during July and August. Purplish-red to violet-rose spotted with deep red at the base. Also white and purple varieties.

L. PARDALINUM—The Leopard Lily. Grows to 8 ft. Reflexed flowers which droop on the stalk are bright orange-red with dark crim-son spots. Requires shallow planting.

L. REGALE—Regal Lily. Perhaps the favorite lily. Produces 10 or more fragrant white funnel-shaped flowers on a single stem in July. The white flowers have a canary-yellow throat with rosy-purple markings on the outside. Grow from 3 to 6 ft. Like sunny location. Set bulbs 8″ deep. Can grow a flowering bulb from seed in 2 or 3 years. Easy culture.

L. SPECIOSUM—Rubrum Lily. Blooms in late summer and fall. Its lovely white flower flushed with rose with crimson spots is re-flexed and slightly drooping. Four to ten blossoms are borne on sturdy $2\frac{1}{2}$ to 4 ft. tall stems. There are many exquisite varieties, some in pure white, others crimson.

L. TENUIFOLIUM—The dainty Coral Lily is choice with slender, graceful stems not over 2 ft. tall. The coral-red blooms appear in June and are fragrant. Plant bulbs 5″ deep. Can raise from seed. Also yellow flowered form.

L. TIGRINUM—Tiger Lily. Large and showy recurved orange blooms with dark spots borne on sturdy 4 ft. stems. A garden escape in many parts of New England. Plant 6″ deep.

Lycoris—Summer Amaryllis. Sometimes called Magic-lily-of-Japan. Its strong, handsome strap-like, gray-green leaves come up in the spring and then ripen quickly, dry off and disappear. The fragrant orchid-pinkish flowers come up without any foliage in August on stems 2 to 3 ft. high. The lily-like flowers 6 to 9 to a scape are most useful in the garden because they bloom after many perennials are through, making a handsome garden display. Plant among ferns or any foliage plant that likes part shade to hide their lack of foliage.

Excellent in arrangements, they keep best if cut half open. Split stems and condition in water overnight. Remove faded flowers from clusters as buds continue to open.

Plant 5″ deep in rich soil with humus. Do not disturb once planted. When established they will go on blooming, year after year.

Tritonia—(Montbretia). Of the iris family, a half-hardy bulb with narrow sword-like leaves deeply grooved and 1 to 3 ft. stems bearing long, simple or panicled spikes of yellow, orange, copper, red or white tubular flowers. Buy the corms and grow as you would gladiolus. They will endure light shade but do better in the sun. Bring indoors to decorate the house.

Tuberous Begonia. Most valuable for summer bloom in shady places and very desirable for cutting. Starting in July, they carry gorgeous flowers in a wide range of colors from pure white to yellow, orange and apricot, and from pink to rose, salmon, red and a deep, rich crimson. Some have enormous flowers 4″ or more across, held well above the broad attractive foliage. Some are single and crested in form, others double and frilled, there are fringed and ruffled novelties and blooms that look like delicate camellias. Excellent planted in a shady border or along a shaded porch. Good winter house plant. The hanging types are excellent in terrace boxes or hanging baskets.

AS CUT FLOWERS

To cut for arrangements choose fully open blooms and a few well-developed buds. Well-developed buds will open in water but will be smaller. Split stems of both foliage and flowers. Condition in cold water using one tablespoon of salt to each quart of water. Avoid breaking the brittle stems. Spray decorative begonia leaves on the underside with a clear plastic to keep from curling. Lay a begonia blossom in the palm of your hand, lower it into a container of clean, cold water until submerged. Bring to the surface, gently turn it over and let the excess water run off. Never shake. The water that stays in the base of the petals will help keep the flower fresh. Florists syringe the blossoms with a fine mist of cold water. Short-stemmed flowers and the long sprays cut from the hanging types will last up to a week cut. Foliage will last a week or more. Some types root in the water. Cut foliage when size and color you like.

CULTURAL REQUIREMENTS

Purchase growing plants or use dormant tubers which may be started indoors in early spring in pots, shallow boxes or flats in a light soil. Water sparingly, until the first leaves show. Then, increase water so soil is on the moist side, but not wet. When all danger of frost is gone, set outdoors in a rich, well-drained soil in a shady spot. When planted in masses set a foot apart. Tubers will last for years and may be used over and over again. Take plants up before danger of frost, with all adhering soil and with tops left on. Spread out under cover to dry off for a week or two. Cut back tops leaving 3 or 4" of the fleshy stems and roots to dry up gradually. When completely dry, shake off soil and stem stubs. Pack for winter storage in peatmoss, vermiculite or sand and store in a cool (45°-60° F.), dry, frost-proof place. The indented side of the flat tuber is the top.

VARIETIES

Tuberous begonias are listed under various descriptive names such as Camellia Flowered, Double Frilled or Carnation Flowered, Single Crested and Fringed or Ruffled Novelties. Among the species are B. sutherlandi and B. evansiana.

LATE SUMMER AND FALL FLOWERING

The Dahlia and Gladiolus are two of the most important of the late flowering bulbs. Both supply the arranger with a quantity and variety of material in color, form and size.

Cyclamen europeum. Autumn flowering hardy species will grow freely beneath trees, on half shaded rock-work, in clumps in flower borders. Likes well-drained site with some lime in the soil. Dwarf habit with lovely foliage, rosy-crimson, sweet scented flowers in September and October, charming in effect. Plant corms when you get them in September 4" deep, 2" to 4" apart.

Dahlia. Many of the modern, small and single flowered varieties and dwarf sorts are very attractive. Planted in front of broad-leaved evergreens or a group of shrubs, their lovely autumn hues, when judiciously choosen, make a handsome display. Dahlias furnish the arranger with colorful flowers from late July until frost. Many varieties are lovely cut in graceful sprays and will last a week. Cut sprays just after flowers have fully opened and scar stem ends to stop flow of juicy sap. Remove any leaves that go below the water level in the final arrangement, since dahlia foliage deteriorates rapidly in water. Place stems in cold water using a pinch of potassium nitrate (drugstore) to each quart of water and leave overnight in a dark, cool place. Prematurely wilted dahlias may be revived by recutting stems and placing in hot water.

When cutting large-flowered dahlias for exhibition purposes, place stems in cold water for a couple of hours, then place stems in a container with 2 to 3 inches of boiling water. The heat destroys air pockets that might hinder water uptake. Place in deep container of water in a cool spot overnight.

CULTURAL REQUIREMENTS

Dahlias are tender plants, so do not set out until after danger of late frost. Thorough watering is essential. Gross feeders, they need plenty of food. When the plants have 3 or 4 sets of leaves, pinch out the top above the second pair of leaves. This will produce a lower and heavier plant with better branches and mass flowering. After topping, tie the plant close to a stake. Keep dead blooms removed for successive flowering. Dahlias like a good neutral or slightly acid, well-drained soil with a pH value of 7 to 6. Nurserymen offer dormant roots or tubers and "green plants." The root is a single division removed from a clump and must have a live eye. The green plants are obtained by propagation of cuttings from a rootstock, made in the late winter and grown in small pots, long enough to form a fairly good root ball. A green plant costs less but if damaged is a complete loss. An accident to a sprout or root will merely delay growth as another sprout will start. The root is easier to handle and plant. Green plants give a few more flowers but will not have as good rootstocks at digging time. The dahlia root, being a root and not a bulb, is likely to become dried out, so it's a toss-up. Once you have a supply it is easy to start plants from cuttings. Root divisions are obtained by dividing clumps in April or early May.

CLASSIFICATION AND VARIETIES

Well over one hundred novelties are offered by dealers every year showing a wide range in size and form of bloom, habit of growth and coloring. The Involutes are turned inward, forward or toward the face of the ray and the Revolutes are turned outward, toward the back of the ray. The present Dahlia classification is as follows:

Single Dahlias. Open centered flowers with only one row of ray florets, margins flat or nearly so Ex: Pequot Yellow; Purity.
Mignon. Do not exceed 18″ in height. Ex: Coltness Gem; Torquay Gem.

Orchid Flowering. As in Singles, except rays more or less tubular by the involution of the margins. Ex: Dahlia del Twinkle; Imp.

ANEMONE: Open centered flowers with one row of florets, with tubular-disk florets elongated forming pincushion effect. Ex: Croix du Sud; Vera Higgins.

COLLARETTE: Open centered flowers with one row of florets, with addition of one or more rows of petaloids (usually of different color) forming collar around disk. Ex: Sparkle; Tribune.

PEONY: Open centered flowers with 2 to 5 rows of ray florets, with or without smaller curled or twisted floral rays around disk. Ex: Susan Coe; The U.S.A.

INCURVED CACTUS: Fully double flowers, margins of most floral rays fully revolute for $\frac{1}{2}$ their length or more, tips of rays curving toward center of flowers. Ex: Ohio; Nightfall.

STRAIGHT CACTUS: Fully double flowers, margins of most floral rays fully revolute for $\frac{1}{2}$ their length or more, rays straight, slightly incurved or recurved. Ex: Miss Belgium; Zenith.

SEMI-CACTUS: Fully double flowers, margins of most floral rays fully revolute for less than $\frac{1}{2}$ their height. Rays broad below. Ex: Amelia Earhart; Edith Willkie.

FORMAL DECORATIVE: Fully double with margins of floral rays slightly or not all revolute, rays generally broad (pointed or rounded at tips), outer rays tending to recurve and central rays tending to be cupped, all rays in somewhat regular arrangement. Ex: Commando; Five Star General.

INFORMAL DECORATIVE: Fully double with margins of floral rays slightly or not all revolute, rays generally long, twisted or pointed, usually irregular in arrangement. Ex: Jane Cowl; Murphy's Masterpiece.

BALL: Fully double, ball-shaped or slightly flattened, floral rays blunt or rounded at tips and quilled or with marked involute margins in spiral arrangements, the flowers $3\frac{1}{2}''$ or more across. Ex: Mary Helen; Rosy Dawn.

MINIATURE: Dahlias which produce flowers that do not exceed 4" in diameter (pompons excluded). Ex: Fugi San; Pink Lassie; Betsy T. Kay; Little Diamond; Little Lemon Drop; Rapture; Dusky.

POMPONS: Same characteristics as Ball Dahlias but not more than 2" in diameter. Ex: Atom; Johnny.

Gladiolus. Gladiolus are useful as an edging along walks or in flower borders, used with other flowers to provide vertical effects and color during the late summer and early fall. Excellent as cut flowers, they may be used for height or cut into short lengths for low arrangements.

Choose stems for cutting when the second blossom on the spike is ready to open. It is better to cut gladiolus in the middle of the afternoon, when the flowers are less turgid. If you must cut in the early morning or late evening, let them remain out of water for about thirty minutes. When the tissues soften, the opening of buds is delayed which means longer lasting. If the corms are to be saved, leave at least four leaves on the plant below the cut. When cutting off dead blooms make the cut directly beneath the flower head, leaving all the foliage on the corm. Cut carefully, to avoid disturbing the roots. Any foliage the corms can spare is excellent either fresh in arrangements or dried for winter designs.

INDOOR DECORATION: Recut and split stems and condition at room temperature until the next morning. Gladiolus will not last well if cut in bud stage, stored immediately in a cool place and then brought into a warm room. Never crowd flowers in container for conditioning, as petals may bruise and buds need space to expand into shapely blossoms. Tiny buds at tips seldom open, so remove at once or leave, whichever does most for your arrangement. Place some stems slantwise in the container while conditioning, to avoid having all stiff and straight. Tips will then curve upward.

For low arrangements, cut stems into shorter lengths, with 1, 2, 3, 4 and 5 flowers to a length. Remove the outer green covering from several of the buds, just above the highest open flower, for more color and to extend color further up the spike. The cut open flowers last 1 or 2 days, but the spike goes on blooming for 1 to 2 weeks.

CULTURAL REQUIREMENTS

Plant corms outdoors as soon as danger of frost is over. Plant 3" deep and 6" apart. May be grown in almost any type of well-drained soil, but prefer sandy loam. Will flower 75 to 90 days after planting. Make successive plantings every 2 or 3 weeks for continuity of blooms over an extended period. When the foliage has died down corms should be lifted with a spading fork, usually 4 to 6 weeks after blooming and in the North always before frost. Cut off tops, remove old withered-up corm, thoroughly cure or dry the new ones and then store in a frost-free but cool, well-ventilated location for the winter.

CLASSIFICATION

Formerly classified according to the shape of the individual flower as large-flowered, hooded (Primulinus), ruffled and orchid-flowered. This system was abandoned in favor of a classification according to size and color. They are available in miniature, small, medium, large and giant sizes, the miniatures

Lilies, hosta leaves and branches of Rivers Beech were all grown on the Merrys' place. Lilies, decorative and long lasting for cutting, are often fragrant. Hosta foliage is invaluable for use in arrangements, both fresh and dried. The decorative beech leaves may be preserved by means of a glycerin solution, either while green or after they have turned color in the fall.

ARRANGEMENT BY RUTH MERRY   PERCY MERRY PHOTO

Two large spider chrysanthemums are combined with decorative kale, a cup and saucer squash and white grapes. Line material of deformed daylily stalks repeats the twist and form of the chrysanthemums. A rough cut finished base of wood completes the composition.

ARRANGEMENT BY VERA T. BAYLE   JOHN C. BAYLES PHOTO

having florets less than $2\frac{1}{2}''$ in diameter, the giant having florets larger than $5\frac{1}{2}''$. Varieties of the Primulinus type and the Miniature glads, are popular and useable for the small home and lot.

The colors range from white to deep yellow, buff, orange, light to deep salmon, scarlet, light pink to an almost black red, rose, lavender and purple. With thousands of new varieties on the market there is a gladiolus to suit every need.

QUESTIONS AND ANSWERS

What causes the lower leaves of tomato plants to curl? Plants are otherwise healthy.

The curling of the lower leaves of tomatoes is characteristic of these plants and is caused by the fact that the leaves give off water during hot weather quicker than they can replace it. Some varieties also apparently do it more than others, but it should not be cause for alarm if plants are kept moist and in healthy condition.

What can I do to make my wisteria bloom? It is healthy and luxuriant.

This is a common problem with many gardeners. Dig a three-foot trench, 18 inches deep, around the plant (when possible), keeping a safe distance from the trunk. Then mix superphosphate or bonemeal with the soil as it is replaced in the ditch, since these are phosphorous fertilizers which promote the production of flowering beds. In addition, pruning, in some cases severe in nature to cause shock, is also advised. This treatment, best done in the spring, is recommended for flowering dogwoods which fail to bloom.

(See index for scientific names)

What kinds of annuals can I grow in my tulip beds? Bulbs will not be lifted after flowering is past.

Many kinds of low growing annuals, with shallow root systems, can be grown without interfering with the bulbs. Restrict the variety to kinds that grow about a foot tall, and if you plan to sow seeds directly in the ground rely on sweet alyssum, California and Shirley poppies, bachelors-buttons and candytuft. If you prefer to set out young plants after warm weather arrives, consider dwarf marigolds and zinnias, petunias, nemesia, verbenas, ageratum, lobelia, low growing snapdragons and periwinkle.

What control do you suggest for slugs that are eating my perennials?

Slugs can be effectively controlled with poison bait, which contains metaldehyde the attractant and calcium arsenate as the poison. Bait is available in either meal or pellet form from most garden supply stores. Spread it on the ground around the plants late in the day or in the early evening, since the slugs do most of their feeding at night. Sanitation in the garden, cleaning up all hiding places, such as garden debris, rotting boards and logs, will also help to keep slugs and snails under control. A 5% chlordane dust can be used, although it is less effective than bait.

6

VEGETABLES, HERBS
AND GOURDS

Do not overlook the possibilities of using vegetables, their leaves, flowers and seed pods in arrangements. For arrangers with imagination and ingenuity, the vegetable garden is a source of valuable material, and much can be dried for use in winter bouquets. If you do not grow your own vegetables for eating, perhaps you buy them from a nearby roadside stand or local commercial grower who will be cooperative, letting you have some edible pea vines or similar material you might want for arrangements.

Any material used in fresh arrangements must be properly conditioned. Large leaves with practically no stems should be submerged in very cold water for 1 or 2 hours. With plenty of stem, submerge for $\frac{1}{2}$ to 1 hour, until crisp and then condition overnight. Before arranging, to prevent curling, spray the underside of the leaf with clear plastic.

THE VEGETABLE GARDEN

Arrangers may want to grow a few vegetables which are not easily bought on the market. Grow old-fashioned tiny husk tomatoes and arrange cut vines and all. Or grow a clump of wheat for height and graceful curves in fall arrangements or swags. Collect grain in two or three stages, green to tan, and hang to dry. Dwarf ornamental corn is useful; even the husks, leaves and tassels are decorative. You may plant these with flowers if you do not have a separate vegetable garden. The same is true of herbs.

If you have the space, you may want to have a small vegetable garden. Good managers no longer grow quantities of material they do not need. It's too expensive and time consuming. Decide first what you want to grow and how much. If you're a beginner, start in a very small way and learn all you can through reading, conversation and experience. Keep your garden space to a minimum, getting production through successive plantings, which will furnish you with a continuous supply of young, fresh products. Use a minimum of space and efficient methods to cut waste and work to a minimum. Edged by a border of annuals, perennials and herbs for cutting the vegetable garden can be a very pleasant sight. Mulch with grass clippings or some other inexpensive material to keep down weeds. This will also conserve moisture and give a neat appearance to the garden.

IN ARRANGEMENTS

Corn tassels are very popular with arrangers, particularly to use with harvest arrangements. They dry well, too. During the fall and autumn through Halloween and Thanksgiving, arrangements using vegetables combined with fruit or flowers, berried branches, nuts, cones, leaves and vines are timely. Spilling out of baskets and cornucopias, these garden products typify the glory and vivid coloring of autumn. Arranged on a sideboard or dining room table, or designed for a game room buffet, outdoor barbecue or combination kitchen-dining area the bright colors, interesting shapes and textures have great appeal, especially so for men.

Globe or French Artichoke, Cynara scolymus. Resembling a large thistle, this is grown for its interesting flowering head, usually gathered before the flower expands. In special varieties the head attains an enormous size. Those we buy locally in the grocery store are usually a bluish-green and much used by arrangers both fresh and dried. For use in fresh bouquets, recut the short, thick stem and submerge the head in cold water for an hour. The fresh artichoke should keep about a month before noticeably shriveling. Attractive in fruit and vegetable arrangements.

Dried, you may want to coat the fleshy bracts or scales with a clear shellac or plastic for longer keeping, or paint the heads silver or gold, for silver and gold arrangements during the holiday season. If necessary, a false stem may be made by wiring a plant stake to the short stem.

The large, purple thistle-like flower is excellent in arrangements as is its fern-like foliage. Condition overnight in cold water. The flowers also dry well, retaining most of their purple color, if gathered and cut when fully open and then hung to dry. Left on the plant to dry they turn lovely tans. If left until the flowers go to seed they are equally interesting and tan in color.

Cabbage Family. Use the young, small heads of the red-purple cabbage with its glossy sheen or the Savoy, with its crinkly leaves; a choice white head of cauliflower or the more interesting strain tinged with purple. This type is easily grown, but not often found in the markets. The slender, tall head of Chinese cabbage, with its long, crinkly leaves may be choosen in various heights and sizes. The individual leaves have an almost translucent quality and are useable in leaf arrangements.

Leaves, Flowers and Seed Pods. Beet tops with their red veined and shiny green leaves with reddish tinge cut in various stages of development may be just what you need in green, with a suggestion of red for your arrangement.

The rich, dark green leaves of swiss chard, much crumpled or savoyed may be used in many ways. As a rosette at the base of a low arrangement it is attractive and useful. The older leaves are thick and fleshy, suitable where a coarse texture is desired. They have prominent pearly-white mid-ribs. Rhubarb Chard has beet-like leaves. The leaf stalks are bright but delicate, translucent crimson; the rich color extends out through the veins into the dark green, heavily crumpled leaves.

The crinkly texture of kale in both the dwarf, compact or spreading, and tall forms, is effective. The Blue Curled Scotch variety which grows 12″ to 18″ tall, has finely curled, bluish-green leaves, while the Dwarf Siberian 12″ to 16″ high, has broad, thick grayish-green plume-like leaves, plain at the center and slightly frilled at the edges. The variety Flowering Kale in autumn develops remarkably beautiful colors from white-cream, pink, rose to magenta, with leaves edged dark green.

The interesting, young, crumpled green leaves of rhubarb, with reddish colored ribs, are admired in arrangements and rhubarb flowers are attractive. Cut flowers when fully open and hang to dry for use in winter arrangements.

The leaves and tassles of the ordinary garden sweet corn are in demand by arrangers. Hang tassels to dry for winter use. Paint dried foliage silver or gold and use in designs during the Christmas season.

There are several varieties of parsley on the market, some with plain, dark green, deeply cut, flat leaves, others with handsome, uniformly curled dark green leaves. Excellent for small-scaled arrangements when a deep, dark green is needed. Use the varieties with tall, stout stems.

Even the leaves of the ordinary parsnip may be used to good effect. In choosing leaves, use variety in sizes and different stages of development, as well as color for added interest.

Pick the green ridged pods of the okra which grow from 4″ to 12″ long, when they are the size you want, and select those which have interesting curves for pleasing effects. Hang to dry. These pods may also be gilded or silvered for use during the holiday season.

Pumpkin Family. The pumpkin family offers variety and interest in both form and color and includes the pumpkin, as well as ornamental gourds and many interesting squash. The long lasting quality of these products is a big advantage in vegetable arrangements.

Tomatoes. The arranger, if she grows her own, may choose from the "currant" (growing currant style in long clusters) which weigh less than an ounce on up to the giant size, weighing over a pound. There are shapes resembling the cherry or grape borne in bunches, the plum and the pear, as well as the ordinary round and oblong forms and there are colors from the green to the ripened hue of the fruit, varying from yellow-red and purplish-red to yellow and orange. The common husk tomato of our grandmother's day (Physalis pruinosa) has fruit the size of a cherry, orange-yellow or red and matures in a large hairy calyx. A vine of these tiny fruits is highly decorative.

When using tomatoes on the vine in a decoration, it is interesting to have some green and others partially ripened, as well as the fully ripened fruit. Too ripe, of course, the tomatoes will not keep long. Grow some of the yellow varieties for interest in decoration.

Miscellaneous Vegetables. Do not overlook some of the heads of lettuce which are delightful. Try Oakleaf in your next arrangement, placing the stem end in a shallow container of water for longer lasting. Curly endive and the smooth broadleaved type are effective but wilt quickly in a dry atmosphere.

The shiny, rich purple, pear-shaped eggplant is ornamental and cut with some of the stem and leaves, it is even more decorative. Interesting spears of asparagus, peas in the pod cut with the vine and bright red radishes, some cherry-like in shape, or the white type shaped like icicles all have possibilities.

The tiny ears of mahogany-red strawberry popcorn and miniature varieties of Indian or ornamental corn variously variegated are decorative and lasting, often used with gourds.

Use the colorful green and red peppers. The long, thin, hot ones dry well and hold their bright red color. They may be strung and used as swags and are popular used that way in Mexico.

THE HERB GARDEN

Perhaps no arranger gets more pleasure from a hobby than the possessor of an herb garden with its fascinating history and many present day uses. Excellent for fragrance, miniature and foliage bouquets, herbs supply the best possible material for dried arrangements, including leaves, flowers and many exciting seed pods. Most herb gardens are laid out in very simple, geometrical patterns, some informally along a wall or kitchen walk. Constant pruning and dividing is necessary to keep the garden neat and under control. Plants, like the chive, mint and angelica need constant care to keep them under control since the clumps increase rapidly. Herbs are easily grown in a sandy loam soil, given a sunny, well-drained location.

The outstanding charm of the herb garden is its spicy fragrance and the unusual patterns made by its leaves. Some are glossy green, others have a hairiness which gives them a shimmering gray appearance. The all over gray-green effect is cool and pleasing. The spear-like foliage of chives and sweet flag (Acorus calamus) offer an interesting contrast in form to the frothy growth of the savories and sages.

Although some people think of herbs as plants grown principally for the leaves, seeds or fruits, and roots used in flavoring food, many of the plants are ornamental in the garden and decorative used with cut flowers or alone. Mainly of the mint family (leaf herbs) and parsley family (seed herbs) with some alliums (smelly bulbous herbs of the lily family, including chives, garlic and shallots) they have decorative foliage. Avoid cutting the new tender growth, which is soft and hard to condition. Old growth is woody. Strip the excessive foliage from the base of the stems, then split the woody stem and place in warm water. Allow to condition overnight. Herbs are cut for their decorative foliage in most cases, since the flowers are as a rule small and inconspicuous in white, soft pink, lavender or pale blue colors. For best keeping, cut the flowers after they have started to open, about $\frac{1}{3}$ of the way. Cut foliage from older growth any time and it lasts well, longer than most cut foliage. The herb garden is perhaps at its best for color during the month of July, but will continue to flower until frost.

Achillea millefolium—Yarrow. Grows to 18″. Red Yarrow has colorful red flowers and white centers. Likes rich, moist soil and sun. Good in flower arrangements.

Allium schoenoprasum—Chives. Plant in clumps in the general border. Use in soups, scrambled eggs, soft cheeses and mashed potatoes. Grows to 12″. Lavender clover-like flowers. Likes average soil and sun. Divide every three years.

Anethum graveolens—Dill. Annual. Self sows easily. Grows to 3 ft., terminating in flat flower heads with small, yellow flowers and has attractive fine, feathery foliage. Good for cutting. Leaves used in potato salad, sprinkled over steaks, chops and boiled potatoes. Likes well-drained, average soil.

Artemisias—Grown for their gray-green foliage.

ARTEMISIA DRACUNCULUS—Tarragon. A perennial 24″ tall and 12″ across, with long, narrow, smooth gray-green leaves. Plant in clumps in the general border. Use in vinegar, over chops, steaks, in salads and fish sauce. Transplant every three years.

ARTEMISIA SCHMIDTIANA NANA—Silver Mound. Prettiest of artemisias, dwarf plant with stems clothed in rosettes of frothy gray-green leaves. Good as a border plant or accent plant in rock garden.

Anagallis arvensis—Scarlet Pimpernel. Plant lies on ground, prominent flowers in all shades of red facing up, close in mid-afternoon. Hard to transplant. Likes dry, well-drained soil and full sun.

Angelica archangelica—Angelica. Perennial planted in borders for bold effects. Grows to 3 ft. Small white or greenish and yellow flowers. Must discipline to keep within bounds. Likes moist rich soil and partial shade. Propagation by seed and division.

Asperula odorata—Sweet Woodruff. Beautiful ground cover. Tiny, white, star-like flowers. Likes partial shade, loose, moist, well-drained soil. Grows to 6″.

Chrysanthemum cinerariaefolium—Pyrethrum. Good in masses for bright spot in garden. Good for flower arrangements. Likes a limy, well-drained soil and sun. Grows to 2 ft. Propagation by seed and division.

Chrysanthemum majus—Costmary, Sweet Mary. Plant in clumps in the general border. Grows 2′-3′. Propagate by seed and division. Aromatic, yellow flowers. Strong underground runners. Likes dry soil. Needs sun to flower.

Eupatorium perfoliatum—Boneset, Joe Pye Weed. Fragrant, showy, fluffy, purple flowers. Good in borders or for arrangements. Likes a light rich, moist, well-drained soil and sun. Grows to 4 feet.

Foeniculum vulgare—Fennel. Tall, feathery, bright green foliage, quite like dill in appearance. Grows to 4 ft. Good for cutting. Likes fertile, dry soil in sun.

Hyssopus officinalis—Hyssop. Shrubby plant 18″ tall and across. Good for edging and low hedges. Upright branches clothed with dark aromatic green leaves, almost evergreen, which stand out stiffly. At the tips of the branches are spires of bloom in white, pink or two shades of blue. Likes sun or partial shade.

Lavandula officinalis—English Lavender. Ornamental perennial, grows to 3 ft., good border plant. Indispensable in herb garden, with pleasant scent. Flowers blue, violet or lilac. For use in fresh arrangements, cut when almost $\frac{1}{2}$ flowers on spike are open. Flowers will last around ten days. For drying, cut when $\frac{3}{4}$ flowers are open. Fragrant, silvery green foliage grows to 15″.

Majorana hortensis—Sweet Marjoram. Bushy, little plant with soft foliage. Grows from 6″ to 1$\frac{1}{2}$′. Good for cutting. Annual. Fragrant. Use in egg dishes, as garnish for meats, in salad and soft cheese. Prefers light, average soil and full sun.

Melissa officinalis—Lemon Balm. Grows 1 to 2 ft. high and has small 2-lipped flowers in late summer. Leaves of a decided fragrant lemon odor and flavor. Var. with variegated leaves. Likes dry soil in partial shade. Use in tea, soup, salad and iced drinks.

Mentha—Mint. Perennial with aromatic, attractive leaves and small, inconspicuous flowers. Includes the Spearmint, Peppermint, Pennyroyal, Bergamot Mint (Mentha citrata) and Apple Mint. Must discipline to keep under control. Fragrant leaves. Used in fish sauce, lamb sauce, jelly and tea. Likes a rich, moist soil, preferably shady.

Mentha pulegium—Pennyroyal. Give winter protection. Stems lie on ground. Has small bluish-lavender flowers. Said to keep mosquitoes away. Self sows readily.

Monarda didyma—Bee-Balm. Perennial which grows to 3′ or more. Long season of bloom. Scarlet flowers surrounded by red tinted bracts at summit of the leafy stalks. Cut flowers last 5 to 7 days, buds and foliage 10. Cut when $\frac{1}{4}$ blooms on a stem are about half open. Remove bottom leaves. Condition overnight. Start with warm water. Alba, white; var. salmonea, yellowish-pink blossoms.

Myrrh or Myrrhis odorata—Sweet Cicely. A perennial, will grow 2 to 3'. Decorative in border with its finely cut leaves. Has fragrant, small white flowers in umbels. Plant in clumps in the general border.

Nepeta cataria—Catnip or Catmint. Perennial 3' high, with wooly, gray foliage. Frothy growth. Pale purple to white flowers. Pungent odor liked by cats. Catmint (Nepeta mussini), low branching perennial 12" to 24" high. Gray-whitish down foliage. Flowers blue with dark spots.

Ocimum basilicum—Sweet Basil. Grown as annual. Pleasing fragrance. Good for cutting. Bush Basil preferred by many, makes a small, compact plant. Purple Basil (O. b. purpureum) is the tall variety grown for its reddish-blue-brown foliage.

Rosa damascena—Damask Rose. Good accent and background plant, with fragrant pink flowers. Likes well-drained soil. Grows to 5 ft. Propagate by seed or division. One of the perfume roses, source of attar of roses.

Rosmarinus officinalis—Rosemary. Gray-green foliage, almost evergreen, blends well with many flowers. Cut at any time. Lasts 2 weeks. Easily bent into desired curves with warm hands. Needs winter protection.

Ruta graveolens—Rue. Grows to 2 ft. Lacy blue-green leaves, yellow flowers. Good for hedge or path borders. Likes limy, poor, heavy, well-drained soil. Flowers last 5 to 7 days, foliage up to 12 days. Cut when clusters have 3 to 6 fully opened flowers. Foliage at any stage. Collect fruits while green or later in fall when they turn tan. Dry for winter use.

Salvia in variety. Many handsome sage perennials. S. officinalis, Common Garden Sage. Rough-textured, shrubby, gray leaved plant, very highly decorative. Grows to 3 ft. tall and 24 to 36" across. Cut well-developed foliage any time. Cut purple or white flowers when $\frac{1}{3}$ the spike is open. Flowers last 5 to 10 days.

Satureia hortensis—Summer Savory. An annual preferred by many to Winter Savory. Yellow to red flowers. Frothy growth. Plant in clumps in the general border. Likes a moderately rich soil and sun. Use for seasoning meat, eggs, green beans and peas.

Satureia montana—Winter Savory. A perennial or green shrublet 15" high with lavender, pale pink to white flowers scattered along the stems; branches will trail gracefully over a wall or along a slope where there is space to spread out. Glossy, dainty leaves have a spicy flavor and can be picked all winter long. Likes a poor, light, well-drained soil in full sun.

Symphytum officinale—Comfrey. Plant in clumps in the general border. Early bloom in many colors. Grows to 1½'. Propagate by division.

Thymus—Garden Thyme. Perennial essential in any herb garden. Many varieties. Some like T. serpyllum, Creeping Thyme, good as a ground cover. T. vulgaris, Common Thyme, is an erect shrubby plant with white hairy branches and small leaves. Grows to 8". Good in front of a border or for cutting. Divide every few years because of tendency to get woody. Protect with a mulch so won't winter kill.

GOURDS

Gourds are tender annuals which trail or climb by means of tendrils. They like a light, rich well-drained soil in full sun. Sow the seeds where the plants are to remain, as they do not transplant well. The plants are rapid growing and have good foliage, so they make good summer screens, trained on trellises or along porches facing south. The odd shapes, markings and colorings of some of the varieties make them attractive and ornamental. They are popular in late fall arranged with ornamental corn, grains, millet, autumn leaves or evergreens.

Pick the fruits when they are ripe, when the outer shells are hard, just before frost. Leave some of the stem or vine attached and they will be more decorative. Thoroughly clean and then dry in the sun for a few days, if possible, then store in a dry cold place where there is good circulation of air to prevent decay. Make a small hole through the outer shell into the center using a fine electric drill or a very thin nail. When the gourds are well dried you may coat them with a clear plastic or shellac if you wish. Many prefer them natural, some rub them with floor wax. For definite color schemes you may cover with a dull, flat paint or glossy highlighted enamel.

Large gourds may be dried and hollowed out, waterproofed and used as dippers, bowls, wren houses or for hanging containers. Thin leather straps or an appropriate cord may be used to hang them up. Smaller gourds are often strung together and used for ornaments. Combined with wheat and magnolia leaves an attractively designed Thanksgiving door swag can be dreamed up using perhaps yellows, both light and dark, combined with some lovely green gourds for contrast. Gourds are listed in seed catalogues as Small Gourds, Mixed; Big Gourds, Mixed; All Kinds, Mixed or by such descriptive names as Hercules Club, Dipper, Turk's Turban, Bottle, Spoon and Warted Sorts.

QUESTIONS AND ANSWERS

I have some peony plants that develop small buds, which dry up before flowering. What causes this? Other plants nearby bloom prolifically, so I doubt if a disease is to blame.

If peonies are planted too deep, buds will fail to develop properly. Since your other plants flower normally, too deep planting might be responsible for this condition. Check your nonflowering specimens, and if the crowns are more than one or two inches below the surface of the soil, lift and set the roots higher this fall.

What is the best time to move or plant Christmas roses?

In the fall when cool, moist weather enables them to make strong root growth and thus become established before winter sets in.

For the past several springs, I have noticed that the stems of some of my tulips shrivel at a particular point so that the flower heads flop over and die. What causes this? Bulbs bloom well the following year.

The condition you describe is caused by too much water and is particularly prevalent during rainy seasons. There is nothing that can be done about it, except to improve drainage if it is poor. At least bulbs are in no way affected.

How can I prepare herbs for drying? Which are particularly fragrant?

Herbs should be gathered just before the flowers open. Strip the lower leaves from the stem and place on a screen or hang upside-down in a dry, airy place away from the sun. Bee-balm, mints, lavender and lemon-verbena are a few of the more fragrant kinds. See Chapter 9 for other herbs which dry well.

7

HOW TO CUT AND
CONDITION PLANT
MATERIAL

The remarkable beauty of some of the bare branches, both in color and line, should not be overlooked during the winter and early spring. Choose a few well-shaped branches and arrange them to emphasize their natural beauty. Most plants need pruning each year to shape them and keep them within bounds. Also, thinning out the dense growth allows more air and sunshine to enter and a stronger plant to develop. Learn all you can about pruning, so you can enjoy cut branches for arrangements indoors and enhance the beauty of the plant from which you cut. If you cut in the woods, observe the state conservation laws and never for a few branches or flowers, do anything to harm our woodland treasures. Continual snatching of flowers as dogwood and mountain laurel soon leaves heavily traveled highways completely barren.

PRUNING TREES, SHRUBS AND VINES

Ornamental plantings are pruned to keep them shapely, within bounds and to increase flower production. It is a wise homeowner who annually or semi-annually does a light pruning job, keeping vines, shrubs and trees under control, especially on the small lot. Well pruned plants are bushy and more attractive. Cutting here and there as necessary you will acquire a wealth of branches for arrangements indoors and at the same time maintain the natural shape of the plant, a part of its particular charm. If a shrub naturally sends up new growth from the base, cut away old wood near the ground line. Prune sufficiently, shrubs with branching habits, to prevent overcrowding of growth. Cut flowering branches one-fourth inch above a node or bud to encourage good branching. Deciduous trees and shrubs may be cut back more severely than evergreens. Learn to know how and where the individual species produce their blossom buds, for this will tell you when and how to prune.

Pruning Details. Use clean, sharp tools, a sharp knife, pruning shears or saw for a large branch. Remove any dead or diseased branches as well as those lacking in vigor or branches that cross or rub each other. Thin and open up where growth is too thick to allow air and sunshine to enter. Remove suckers at the base of a plant and "water sprouts" along the branches. All large cuts should be flush with the trunk or branch, as stubs rot and may spread decay. Cover any cut, an inch or more in diameter, with tree wound paint to prevent diseases from entering open cut.

When to Prune Early Blooming Shrubs. Most early spring-blooming plants develop their flower buds the year before on the wood of the preceding year. Pruning these plants while dormant would cut off the flower buds and lessen the amount of spring bloom. Pruned just after the plant flowers, the new growth, as it comes, will develop flowering buds for the following year. This group includes a host of favorites like the azalea, deutzia, dogwood, flowering almond, forsythia, kalmia, kerria, leucothoe, lilac, pieris, rhododendron, wisteria and the early spring-blooming honeysuckles, philadelphus and white flowering spirea. Excellent material for forcing in early spring if you cut a branch here and there, the length you want, thinning out where growth seems overly crowded, you will have material for forcing indoors as well as an effective outdoor display. Actually you can do a good pruning job in this way.

Take as many of these branches as you wish just before the blooming period, for forcing, so long as you enhance and do not destroy the beauty of the plant. Never hesitate to cut flowers of the lilac, mountain-laurel or similar shrubs from well-established plants, as the flowers that are allowed to go to seed take much from the strength of the shrub. Cutting this year's flowers helps develop better flowers the following year and insures a stronger more vigorous shrub. Then, if the shrub needs further trimming, prune the plant just after it has finished flowering. The new growth develops flowering buds for the following spring, so do not cut branches later in the year or you will be cutting away next year's flowers.

When to Prune Late Blooming Shrubs. Shrubs that bloom late in the season, say any time after June, form their flower buds early on new shoots, or wood, which develop the same season. With these plants, it is advisable to prune while they are dormant in winter or early spring, just before the leaf buds open, just as growth is starting, to encourage the growth of more strong shoots which will bear flowers the same summer. The greater the quantity of strong new wood produced in any season, the greater the bloom you will have that season. Prune rather heavily in winter and early spring.

Late flowering shrubs to be pruned while dormant include buddleia, campsis (trumpet creeper), caryopteris (blue spirea), most of the clematis, clethra (summersweet), the shrubby hibiscus, some of the late blooming honeysuckles, hydrangea, the rose, late red flowering spirea, and vitex (chaste tree). In fact, with plants like buddleia, caryopteris, the rose and vitex, old growth may be cut back to the ground, retaining any new young shoots which will produce flowers. This is advisable where plants are doubtfully hardy. Branches of late flowering shrubs are not forced out of season as they bloom when flowers are plentiful. If you have well-established plants, cut branches when they are in bloom for arrangements, using care to thin where growth is thick and to enhance the shape of the bush.

Pruning Evergreens. Evergreens should never be pruned as drastically as deciduous plants. Keep evergreens down to the desired size by semi-annual pruning. Shape plants nicely by cutting short ends here and there around the entire plant. Prune where plant is crowded and needs thinning to admit air and sun for good health.

Pruning Vines. Vines which flower early as some of the early spring blooming honeysuckles (lonicera) and wisterias should be pruned directly after flowering. Shorten some of the lateral or side branches and some of the old main shoots if they seem too numerous, to make way for young growth.

Vines which flower on shoots of the current season's growth, like the trumpet creeper (campsis) and most of the clematis are pruned in the spring, just before new growth starts.

Occasionally it is advisable to give old plants like English ivy (hedera) a severe spring pruning. They will soon be covered with new leaves. Old plants of evergreen bittersweet (euonymus vegetus) will stay more compact and attractive if some of the laterals are shortened or cut back each spring.

A rampant grower like the fleece vine (polygonum) planted in a small area will need a lot of cutting back while a slow grower like the climbing hydrangea will require little. Use pruning shears with discretion to retain the natural beauty of the growing vine.

Cutting Back Annuals and Perennials. Perennials like the aster, artemisia vulgaris (mugwort), delphinium, helenium (sneezeweed) and phlox are likely to produce too many stems for the area the roots occupy after the first season. This will curtail the size of the flower clusters unless in May you go over the plants and remove all but the strongest shoots. Leave two or three delphinium shoots and cut the weak ones out low. Six strong shoots are sufficient for the other perennials. In many cases weak growth can simply be pulled out. Three and four year roots will produce excellent good-sized flowers handled in this way or you may prefer to divide these perennials every three or four years whichever method seems most practical to you.

With annuals like African marigolds, China asters and zinnias, after the center flower bud starts to develop the plants usually branch naturally. If they don't remove the center bud. The side branches in turn develop a bud and make laterals or side branches. Pinch out the surplus laterals if you want larger flowers.

If a dahlia plant with one stem has the top pinched out when it is about a foot tall, it will send out several laterals, each of which will produce a cluster of buds. If a large flower is wanted, retain only the best bud. Several stems will start pushing forth laterals at the upper leaf joints. Nip these out allowing only those at the base to develop for a better shaped plant. With large flowered chrysanthemums leave only two or three stems and one flower bud to a stem if you want large blooms.

CUTTING FOR ARRANGEMENTS

Most arrangers will cut when they need the material, but certain precautions will insure good flowers in the future. Do not cut from a plant until it has had sufficient time to become well-established and never cut too drastically from any one plant during a season.

Plan your arrangement before you cut flowers and foliages, so you will not waste precious material. Know how long a branch is needed for the design, then measure with your mind's eye or a tape measure if you have to. A suggestion for beginners is that the longest branch be two and a half times as high as the container, or as wide, if the container is a horizontal one.

Clean equipment is vital. A sharp knife for flowers and larger pruning shears or even a small saw may be necessary for woody and heavy branches. Gardening gloves will protect your hands from thorns.

Annuals and Perennials. Carry a clean pail filled with fresh water to the garden with you. As soon as a flower is cut place it in water. Choose only good quality material if you want it to last. Cut either in the early morning or late evening when the stems are most turgid or inflated with moisture. Never cut during the heat of the day. From a practical viewpoint early evening is an excellent time for cut flowers can be conditioned in water through the cool night, when little transpiration takes place, and arranged first thing after breakfast.

In general, cut flowers when they are sufficiently mature, about half open, so they will finish opening in water. Buds should be advanced enough to show their petal color. Flowers cut past their prime do not last long enough to warrant the effort spent in arranging them.

Flowers like the peony, rose, iris, and gladiolus should be cut when buds are less than half open, while the aster, dahlia, marigold, zinnia, and chrysanthemum should be three quarters or almost fully open. For effect in arrangements and from the standpoint of interest you may want to use buds as well as partially open and fully opened blooms, regardless of keeping quality.

Some authorities say flowers keep just as well if the stems are cut straight across but we still like to make a slanting cut to increase the surface exposed to the water. The slanting cut also keeps the stem from resting on the bottom of the container.

Flowering Branches for Indoor Forcing. Flowering branches properly handled, will bloom several weeks ahead of their normal flowering time, filling the house with touches of preseason color. Excellent combined with flowering bulbs or evergreen branches. Make a slightly slanting cut which will heal quickly. Cut the branches during a thaw on a mild day around midday, when the branches are full of sap. On a freezing day, the branches may split and there is more danger of injuring the plant. The larger and fatter the buds, the more sap in the branches, so the better the blossoms will be. A sufficient amount of sap is necessary to produce good blooms. All branches in order to force must have completed a period of dormancy before they will produce best results, hence a period of frost, which produces rest, must precede forcing.

Start cutting a few well chosen branches during the January thaws. February is likely to be a bad month, weatherwise, with lower temperatures and often ice and snow. A good time to cut is immediately after a rain, as the heavy wetting and extra moisture helps the flow of sap and swelling of the buds.

Varieties that bloom early outdoors force more quickly indoors but do not last as long as those that bloom later and force more slowly. Shrubs like forsythia and the cornelian-cherry that produce blossoms before the leaves come, force more readily than those, like weigela and deutzia, whose leaves appear before the blossoms. The later plants bloom out of doors, the longer the time required to force them indoors, but they last over a longer period of time. The nearer to the natural blooming season outdoors the cutting is done, the less time is required for forcing indoors. Some branches cut in the woods, like the pussy willow, spicebush and shadbush, have already pushed their buds upward to the sun by February, so they need only a short time to force. *Cut for indoor forcing six to eight weeks ahead of the normal flowering time.* Please see page 166 for list of flowering branches that may be forced.

Evergreen Branches. Garden club members all over the United States cut all types of evergreen branches the entire year for use in flower arrangements, whatever they have in sufficient quantity. In planting a new home, arrangers should keep this in mind.

Evergreen branches are beautiful throughout the year but during the winter when flowers are scarce and other trees and shrubs are barren, their rich green branches with an interesting variety of color, texture and form are particularly welcome.

A line composition of branches of sprays of new young growth with a grouping of some of the early bulb flowers can be charming. As the flowers fade they may be replaced by a cluster of broad-leaved evergreens. These arrangements will remain fresh for weeks. The new growth on pines and cedars is useful and the firs are pliable with either gray-green or dark green needles which do not shed readily. The Japanese larch (Laris leptolepis), early in the season furnishes new growth which is soft in texture and particularly pleasing in its delicate effect. Juniper, yew, arbor-vitae and ilex supply wonderful foliage all year. At Christmas time short clippings cut from the tips of branches are excellent for wreaths, swags and in centerpiece arrangements. Longer branches may be had by shortening over-long tip end growths.

Branches from the mountain laurel, rhododendron, andromeda, mountain pieris and the graceful curving branches of the leucothoe or sweetbell are useful and rather long stems may be cut from overgrown plants. Make the cut back to the first side branch or first cluster of leaves below the tip. Do not cut stems which bear plump flower buds at the tip ends and waste precious flower buds unless it is flowering time. Cut from crowded plants that need thinning and where cut areas will not show. It takes very little material if cut judiciously to be useful in the average sized home.

Vines. Cut a flowering vine with a few open flowers and many well developed buds about ready to unfold or those with flowers in clusters when cluster is about one-third open. If possible, cut some of the old wood with each spray for better keeping.

Some of the non-flowering vines are versatile, their foliage blending well with flowers, fruits or vegetables. For added interest cut both old and tender pale-green new growth. Cut just above a node for good branching.

CONDITIONING ANNUALS AND PERENNIALS

Hardening Off

Leave the flowers in the pail you carried to the garden if you wish, since the less handling the better, but do not crowd them for conditioning. You may have to add more water to the pail. If you don't have warm water, room temperature is next best. Wash and clean all foliage to look crisp and fresh and last longer.

You will add hours to the flowers in an arrangement by "hardening off" or conditioning the cut material properly, which means getting it into the best possible condition of crispness to increase its lasting qualities. Cut flowers keep best when the stem, leaves and flowers are filled to capacity with water and there is a minimum of transpiration. Since stem structure varies with different plants, it is necessary to consider this and to give flowers with special stem structure special treatment. However, the following procedure applies to most cut flowers and will add to their life.

Use Warm Water

Perhaps the most radical change in handling cut flowers in recent years is the recommendation that flowers be placed in warm to hot water (80°-100° F., just warm to the elbow). The water then cools as the room temperature normally reduces it. Add more tap water to the container if the water level lowers. The warm water does not give the sudden shock or change in temparature that cold water does and moves up into the stem more readily. Run faucet water for flowers five or ten minutes before needed, so all air bubbles will be gone as these bubbles may obstruct the passage of water into the stems. Place the pail or container of cut flowers with stems in water in a cool dark room such as a shower stall overnight or for at least several hours. This enables them to regain their turgidity and last much longer. High humidity may be encouraged by spraying a fine mist of cold water into the air above and around the flowers or by wrapping a piece of paper around them to reduce water loss. Good circulation is important, but avoid cold or hot drafts, blowing from fans, direct sunlight, heat from radiators or anything that will

CUTTING and CONDITIONING for ARRANGEMENTS

Enjoy Rhododendron blossoms indoors. Cut branches from crowded places that need thinning. Where branches will not be missed. From long shoots that need shortening. Just above a node for good branching.

Use boxwood or yew clippings decoratively at Christmas time Cut short ends here and there around the entire plant. Good way to keep plant the desired size

Carry pail of warm water to garden. Cut flowers with sharp knife (NOT SCISSORS) Use diagonal cut. Remove unnecessary leaves. Place stems in warm water at once. Leave in pail overnight in cool place

Cut berried spray of Pyracantha. Choose one that wont be missed. Cut above a node. Remove thorns any leaves that hide colorful fruit.

Revive prematurely wilted flowers. Recut stem ends. Place in warm to hot water (80° to 100° F) Recondition overnight.

80°-100° WATER

To condition evergreen branches Wash in warm soapy water. Rinse in cold water Remove defective leaves, thin if too full. Split stem ends 2"-3" Place in warm water, condition overnight or longer. Use one tablespoon of glycerin to each quart of water.

To condition Ivies Cut just above a node for good branching Submerge mature foliage in cold water for 4 hours. Young tender foliage 1 hour. Insert stems in water filled orchid tubes for vegetable and fruit arrangements

ONE TABLESPOON   ONE QT.   TO EACH QUART

Scotch Broom, Cut branches desired length clean in cold water Split woody stems. Tie branches bent to curves wanted. Submerge in cold water several hours Dry, then untie.

Spray berried or needled branches with a clear plastic to decrease the shriveling and falling of berries or needles.

increase the evaporation of moisture from the cut material. You can double the life of cut flowers by placing them in a cool location at night when not in use, as a high temperature decreases their life time.

Flowers with hollow stems like the hollyhock, some with herbaceous woody stems like lantana and others with hairy stems like calendulas keep better if first placed in warm to hot water, 80°-100° F. Let them remain in this same water to condition overnight as it cools. Add more cold water if water level lowers. Following is a list of flowers that keep best if first placed in warm to hot (80°-100° F.) water.

Acer, Maple
African Violet, Saintpaulia
Ageratum
Althaea rosea, Hollyhock, sear
Antirrhinum, Snapdragon
Artemisia stelleriana, Dusty Miller, sear
Asclepia, Milkweed, sear
Aucuba
Buddleia davidi, Butterfly-Bush
Calceolaria, Slipperwort
Calendula
Calluna, Heather
Campanula, Canterbury Bell, sear
Centaurea americana, Basket-Flower
Centaurea montana, Mountain-Bluet
Cercis, Redbud
Chrysanthemum, perennial, sear
Chrysanthemum parthenium, Feverfew
Cineraria
Citrus, Orange Blossoms

Cleome, Spider Flower
Digitalis, Foxglove
Dogwood
Euphorbia corollata, Flowering Spurge
Euphorbia epithymoides, Cushion Spurge, sear
Euphorbia marginata, Snow-On-The-Mountain, sear
Evergreens
Fagus, Beech
Geum
Gomphrena globosa, Globe Amaranth
Helianthus, Sunflower
Heliotrope, sear
Hepatica, Liverleaf
Herbs, many of them
Hesperis, Sweet Rocket
Iberis, Candytuft
Jacobinia
Kalmia, Mountain-Laurel
Koelreuteria, Golden-Rain Tree
Laburnum, Golden-Chain Tree
Lagerstroemia, Crape-Myrtle

Lantana, sear
Lathyrus, Sweet Pea
Lavandula, Lavender
Linum, Perennial Flax
Lippia citriodora, Lemon Verbena
Lobelia cardinalis, Cardinal Flower, sear
Lunaria, Honesty
Lychnis chalcedonica, Maltese Cross
Lychnis coronaria, Dusty Miller
Lychnis dioica, Morning Campion
Lychnis viscaria, German Catchfly
Lythrum, Purple Loosestrife
Macleays cordata, Plume-Poppy, sear
Mertensia virginica, Virginia Bluebell
Monarda, Bee-Balm, Oswego Tea
Nerium, Oleander, sear
Nicotiana, Flowering Tobacco
Osmanthus, False Holly
Paulownia, Empress Tree
Pelargonium, Rose Geranium
Perillia
Philadelphus, Mockorange
Platycodon, Chinese Balloon Flower, sear
Polygonum, Fleece Flower
Primula, Primrose
Prunus, Cherry Blossoms
Pryracantha, Firethorn
Ranunculus, Wild Buttercup
Reseda odorata, Mignonette
Ruta, Rue
Salvia farinacea, Blue Sage
Salvia officinalis, Garden Sage
Salvia patens, Gentian Sage
Salvia splendens, Scarlet Sage
Spirea, Bridal Wreath
Stachys, Woolly Lambs-Ear
Tithonia, Mexican Sunflower
Tropaeolum foliage, Nasturtium
Valeriana, Garden Heliotrope
Verbena
Veronica, Speedwell
Vinca, Major Periwinkle

Close Stem Ends With Heat

Some flowers with a milky or colorless fluid in their stems like the poinsettia and poppy need their stem ends seared with heat using either boiling water or a flame to stop flow of fluid from stems. Place stem ends in 1″ to 2″ of boiling water for 1 minute. Protect upper leaves and flowers by pushing stem ends through a thickness of heavy paper to keep steam from rising. Or split stem ends for an inch or more and sear each stem end in a lighted candle or with a cigarette lighter while counting to thirty. If the stem was not cut to the correct length for the arrangement any new cut must always be seared. With boiling water or a flame sear the stem ends of the following; place flowers in hot water (80°-100° F.) to condition overnight, to start with, unless cold water is indicated.

Althaea rosea, Hollyhock

Artemisia stelleriana, Dusty Miller

Asclepia, Milkweed

Campanula, Canterbury Bell

Chrysanthemum, perennial

Daffodils—condition in 3" to 4" cold water

Dahlias—condition in cold water

Euphorbia epithymoides, Cushion Spurge

Euphorbia marginata, Snow-On-The-Mountain

Euphorbia pulcherrima, Poinsettia—condition in cold water

Fuchsia—condition in cold water

Heliotropium, Heliotrope

Hydrangea—condition in cold water

Lantana

Lobelia cardinalis, Cardinal Flower

Macleaya cordata, Plume-Poppy

Myosotis, Forget-Me-Not, condition in cold water

Nerium oleander, Oleander

Papaver, Oriental Poppy, cold water

Platycodon, Chinese Balloon Flower

Plumeria, Frangipani, cold water

Stephanotis—condition in cold water

To Revive a Wilted Flower

If a flower wilts recut the end of the stem, place it in warm to hot water (80°-100° F.) and recondition. This will often revive prematurely wilted blooms. Of course a completely wilted flower can never be revived.

CONDITIONING FLOWERING BRANCHES

Woody flowering branches (see list in the chapter which follows) last longer if the stem ends are split vertically two to three inches with a sharp knife, so they open and can take up water more readily. Hammering is likely to bruise and pound together some of the tiny water tubes and prevent water from entering. Set the cut branches with split ends deep in a bucket of warm water in a warm room (70° to 75° F.) for a few days until the sap has warmed within the branches, then arrange. To hasten bloom, fine spray the branches each day with lukewarm water for added humidity. This warm moisture will swell and encourage bud development. With branches that require several weeks to force, store in a humid, warm atmosphere. A warm, humid atmosphere with the use once a day of 100° F. water will considerably shorten the forcing time.

To retard branches, keep them in deep, cool water in a cool room until needed. If it is not necessary to force quickly, a 60° to 65° F. temperature will hold blooms well. Avoid direct sunlight as the intense heat may cause the buds to dry up. However, good light is necessary to develop good color, a dark room pales the color of the blossoms. A continuous supply of lovely branches may be provided by cutting at regular intervals or by retarding the development of some, under the proper cool conditions.

If an immediate arrangement is desired, cut the stem lengths to suit the arrangement, split the ends a couple of inches and place in warm water to encourage swelling of buds. Coax the branches into graceful curves by gently bending each branch between the thumb and forefinger. Run warm water from the faucet over the part you want to bend, if it is stubborn. Place the finished arrangement in its proper setting. A piece of charcoal in the water will help keep it sweet. Change the water once a week or as necessary and at that time cut the stem ends if they look as though they need it. Add a few daffodils or tulips at the base for color while you're waiting for the buds to open, or cuttings from house plants may be used with pleasing results.

There are several commercial preservatives on the market which added to water encourage blossoms to bloom sooner and last longer. You may wish to use them and make comparisons. Always follow the directions on the package for best results.

CONDITIONING EVERGREEN BRANCHES

Garden club women who answered our questionnaire wrote us that for best results they condition evergreen branches in a cool place for at least a day and night before bringing into heated rooms. Also they spray with a colorless shellac spruce and hemlock, which ordinarily quickly shed their needles in the dry atmosphere of the home; so treated they will hold their needles a couple of months or more.

It will be necessary to brighten and clean the cut evergreen branches. Place them in warm soapy water and wash thoroughly to remove dust and dirt. This cleans and also gives a glossy, fresh look. Now rinse in cold water. Remove any leaves that have turned brown and if the branches seem too full, thin out for more lacy effects. To bend evergreen branches to a desired curve, immerse and soak the branch in water to make the stem pliable. Then tie it to the desired curve while still wet. When dry, unfasten, it will spring back some; so curve more than you need for the arrangement when tying the wet branch.

Split the stem ends of evergreen branches several times vertically for two or three inches and place in warm water to condition, overnight or longer. To condition evergreens use one tablespoon of glycerin to each quart of water. Keep the water level high by replacing the water in the container as it evaporates. Use a piece of charcoal to .absorb odors and keep the water sweet. Change the water weekly for longer keeping.

CONDITIONING VINES

With vines like English Ivy (Hedera helix) thoroughly wash all foliage. Submerge mature foliage in cold water for a couple of hours, young tender foliage only an hour. Then, place stems in cold water with no leaves below the water line. Sprays are long lasting and will take root. If you wish tie sprays in desired curves before submerging, then dry while still tied. Place spray ends in water filled orchid tubes for use in fruit and vegetable arrangements.

With flowering vines split woody stems and condition overnight in cold water. Submerge foliage about a half hour in cold water if necessary to firm and crisp it.

HOW TO KEEP ARRANGEMENTS FRESH

Pinholders, scissors, containers—all the equipment you use—should be spotlessly clean to keep down the bacterial count of the water. Use fresh clean water. Any decayed material or foul water will clog the tiny water tubes and decrease the water intake. Plastic foam is popular with arrangers and florists since it is so easily used. Flowers can be quickly adjusted to any angle. It is ideal for hospitals and gifts, as arrangements can be transported easily without dislocating the placements. It may be washed and reused if you care to go to that trouble.

Remove Unnecessary Foliage

Submerged foliage decays readily. It is best to remove all foliage below the water level unless you are using a glass container and leaves are part of the design. When using a glass container choose a flower with sturdy foliage that will not decompose readily in water, like the rose or carnation. Experiments prove leaves are an asset to the keeping quality of chrysanthemums and pansies, so remove only those well under water. Some flowers like the zinnia seem to keep better the more defoliated they are.

Remove all foliage from the lilac (syringa) and mockorange (philadelphus) branches to make the flowers last longer and display them better. Cut a few non-flowering branches, split and condition, to arrange with the flowering stems. Then as the foliage wilts it may easily be replaced without upsetting the arrangement.

Cut Some Stems Under Water

The floriculture departments at several of our state universities have carried on extensive experiments in keeping cut flowers. In England the Journal of the Royal Horticultural Society reported that recutting carnations under water and then leaving them to condition overnight definitely prolongs their life.

From experiments it would seem that the following flowers do benefit by recutting under water. In the case of most other flowers the practice seems ineffective.

African Violet, Saintpaulia
Antirrhinum majus, Snapdragon
Aster, Michaelmas Daisy

Callistephus chinensis, China Aster
Carnation
Chrysanthemum, Annual

Chrysanthemum frutescens,
 Marguerite
Dianthus chinensis, Garden
 Pink

Lathyrus, Sweet Pea
Nymphaeaceae, Water-Lily
Tagetes, Marigold

Acid and Alkaline Water

Most annuals, perennials and shrubs grow best in slightly acid to neutral soil. Bird-of-paradise flower, this can be bought cut at florists and will last for about a month, carnation, delphinium, hydrangea, larkspur, rose, snapdragon, stock and wisteria are some of the many flowers that like acidity. Plants like the mountain laurel, rhododendron, azalea and most of the needled evergreens prefer an even more acid condition. Plants like the peony, iris, hollyhock, lilac and mockorange thrive best in a neutral to slightly alkaline condition. Acid-loving plants when cut will keep best in slightly acid water and alkaline loving plants like water slightly alkaline. You may call your water department to find out how your local water tests.

If you have alkaline water you may make it acid by using 1 heaping tablespoon of sugar and 2 tablespoons white distilled vinegar to each quart of water. If you are having no difficulty in keeping flowers your local water supply is perhaps acid enough.

Table Salt and Sugar

The use of table salt helps some flowers absorb water more readily and hence last longer. Use 1 tablespoon of salt to each quart of water. Use it for achillea (yarrow or milfoil), begonias and coreopsis. Salt is also recommended by some people for asclepias (milkweed), althaea (hollyhock), antirrhinum (snapdragon), gaillardia, macleaya (plume-poppy), rose and tagetes (marigold).

Sugar, which acts as a nutrient, also prolongs the life of cut flowers. Use one rounded tablespoon of sugar to each 1 quart of water for the following.

Acer, Maple
Asclepias tuberosa, Butterfly-
 Weed

Aster (hardy), Michaelmas
 Daisy

Callistephus chinensis, China Aster

Chrysanthemum, annual and perennial

Gaillardia

Lathyrus, Sweet Pea

Lychnis chalcedonica, Maltese Cross

Nigella, Love-in-a-Mist

Petunia

Verbena

Other Chemical Aids

One tablespoon of household ammonia to two quarts of water is used by some with amaryllis to check bacterial growth, a tiny pinch of zinc sulphate crystals in one quart of water will retard decay of stems and foliage with marigolds, a pinch of potassium nitrate is advised for dahlias and hollyhocks and so it goes. More attention is being given to experiments in keeping flowers, so we should be getting more information along that line as results are obtained.

There are many trade-named chemicals on sale at flower shops and hardware stores for keeping cut flowers. They will help flowers last longer if added to the water and used as directed on the package. Composites of sugar and other materials which act as a nutrient and acidifier, check bacterial growth and also act as a mild fungicide to inhibit the growth of fungi, so help keep water fresh. Charcoal aids in keeping water sweet and odorless. It may be purchased from a florist or garden shop. Aspirin and the copper penny have been found to be of no value.

The primary considerations in keeping cut flowers fresh are clean utensils, good quality flowers, clean fresh water, proper conditioning, cutting the stems as necessary, keeping the stem ends always well covered with clean fresh water, fresh air, no direct sunlight and maintaining a cool humid atmosphere. There is no magic chemical that will take the place of these important factors.

8

FLOWERING BRANCHES
THAT MAY BE FORCED

Flowering branches forced indoors (see page 154) give a pre-season display of bloom, supplying the arranger with decorative branches when material is scarce and expensive. Forcing results will vary depending upon plant varieties grown, weather, soil conditions, stage of dormancy, chemical content of water, temperature, section of country, etc. but the list should be a helpful guide. The forcing schedule listed below is based on a 72° F. temperature during the day, around 55° to 60° F. at night. The branches available for forcing are endless, but will be determined individually by the sources available to you and your locale.

Acer palmatum—Japanese Maple. Small tree, shows beautiful coloring in early spring, some varieties have attractive, finely cut leaves which come in mid-May. Cut in early March, will force in two weeks; young leaves attractive and long lasting.

Acer rubrum—Red or Swamp Maple. Has shell-pink to scarlet-red blossoms, before the leaves come in April. Cut in mid-March, force in one week; watch young, attractive leaves come out as blossoms dry up.

Aesculus—Horse-Chestnut. Sticky bud on terminal twig develops into showy cluster of flowers ranging from white through yellow and pink to shades of purple and red which bloom in late May. Cut in mid-March, force in five to six weeks, last two weeks.

How To Force Flowering Branches

Soak branches in bath tub for 24 hours

Cut branches with sharp tool on a mild day

Place branches deep in water until buds break

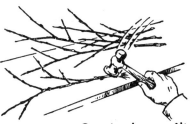

Crush stems with hammer to aid water intake

Place in sunny window for flowering

Alnus—Alder. Catkins come in advance of foliage in early April. Cut in January, force in two to three weeks, catkins long lasting.

Amelanchier canadensis—Shadbush. White flowers which come in late April before foliage. Most conspicuous of woody plants. Cut late January; force 3-4 weeks; last 1 week.

Azalea. Branches cut end of January or early in February; force in 3-6 weeks; last 5-10 days.

Betula—Birch. The unfolding of its pale green foliage and its delicately hanging catkins is interesting to watch. Catkins come in mid-April. Cut in early February; force in 2-4 weeks, long lasting.

Carya—Hickory. Attractive drooping catkins in early spring. Tender, new growth of foliage also attractive.

Cercis canadensis—Red Bud. Rosy-pink flowers come in clusters in mid-May before the leaves. Cut in early March, force in 2-3 weeks; leaves will come out and keep as blossoms dry.

Chaenomeles lagenaria—Flowering or Japanese Quince. Keeps 4-7 days; forces readily, cut in early February it forces in 4-5 weeks, in mid-March 2 weeks.

Cornus florida (white) and **rubra** (pink)—Flowering Dogwood. Cut mid-March will force in 2-4 weeks; last 7-10 days.

Cornus mas—Cornelian Cherry. Cut in late January; force in 2-3 weeks; lasts 1 week.

Corylopsis spicata—Winter Hazel. Cut in early February will force in 2-3 weeks; last 1 week.

Corylus—Hazelnut or Filbert. Related to the birch, has equally interesting drooping, bronzy-yellow catkins, which come in March. Cut in late January; force in $2\frac{1}{2}$ weeks; catkins long lasting.

Crataegus—Hawthorn. White, pink or scarlet flowers bloom in May. Cut middle of March will force in 4-5 weeks; last 1 week.

Cytisus scoparius—Scotch Broom. Cut in late January will force in 4-6 weeks; cut mid-March will force in 2-3 weeks. Leaves outlast blossoms, which go quickly, valuable as line branches.

Dogwood is one of the most completely satisfactory and long-lasting of flowering trees for arrangements. Its creamy bracts, being in fact modified leaves, are much more durable than true petals would be. Split the stems of this and other hardwooded arrangement material, to permit better water take-up.

Arrangement by Myra J. Brooks   Roche Photo

The branches available for indoor forcing will depend on the locale but there should be an ample supply to give the arranger preseason decorative material when it is scarce and expensive. This tulip arrangement is simple and highly effective.

ARRANGEMENT BY MYRA J. BROOKS   ROCHE PHOTO

Daphne mezereum—February Daphne. Fragrant lilac-purple flowers appear in early April before leaves. Cut in late January will force in 2-3 weeks; last 1 week.

Deutzia. Cut mid-March will force in 5-6 weeks; last 2 weeks.

Forsythia. Cut in early January; force in 3 weeks; cut in early February, force in 2 weeks; cut in mid-March force in 1 week. Last 1 week.

Fothergilla. Cut in early March will force in 2-3 weeks; last 1 week.

Hamamelis mollis—Witch-Hazel. Fragrant yellow flower clusters with purplish-red calyx, occasionally bloom in December, mostly February and March. Cut in January will force in a week and last a week.

Juglans cinerea—Butternut. New growth attractive in arrangements, creates oriental feeling. Cut branches in early spring when new growth is at stage you like it.

Kalmia latifolia—Mountain Laurel. Cut in mid-March will force in 5 weeks; flowers last 2 weeks, foliage 4 weeks.

Kerria japonica—Kerrybush. Cut in early March will force in $2\frac{1}{2}$ weeks. Flowers last 5 days but buds continue to open.

Kolkwitzia amabilis—Beauty Bush. Cut mid-March, will force in 5-7 weeks, last 2 weeks.

Leucothoe. Cut in March will force in 4-5 weeks. Flowers last 1-2 weeks; foliage longer.

Lindera—Spicebush. Cut in woods in early February, will force in 2-3 weeks, and last 10 days.

Lonicera—Honeysuckle. Cut in early March will force in 1-2 weeks and last a week.

Magnolia. If frost threatens as flowers are ready to burst cut branches and open indoors. Branches cut in early March will force in 4-5 weeks. Flowers last 3-4 days.

Malus. Cut branches when buds are well developed and just ready to burst for short forcing period. Cut in mid-March will force in 2-3 weeks and last a week.

APPLE BLOSSOMS: Bloom in early May. Branches cut in late January or early February will force in 4-5 weeks, last 1 week or more.

FLOWERING CRAB-APPLES: Bloom in May. Branches cut in early March will force in 2-4 weeks and last 5-6 days.

Philadelphus—Mock-Orange. Cut middle of March will force in 4-5 weeks. Single flowers last 2-3 days, double 4-6.

Pieris—Andromeda. Cut in early February they force in 3-4 weeks, in mid-March 1-2 weeks. Flowers last 10-12 days.

Populus—Poplar. Drooping catkins appear in early April. Cut in late January will force in 3 weeks, in mid-March in 1 week. Catkins long lasting.

Prunus—Flowering Fruit Trees. Cut in mid-March may be forced in two to three weeks. Last a week.

P. DAVIDIANA—Flowering Almond. Cut in January will force in 3-4 weeks, in mid-March 2 weeks, last 1 week.

P. MARITIMA—Beach Plum. Cut in late January or early February will force in 4-5 weeks, last 1 week.

P. MUME—Flowering Apricot. Cut late January or early February forces in 3-4 weeks, last 1 week.

P. PERSICA—Flowering Peach. Cut in late January will force in 4-5 weeks, last 1 week.

P. SIEBOLDII—Flowering Cherry. Cut end of January will force in 3-4 weeks, mid-March 2-3 weeks. Will last 2 weeks.

P. TRILOBA—Flowering Plum. Cut in late January will force in 3-4 weeks, last 10 days with buds opening.

Pyrus communis—Pear. Cut in late January or early February will force in 4-5 weeks, in mid-March 2-3 weeks, will last 2 weeks.

Quercus—Oak. In the spring the young pink leaves of the oak are soft and velvety looking and its branches bear slender, drooping catkins, a spike of tiny, minute flowers, which appear in mid-May. Cut in early March they force in 2-4 weeks and the catkins are long lasting.

Rhododendron. Flowers in color range from white through pink, lavender, lilac to red. Bloom from mid-May until mid-June. Cut in February or March will force in 4-6 weeks, last 7 to 10 days.

Rhus canadensis—Sumac. Yellowish flowers in clustered spikes come in early May before the leaves. Cut in mid-March will force in 2 weeks, last 5-8 days.

Ribes odoratum—Currant. Fragrant yellow flowers in early May. Cut in early April when buds are breaking, will flower in week to 10 days, last 1 week.

Rosa hugonis. Cut in early April as yellow shows in buds, will force in a week. Shatters quickly but effective for day or two.

Salix—Willow. Another of the group of trees with interesting drooping catkins in early spring.

SALIX DISCOLOR. Pussy Willow. Cut in February, will force in 1-2 weeks. Keeps well. To stop "pussies" from developing long yellow, pollen-filled catkins, remove bud scales. Cultivated varieties have larger, more striking "pussies" than swamp varieties. When fully developed unless you want them rooted, use container without water to eliminate tendency to drop as roots develop.

Spirea—Bridal Wreath. Cut in mid-March will force in 4 weeks, last 4-10 days.

Syringa—Lilac. Lilacs which bloom in May and June are found in most yards. Will force well if large or long branches are selected. Cut in early March a long branch will force in four to five weeks and will keep a week. Free flowering and very ornamental, the wonderful new hybrids range in color from pure white to deep crimson, through many shades of lilac, with some soft pinks, some almost blue. Single or double, they are usually very fragrant and offer many possibilities for the arranger.

Wisteria. May be forced in 5 weeks if cut in mid-March. Will last a week.

9

PLANTS WHICH DRY WELL

Nature has a wonderful way of distributing her wares. Each season has its beauty from the rich, lush colors of summer and early fall to the lovely more somber hues of the seed pods, fruit cones and grasses of late autumn. When you no longer have fresh flowers from the garden, the "winter" or dried bouquet, made from natural materials, well designed and well executed, and planned for its specific place, can add beauty and charm to a front entrance, living room or library. Do not keep the same arrangement out too long, however, no matter how lovely it is. After a few weeks tuck it away in a closet or drawer, whole, or take it apart and save the materials. Then another year, as with children's toys, it will evoke the same happy response.

WHEN AND WHERE TO FIND MATERIAL

For dried arrangements, start collecting as early as June and continue until fall or frost to obtain variety. There is a wealth of material available. Collect from the flower, herb and vegetable gardens; from shrubs, trees and vines; from roadsides, meadows, fields and woods; from swamps and seashore. In fact, gather wherever things grow. Even the mosses and lichens will dry and may prove useful. The endless variety of exciting commonplace plant material is astounding and making dried arrangements need not involve any expense except time, effort and ingenuity. If you wish, however, a wide assortment of exotic, dried material shipped in from the tropics, may be purchased from the florist. Hawaii, California, Florida and the south supply magnolia and eucalyptus leaves, lotus seed pods, Hawaiian wood roses, rose-colored California pepper berries (Schinus molle) and many other dramatic and showy items.

Not all flowers dry well, but those that do must be gathered at the right time and conditioned properly to obtain the best results and maintain good color. In general, allow two weeks for material to dry. Most material should be gathered just as it becomes mature, but here again there are exceptions. You may be more successful with some flowers than with others. Experiment. It's fun and keep records. They'll prove helpful for another year.

DRY TWICE AS MUCH AS YOU NEED

When gathering material to dry, if you want six leaves, cut and dry twelve. In other words, dry about twice as much material as you want, to allow for breakage. Dried material must be handled with care and more dexterity is required than in arranging fresh flowers. Of course, once a dried bouquet is constructed it stays as arranged, which is an advantage.

Most enthusiasts who design long lasting arrangements dry just about everything that can be dried from the garden, but for added interest they also buy exotic tropical and desert materials which do not grow locally, especially interesting seed pods and spectacular leaves from local florists. Glycerin treated galax, eucalyptus, salal and magnolia leaves are long lasting and color attractively. The leaves of palms (some cut and trimmed), crotons, dracaenas, tis and branches of the eucalyptus are highly decorative. The long slender beans of the catalpa, the seed pods of the angels-trumpet (Datura), agave, tulip tree, jacaranda and the bowl-shaped, flat-topped lotus pod are all interesting and useful. Dried artichokes are excellent as focal areas; Scotch heather holds its color well. Your florist shop probably has a wide assortment of exotic dried material.

Many flowers dry well. The secret is to pick them at the right time, when they are just mature and properly developed, if too mature they will shatter.

There are many leaves and much branched foliage that offer the substance and solidity so often lacking in poorly designed dried arrangements. Many of the bold, dramatic leaves are highly effective used in contemporary settings.

Make the most of the flower and herb garden throughout the season and then take advantage of what is left for "dried bouquets." Many of the seed pods are excellent. The pods of the lupine, iris, poppy, coneflower, wisteria and trumpet vine are among some of the most interesting and decorative. Hang upside down to dry.

The form and pattern of burrs, cones, fruits, nuts, seed pods and spurs furnish an interesting selection of materials with which to work. Gather when mature and fully developed. Remove the leaves and tie stems with a string, hanging heads down, or stand in a container to dry or simply store in a covered box in a dry place.

Many of the berried branches are decorative in fall and winter arrangements, many have lines of remarkable beauty. Used with either green, autumn or dried foliage pleasing patterns and forms may be created. If thorny wear gloves or wrap branch in sheets of newspaper.

Grasses, grains, reeds and sedges, both wild and cultivated make up a very effective group. They supply the height and graceful curves necessary in large decorations. Gather these grasses when fully developed, from July through September. Remove the leaves from the stems and store in a box. If there is danger of the heads being shattered tie and hang heads down or stand in a container to dry, allowing plenty of space.

The grass family includes the pasture and meadow grasses as well as the cultivated ornamental types, the fodder kinds, the reeds and also the cereal grains. Closely resembling the grasses are the sedges, many of which inhabit swamp and low places.

Do not overlook the vegetable garden, with its wealth of possibilities. Start drying *broccoli leaves* from the middle of July on, when they are mature and green, before frost comes. They dry to warm tans, with delicate mauve tints. The same is true of cabbage and cauliflower leaves, which dry a lovely soft pinkish-purple. Kale leaves also respond well, select different sizes for variety. These leaves have no stems so attach a false stem to the back of the leaf.

When cut green, the leaves and tassels of ordinary garden *corn* become a pleasing chartreuse. Just hang upside down. Miniature corn, crimson strawberry popcorn, maize and the ornamentals, which come in various colors, all add variety and dry

DRYING TECHNIQUES

DRY NATURALLY. Gather grasses, grains, berried branches, cones and seed pods in fall. Remove leaves, store in covered boxes.

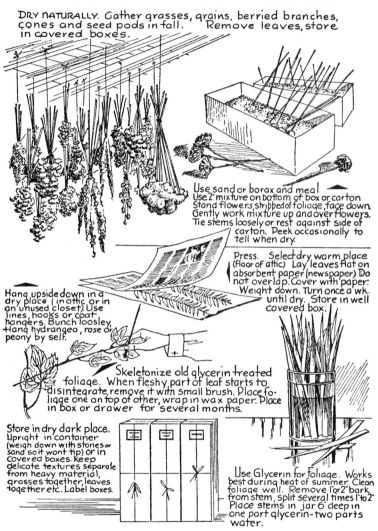

Use sand or borax and meal
Use 2" mixture on bottom of box or carton Stand flowers, stripped of foliage, face down Gently work mixture up and over flowers. Tie stems loosely or rest against side of carton. Peek occasionally to tell when dry.

Press. Select dry warm place (floor of attic) Lay leaves flat on absorbent paper (newspaper) Do not overlap. Cover with paper. Weight down. Turn once a wk. until dry. Store in well covered box.

Hang upside down in a dry place (in attic or in an unused closet) Use lines, hooks or coat hangers, Bunch loosely Hang hydrangea, rose or peony by self.

Skeletonize old glycerin treated foliage. When fleshy part of leaf starts to disintegrate, remove it with small brush. Place foliage one on top of other, wrap in wax paper. Place in box or drawer for several months.

Store in dry dark place. Upright in container (weigh down with stones or sand so it wont tip) or in covered boxes. Keep delicate textures separate from heavy material, grasses together, leaves together etc. Label boxes.

Use Glycerin for foliage. Works best during heat of summer. Clean foliage well. Remove 1 or 2" bark from stem, split several times 1 to 2" Place stems in jar 6" deep in one part glycerin—two parts water.

well. Let *okra* pods mature, but pick them before frost. Then hang upside down to dry a grayish-brown, with beige stripes, interesting in both texture and form. The light, gray flower of the *leek* is delicate and effective and the white flowers of rhubarb turn a lovely cream. Gourds, which should be picked after maturity and before frost hits them, are ornamental and add color throughout the Halloween and Thanksgiving seasons.

HANGING METHOD FOR DRYING

One of the easiest and best ways to dry plant material is to tie the stems together with a string or rubber band and hang heads down in a dry place, as our grandmothers did their herbs. In this way the flowers keep their shape and do not shatter. This is the method which is generally used for most flowers. Foliage should be stripped at once, except in a few cases like thermopsis, its foliage dries well. Any dark, dry place like an attic, a dry shed or an unused closet fitted with lines spaced far enough apart so flowers will not touch each other is suitable. Hooks or wire coat hangers may be used. Bunch flowers loosely in groups of perhaps ten, depending upon the size of the flower, but hang larger flowers or those that might shatter easily like hydrangeas, peonies and roses separately, one to a string, so they will not lose any of their petals. In two to three weeks flowers should be dry. They may be left hanging; if you need the space, stand flowers that shatter easily in jars or cans. Put the other dried flowers in boxes until you want to use them.

To curve stems, soak one-half hour in warm water, wire or tie stem to a coat hanger bent to shape you want, dry tied to hanger.

SAND OR BORAX AND MEAL TO PRESERVE COLOR

To keep the shape and color of flowers like the dahlia, lily, marigold, narcissi, pansies, Queen Annes Lace, tithonia and zinnia either use sifted, fine beach sand, thoroughly dried or mix one part powdered borax with six parts white cornmeal and spread either mixture over the bottom of a pan, box or carton, the bottom reinforced with several thicknesses of paper. Use two inches or more of the sand or mixture. Stand the dry flowers, stripped of foliage, face down. Do not let flowers overlap and gently work the mixture around, up and over the flowers until they are just lightly but completely covered. Smooth out any petals that may need it. Stems may be loosely tied together or rested against the side of the carton. Do not cover, store in a dark, dry, cool place from one to three weeks. The mixture may be used over and over again. When flowers are thoroughly dry, gently remove from mixture and with a soft brush carefully wipe away any sand or borax. With limited home space there is always room to tuck a box somewhere. Use the sand or borax with flowers like the following. The lighter textured types like daisies and jonquils will only require two or three days while a tougher texture like the lily may take three to five weeks to dry. Remove a flower occasionally to check and see how it is drying.

Bleeding-heart	Marigold
Candytuft	Nandina Sprays
Canterbury Bell	Narcissus
Chrysanthemum, Pompon	Queen Annes Lace
Coleus Leaves	Pansy
Dahlia	Peach Sprays
Daisy	Plum Sprays
Delphiniums	Quince, Flowering
Deutzias	Roses—all kinds
Dogwood-pink	Snapdragons
Doronicum, Leopards-Bane	Spiraea biliardi
Euonymus Leaves	Stock
Gloxinia	Sunflowers
Leucothoe	Tithonia
Lilac	Violets
Lily	Zinnia
Lily-of-the-valley	

SKELETONIZING LEAVES

This technique, developed in the early days, was lost for many years and is now back in vogue again. Although skeletonized leaves appear airy and delicate, they are in reality durable and hold their shape well. Using the old-fashioned method, boil leaves one-half hour in soda water using one teaspoon of soda to each quart of water. Let the leaves cool in the water in which they are boiled. Then, spread on a newspaper and with a dull knife scrap away the fleshy part of the leaf on both sides. Work carefully, not tearing any of the structural or skeleton framework. Place leaves in a solution using two tablespoons of bleach to each quart of water for one hour or more. Then rinse with clear water. Wipe gently with soft cloth. Place between sheets of absorbent paper, like paper towels. Press between pages of an old magazine for 24 hours.

Some glycerin-treated foliage, like the crab-apple, elaeagnus, galax, iris and magnolia as it gets old skeletonizes naturally. The fleshy part disintegrates, leaving the vein structure. When the leaves start to deteriorate carefully remove the fleshy part with a small brush. Then place the foliage, one on top of the other and wrap together in wax paper, this keeps the leaves slightly moist. Put in box or drawer for several months.

GLYCERINIZING LEAVES

A glycerin solution may be used to preserve foliage and it works best used during the heat of the summer, since the leaves seem to drink up the glycerin solution more rapidly at that time. Clean all foliage to remove any dust or dirt and cut away any defects. Remove one or two inches of bark from each stem end and then split it with a sharp knife for a couple of inches so it will absorb liquid readily. Place the stems in a jar, about six inches deep, in a solution of one part glycerin to two parts water. When full absorption takes place, usually after two weeks or more, remove from the glycerin solution, which may be saved and reused. Store liquid in a covered jar.

Some leaves change color, others are not affected. Green leaves most frequently turn brown as the lovely magnolia does. Reactions in color vary with the type plant, the time of cutting and length of time left in the solution. Elaeganus leaves, at the end of two weeks, are green but left long enough will turn bright yellow. Foliage removed at the half-way stage may be brown in the center, along the large vein with an irregular green outline around the edge. These leaves keep well. Barberry gathered in the spring turns bright red, gathered in autumn it turns brown. For leaves that change color remove from glycerin when color is right.

Beech, crab-apple, forsythia, plum and almost all the bronze-red foliage retain their own texture and color. Thin textured materials which do not change color require less time and must be watched closely since it is more difficult to tell when they have had enough. A week, is as a rule sufficient. However, re-move at the slightest sign of drooping. Unless too saturated re-store foliage by tieing and hanging upside down for a couple of days.

Beech leaves are particularly lovely and useful, cut while green or after they have turned a golden color in the fall. In 3 or 4 days they are soft and pliable, a little darker, yet, hard to tell from fresh leaves.

Glycerin gives a smooth, satiny finish to most foliage, although a coarse textured leaf like the leatherleaf viburnum stays rough and brown. Everything treated with glycerin keeps indefinitely and may be used in fresh arrangements, as well as dried. Water does not hurt glycerin treated foliage. In the case of Boston and English ivy and low growing plants, which may absorb moisture through their leaves, immerse the whole leaf in a thicker solu-tion, using equal parts of water and glycerin.

PRESSING FLOWERS AND FOLIAGE

To dry leaves pick them when green or at height of autumn color. Lay leaves or flowers you want to press flat on several thicknesses of newspaper which is absorbent. Weight down with bricks or heavy books. Choose a warm, dry place. The floor of the attic is perfect. Few basements are dry enough. A little used room or closet will serve the purpose. Place each flower or leaf by itself, so that they will not touch each other and stick together. If they do, they will break when pulled apart after they start drying. Once a week turn each leaf or flower and when *thoroughly dry,* in about three weeks, store until needed. Lay on a newspaper in a large, flat box and cover. Any heavy textured leaf dries well properly handled. Pressed flowers are popular for making flower pictures.

NATURAL DRYING

Many berried branches, grasses, grains, reeds and sedges, burrs, cones, fruits, nuts, seed pods and spurs just dry naturally. Some of the leaves like eucalyptus and lemon or salal, with their lovely soft green color need no treatment. Arrange and then allow them to dry simply by not replacing water.

Bleeding heart, dahlias, daisies, lilacs, narcissus, roses and tulips may be enjoyed first in fresh arrangements. Don't let them go past their prime. Then dry in borax. Bells of Ireland, acacia flowers and foliage and bird-of-paradise flowers may be arranged and then left to dry naturally. Many of the foliages like boxwood, holly, iris, some of the palm leaves, pandanus, sansevieria, sea-grape, teasel leaves and viburnum leatherleaf may be arranged in a small amount of water and then left to dry.

STORING DRIED PLANT MATERIAL

Store all grasses, grains, branches, seed pods and cones in covered boxes in a dry place. Depending upon the space available and the method which is most convenient, plant material may be stood upright without water in large containers. The large tin can used for fruit juices is excellent, but weight the can down with stones or sand so it will not tip. Delicate flowers are best left standing in a container as they might shatter if placed in a box. Always store in a *dark, dry* place. Bright light will fade the colors in time especially blooms like the hydrangea, with soft delicate tones. However, some dried flowers with intense colors, like red celosia become lovelier as they fade taking on softer orange-bronzy tones. Keep delicate textures separated from the heavy materials. Have fruits together in one box, grasses and grains in another and label everything well for easy finding.

MATERIALS TO DRY

Acacia—Mimosa. Golden flowers and fernlike foliage, some bluish-green, steel-blue, some with silver cast and also grayish-green. Both dry well. In spring press or hang upside down. Thin pea-like pods attractive.

Ageratum. Place blue and white flowers in jar using a little water so won't dehydrate too quickly.

Albizzia. Small tree or shrub of pea family. Pale yellow to golden-brown seed pods 8″ to 10″ long. Like mimosa pods, only larger.

African Tulip Pods. 6″ to 8″ long, boat-shaped, black outside, light tan inside.

Alfalfa or Purple Medic-clover—Medicago sativa. Collect from fields in May and June. Small purple clover-like flowers. Hang upside down.

Amaranthus. An everlasting; white, purple or violet globe flowers; branched, graceful stems. Princess Feather has red panicles. Hang upside down.

Ambrosia mexicana—Feather-Geranium (Chenopodium botrys). Pretty, feathery spikes of fragrant green, oblong leaves. Hang upside down or place lengthwise in borax. Both flowers and foliage press well.

Anemone—Wind Flower. Dry buds, flowers and leaves in borax or press. Store tasseled seed pods in box.

Angel Feathers. Lacey and transparent, medium 5″ in white or pastels, large 7″ natural color. Sold by florists.

Angels-Trumpet—Datura arborea. Large white flowers followed by interesting seed pods used in arrangements.

Anthurium. Dries well, upside down method. As cut flower will last a month.

Apple-of-Peru—Nicandra physalodes. Old-fashioned garden favorite with blue flowers. Seed pods useful in dried arrangements. Hang upside down or just store in box.

Artemisia—Silver King. Dried for its finely hairy, silver or grayish-white foliage. Hang upside down.

Artemisia stelleriana—Dusty Miller. Pick at the seashore from August until frost. Small white heads of disk flowers and densely woolly foliage appear almost white. Showy and fragrant. Foliage more useful than flowers. Hang upside down.

Artichoke. Can buy dried by dozen from supply house, 2″-4″ in diameter, light tan in color. Dry fruit or thistle-like buds, using upside down method.

Ash, Red—Fraxinus pennsylvanica. Canoe-shaped seed pods, excellent for miniatures.

Aspidistra—Iron Plant. Stiff, shining basal leaves, green or striped, may be hung upside down or treated with glycerin. Effective in contemporary settings.

Aster—Michaelmas Daisy. Wild New England aster found growing in fields, has small blue daisy-like flowers. Some white, pink and lavender. Press flowers and foliage for flower pictures or use borax method to dry.

Astilbe. Wild and cultivated. Feathery trusses of tiny flowers from purple-pink to white. Cut in late fall. Hang upside down or use borax method. Attractive seed heads which dry well, retaining their color. Both flowers and foliage press.

Aucuba. Plain and variegated. Glycerin treatment turns leaves lovely, glossy, very dark brown, almost black.

Autumn Leaves. Clean and brush with two coats of clear shellac to preserve.

Avocado Seeds. Look like large grayish-purple plums. Peel off outer skin for golden-brown color.

Azalea. Press flowers and foliage for flower pictures.

Babys-Breath—Gypsophila. White and pink flowers. Stand in jar to dry.

Balloon Flower—Platycodon grandiflorum. Purple and white flowers. Use borax method.

Ball Teasel. Dark brown color, stems 18″-24″. Can buy from supply house.

Balsam—Impatiens balfouri. Pink, rose and white camellia-like flowers in clusters close to stem. Use borax method, flowers turn rose-beige.

Bamboo—Phyllostachys aurea. Press fernleaf bamboo leaves.

Banana—Musa. Dry leaves on flat surface.

Banana Shrub. Michelia fuscata also known as Magnolia fuscata. Shiny leaves lined with purple. Treat with glycerin.

Banksia grandis. Handsome, long and narrow dark green foliage, silvery white or brownish beneath. Simply store leaves in boxes.

Baptisca australis—False indigo. Save the short, plump medium-sized seed pods which turn from green to gunmetal. Foliage treated with glycerin and water turns a fine dark blue.

Barberry—Berberis. Glycerin method turns leaves bright red in spring, in fall bright orange-scarlet foliage turns brownish-wine color. Attractive red, yellow or black berries.

Barley. Erect flower or grain heads 4″ long, the stout appendages 8″ long. Good for line effects.

Bayberry—Myrica. Gather near the seashore from September to frost. Dull gray-green leaves and grayish-white berries. Remove leaves. Hang upside down.

Bead Weed. Dark brown color, stems 30″, good for line. May be purchased from supply house.

Beauty Bush—Kolkwitzia. Fruit, ¼″ long, and stalk covered with bristly hairs. Simply store in box.

Bee-Balm—Monarda didyma. Scarlet flowers in 2″ long terminal clusters, coarse leaves to 6″ long. Hang upside down to dry.

Beech Tree—Fagus. Cut green branches while leaves are green, from July on, with unopened cups which contain the immature nuts. They will open and look like little starry four petaled flowers. Hang upside down. Retain natural color. For golden tan to brown leaves gather in September, before the sap is drawn and use glycerin method. Easy foliage to work with. May also use glycerin on green leaves.

Bell Pods. 1″ in diameter, 3 to 8 at top of 8″-12″ stem, gray to brown in color; can buy from a supply house.

Bells-Of-Ireland. Cut when they turn silvery-beige. Hang to dry. Will also dry naturally in a bouquet. For variety strip stalk of foliage leaving only bell-shaped calyx.

Birch, Gray—Betula populifolia. Use glycerin treatment to preserve leaves.

Bird Leaves. Exotic 12″ to 14″ long on 12″ stems, green to brown-gray in color, can buy from a supply house.

Bird of Paradise—Strelitzia reginae. Dries very well, even after used in a fresh arrangement.

Bitter-Sweet (American)—Celastrus scandens. Cut berried branches in late fall. Yellow and orange fruits open to reveal crimson-coated seeds. Hang upside down. Oriental Bitter-sweet (C. orbiculatus) more commonly found on home grounds.

Bitter-Sweet (European)—Solanum dulcamara; also known as Nightshade. Cut scarlet berried branches before freezing weather. Berries are poisonous if eaten.

Blackberry-Lily—Belamcanda chinensis. Grow in garden for tan seed pods, which burst to show shiny black seeds resembling a large seeded blackberry. Collect in fall. Hang upside down.

Black-Eyed Susan—Rudbeckia hirta. Gather from the fields and roadsides. Daisy-like head of vivid yellow, ray-flowers around a purplish-brown center. Treat in borax.

Blazing Star—Liatris. Purple, rose and white spike flowerheads. Will last 5 years or more. Strip some stalks of petals exposing the calyx which has pale green segments with yellow centers. Hang upside down to dry.

Bleached Cordone. Small heads 2″-2½″, large 3″-4″, creamy-white, may be purchased from a supply house.

Bleeding Heart—Dicentra spectabilis. Place lengthwise in borax or press between absorbent papers, both foliage and flowers.

Blue Thimble-Flower—Gilia capitata. Has dense roundish heads of light blue flowers. Hang upside down.

Boneset—Eupatorium. Dull grayish-white flowers in flat topped clusters. Cut in bud stage so won't shatter. Hang upside down.

Bottle-brush-grass—Hystrix patula. Tall bristly grass with flat leaves and awned spikelets borne in terminal spikes. Good for line. Store in box.

Bottle-Tree—Brachychiton. Interesting woody pods which split.

Bottle Weed. Light tan, pink, light green, 24″ stems, may be purchased from supply house.

Boxwood. Press or dry in small amount of water. Will hold shape well and remain green.

Brazilian Brown Nuts. Brown in color, branches 24″ to 30″ long, may be purchased from supply house.

Bread-Tree—Adenanthera. Fruit a long narrow, parallel margined pod that coils when ripe, to 8″ long. Seeds used for beadwork. Foliage resembles acacia.

Broccoli. Leaves dry to warm tans with delicate mauve tint. Place on flat surface to dry.

Broom-Sedge—Andropogon virginicus. Collect attractive fruited branches in fields in August-September. Place in jar or store in boxes.

Brown Burr Pods at end of 18″ stems, cinnamon-brown in color, may be purchased from supply house.

Buckthorn, Indian-cherry—Rhamnus caroliniana. Shrub or small tree. Fruit red, then black. Collect in swamps and lowlands in S.E. U.S. in May-June. Nutlets are in groups of three.

Bulbous Buttercup—Ranunculus. Collect in fields and woods in summer. Use borax method. Flowers retain form and brilliant yellow color.

Butterfly-Bush—Buddleia. Showy lavender, maroon or white spikes. Cut when blooms are well colored and place lengthwise in borax to dry.

Cabbage. Leaves dry a delicate pinkish-purple. Cut when leaves are green and mature before frost. Select varying sizes. Lay flat to dry.

Cactus Spoons. Light tan in color, 18″ long, buy from supply house.

Calendula. Orange or yellow flowers. Dry in borax.

Calliopsis tinctoria—Coreopsis. Fruits flattish but become curved, small, dry and crowded. Useful to the arranger. Store in box.

Camellia. Some varieties turn brown dried. Put in borax. Preserve attractive dark green shiny leaves in glycerin.

Candytuft—Iberis affinis. White, pink and lavender flowers. Dry in sand or borax.

Canna. Varies in height and color of foliage, usually sea green, green with a bluish-gray tinge. Pick leaves when frost lays them flat for an excellent brown color.

Canterbury Bells—Campanula. Purple, pink and white flowers may be dried in sand or borax.

Cape-Marigold—Dimorphotheca. White, purple, yellow and orange daisy-like flowers. Use borax method or cut off petals leaving only small amount of color around center and then hang upside down to dry.

Carnation—Dianthus caryophyllus. Pink, red, white, variegated. Virginia Supreme good dark pink, Peter Fisher lighter pink and variegated, Linda. Use borax. Can cut off most of petals leaving just a little color in the pale green calyx.

Carolina Allspice—Calycanthus floridus. Old-fashioned plant. Maroon flowers about 2″ wide, retain fragrance when dried. Dry in borax.

Carolina Sedge—Carex caroliniana. Slender sedge, erect and tall. Cut in fields and meadows in May-July for line in arrangements. Store in box.

Carrion Flower—Smilax herbacea. Bluish-black fruit in handsome long-stalked clusters. Eastern N.A. in May.

Castor-Bean—Ricinus communis. Grown as annual in north. Gather spiny pods in the fall, contain three large poisonous seeds, turn a lovely slate blue, some an orange-red. Hang upside down. Large dark green or red foliage also interesting, creating tropical, exotic effect.

Catalpa. Long slender beans. Collect from September to frost.

Grasses and ferns are among the most commonly neglected of arrangement materials, yet they provide textures unavailable elsewhere. Both may be dried readily. They are shown here with a group of daisies which also dry well.

ARRANGEMENT BY MYRA J. BROOKS   ROCHE PHOTO

Foliage, alone, makes a highly dramatic arrangement. Leaves of such familiar shade trees as oak and beech may be used as well as those of many other ornamental trees and shrubs. Dried beech and oak are practically everlasting.

ARRANGEMENT BY MRS. ANSON HOWE SMITH   GEO. M. CUSHING JR. PHOTO

Catnip—Nepeta cataria. Fruiting branch resembles shrimp plant, green and tan. Use borax method to dry.

Cattails—Typha latifolia. Pick both small and large, found in marshy places throughout the United States, in June or before July 4th if you want them to last. They dry a light tan. Dry the leaves too, which are "Chinesey" in effect. Hang upside down.

Cauliflower. Cut leaves of varying sizes. They dry a soft pinkish-purple. Lay flat on table to dry.

Cecropia. Tropical tree. California and Florida. Large, radiately lobed, shield-formed leaves borne at end of branches. Collect after dry on tree.

Cedar—Cedrus deodara. Graceful drooping branches, 5″ cones. C. libanotica, Cedar of Lebanon, dark green leaves and 4″ cones.

Celosia—Cockscomb. Only flower which can be preserved with glycerin method. Bold and handsome dried. Needs more care in drying than most flowers. Cut at the height of bloom, when at very best, through summer until frost, place in a container with no water, and when the stems are free from moisture, hang upside down in a dry, dark place. If moisture remains in the stems, mildew will appear and the blooms may be ruined. When fades in strong light from red to orange or bronze tones even more attractive. Plumed or feathery and crested; come in wide variety of sizes and colors from pale cream to yellow and gold; pale pink to magenta and deep red, sometimes mixed with scarlet and orange. Dry foliage too.

Century Plant—Agave americana. Leaves 6 ft. long. Three-valved dry, splitting pods interesting in arrangements.

Chaste-Tree—Vitex agnus-castus. Lavender-blue flower spikes. Use borax.

Checkerberry, Wintergreen—Gaultheria procumbens. Oval, leathery leaves, nodding white flowers borne singly. Valued by arrangers for scarlet, berry-like fruits.

China-Berry, Umbrella-Tree—Melia azedarach. Fragrant lilac flowers in loose panicles. Yellow oval fruits hang for a long time. Treasured by arrangers. Seeds threaded as beads.

Chinese Hawthorn—Photinia serrulata. Leathery, dark glossy green leaves, crimson tinted when young. Glycerin method gives leaves satiny finish. Round red berries attractive.

Chinese Lantern—Physalis alkekengi. Inflated calyx of fruit conspicuous in fall. Cut in summer or August for green lanterns and in September or October for bright orange color. Hang upside down to dry. Split some of the paper thin husks into three sections for variety. Cut along veins from tip to base.

Chokeberry—Aronia. A. arbutifolia. Profusion of red berries which ripen in September, remain colorful most of winter. Hang upside down. A. melanocarpa var. grandifolia. Shining black fruits ripe in August, outstanding lustrous leaf.

Chrysanthemum. Yellow varieties dry well. Also compact whites and pinks. Hang or dry in borax.

Clematis addisoni. White and purple flowers. Use borax method to dry.

Clover, Bush—Lespedeza. Found in fields and along roadsides. Graceful plant with white and some rosy-purple flowers. Pick from July to frost for pinky-green color. Dried, it stays a soft green, with a pink tinge. A combination can then be made with last year's supply, which has gone through the winter and has taken on brown tones. Brown picked after frost. Hang upside down.

Clover—Trifolium pratense. Red, Pasture or Meadow Clover. Rose-purple flowers in globular heads. Cut in fields and meadows from spring until frost. Hang upside down.

Coconut Palm—Cocos nucifera. Florida. Use calyx and sheath. Tan in color dried. May buy at supply store.

Coleus. Colorful foliage with varied markings. Press or dry in borax.

Columbine—Aquilegia. Three to five chambered cups or spurs, lovely and interesting in arrangements. Store in box. Press flowers and foliage. Flowers in a lovely variety of shades may be dried in borax with leaves which turn to a delightful sandy tan.

Coffee Tree—Gymnocladus dioica. Kentucky. Greenish-white flowers in large clusters borne at ends of branches, followed by long, thick curved red-brown pods. Large, compound attractive leaves all decorative. Use borax for flowers. Store pods in a box. Leaves may be pressed.

Coneflower—Rubeckia. Showy large yellow and red flowers. Cut from August to frost. R. purpurea has purple to white rays. Remove all petals, leave centers attached to stems. Hang upside down or stand in empty jar, or bury whole flower in borax.

Coral Bells—Heuchera sanguinea. Preserve leaves in glycerin. Bury white or red flowers in sand or borax.

Cordone—Thistle. Light tan with lavender, brown or white centers, when purchased already dried. Heads $1\frac{1}{2}$"-3" diameter, on 24" stems.

Cordyline and Dracena. Include many handsome green and varicolored foliage plants. Ti of Hawaii, a cordyline. Leaves excellent in arrangements. Treat with glycerin.

Corn. Leaves and tassels dry well and add distinction to fruit and vegetable arrangements. Corn is appropriate at Thanksgiving. When green, the leaves and tassels of the ordinary sweet garden corn naturally dry a heavenly chartreuse. Variegated Indian or ornamental types and small crimson strawberry popcorn decorative. Bring in at height of color.

Cornflower—Centaurea cyanus. Blue, pink, red and white flowers. Use borax method.

Cosmos. Rose, pink and white flowers. Use borax method. Also press flowers and foliage.

Cotton. Use fully opened bolls or pods, also flowering bud. Hang upside down. Use borax method for buds. Oval pods when ripe are leathery, contain black seeds wrapped in a mass of white cotton fibers. May buy from supply house. Pods brown-gray on outside, white on inside on 2" to 4" stems.

Crab Apple, Japanese Flowering—Malus floribunda. Single red-tinted buds open to a light pink. Fragrant yellow fruit. M. eleyi reddish-purple foliage. Buds deep purplish red. M. niedwetskyana earliest to bloom. Leaves change to red, flowers bronze to red. All leaves take glycerin well, retain own texture and color. Skeletonize well a few years after glycerin treated.

Crape-Myrtle—Lagerstroemia indica. Cut sprays with buds or showy pink lilac-like clusters in summer. Use borax method or hang upside down. Buds look like berries. Develop lines by wetting stems and fastening to bent coat hanger.

Cucumber Vine. Gather sprays of wild egg-shaped prickly fruit when mature.

Cupids-Dart—Catananche caerulea. Silvery 2″ blooms surmounted by a tuft of dull blue. Cut and hang upside down during the summer. One of best everlastings.

Cycas Leaves. Long, stiff feathery leaves arranged in rosette form at top of a short, stout trunk. Buy dried, light tan in color; small 7″ long, medium 12″ and large 18″.

Cyperus. Low—Cyperus diandrus. Tufted grass-like stems, long and slender with terminal clusters. Cut in marshy places August-October. Store in box. Good for line in arrangements.

Cyperus Balls—Cyperus filiculmis. Slender cyperus found in dry fields and on hills from June to August. Spikelets densely clustered in globose heads. Green at first, then greenish-brown. C. ovularis radiating spikelets July-September. Hang upside down. Seed heads interesting.

Daffodils. All varieties dry well using borax method. Fill large cups with borax to hold flower shape.

Dahlia. Either hang upside down or use borax method.

Daisies. Bury in sand or borax. Will dry in a few days.

Datura stramonium—Jamestown Lily, Jimson-weed, Thorn Apple. Found in fields in June-September. Dries naturally. Erect white or violet flowers, very prickly 2″ long fruit. Store in box.

Day-lily—Hemerocallis. Yellow, orange and gold flowers dry to a maroon and brown. Cut from August to frost. Use borax method. Texture gets thin, color good.

Delphinium—Larkspur. Place blue, purple lavender and white perennial type flowers lengthwise in borax. Gather annual kinds before maturity as they start to bud. Hang upside down. Leave foliage as it stays green, or let flowers reach maturity and use borax.

Desmanthus illinoensis—Mimosa. Press mimosa-like leaves. Oblong seed pods in dense heads, 1″ long and curved.

Deutzia. Long, slender sprays of white blossoms. Place lengthwise in borax.

Digger Pine Cones—Pinus sabiniana. California. A heavy thick cone that looks like a pineapple and grows to 10″ long.

Dock or Sorrel—Rumex. Pick dock in fields, on hillsides and along the roadside from June to October. Effective in dried arrangements. Greenish flowers with a pink tinge arranged in whorled clusters or spikes, followed by fruits of leathery reddish-brown. Pick at various stages, green in July, then variegated orange-pink and green, later in autumn the fruits are rosy-beige, after frost chocolate brown. Hang upside down. If picked too late in season will droop and look worn.

Dogwood—Cornus florida rubra. Large, single, pink flowers. Dry placing lengthwise in borax. For leaves press, use glycerin or borax method.

Dracaena Foliage. Treat with glycerin. After several years dracaena leaves treated this way skeletonize naturally.

Echeveria. Succulent with gray-green broad leaves in rosettes. Flowers of Bronze Echeveria (E. gibbiflora var. metallica) dry easily and keep indefinitely.

Elaeagnus Foliage—Elaeagnus. Gray-green, round leaves which florists sell. Green leaves margined with yellow or white. Keep well for several weeks out of water. Turn lovely brown with glycerin treatment. Will after several years skeletonize naturally so treated.

Elm—Ulmus americana. Leaves will not take glycerin but lovely in autumn, press them.

English Daisy—Bellis perennis. Dwarf hardy perennial with rounded double flower-heads of white and pink. Hang upside down or use borax method or press.

English Ivy—Hedera. Shellac to preserve and stiffen the leaves without drying or submerge in one-half glycerin, one-half water.

Eucalyptus—E. globulus. Lovely branches of spiral gray-green foliage, dries naturally. Other varieties have oval leaves suspended on twigs. Small fruit or pods also used in arrangements.

Eulalia. Tall, bold, broad leaved grass with awned spikelets in large terminal silky panicles. Good for informal arrangement.

Euonymus Foliage. Cut long sprays of highly colored foliage, place lengthwise in borax. Requires only 3 or 4 days to dry, retains color well. May also preserve with glycerin. Orange-red berries useful. E. atropurpureus, Burning Bush, has white, rose and purple flowers. Hang upside down to dry.

Evening-Primrose—Oenothera biennis. Found growing wild in dry places. Yellow flowers may be pressed or dried in borax. Transparent beige seed pods are a dainty contribution.

Evergreens. Broad-leaved. Treat with glycerin or use fresh.

Everlasting. Cut in the advanced bud stage and hang upside down. This group includes several plants which our grandmothers grew and used in "dried bouquets." They represent all shades and colors and many have branching slender stems. Babys Breath (Gypsophila paniculata), Globe Amaranth (Gomphrena globosa), Statice (Limonium and certain species of Armeria), Strawflower (Helichrysum bracteatum) and Xeranthemum (Immortelle) are all included in this group. Excellent for mass arrangements.

False Dragonhead—Physostegia. Long green calyx-covered runners remain green. Calyx resembles huckleberry. Hang upside down.

False Indigo—Baptisia australis. Deep green foliage and profuse indigo-blue flowers resembling lupines in form, in long terminal racemes. Blossoms followed by short, plump pods that become almost black, they are such a deep blue. Gather seed pods in September. Hang upside down.

Fan Palm—Livistona australis. Florida. Large fan-shaped leaves with spiny stalks. Buy from florist already dried. Graceful in tan tones.

Fennel—Foeniculum vulgare. Bright green, feathery foliage. Will dry in a few hours. Hang upside down.

Ferns. Pick before frost for green colors and after frost for browns. Press. Take some out before completely dry and stand in jars for graceful curves.

CINNAMON FERN. Broad, blue-green fronds bearing narrow spikes of spores, olive green when young, cinnamon-like when ripe in early June.

OSTRICH FERN. Palm-like sterile fronds are broad, tapering below. The fertile plume-like, shorter, stiffer, appear in July. The common cinnamon and ostrich ferns, with their brown spores, are interesting and add lightness and grace to any arrangement. Put them one layer deep between newspaper sheets and put a weight over them, press, or otherwise they will curl. Ordinarily, pressing is not recommended, because it flattens specimens and a third dimension is desirable. Ferns are frequently cut when the fertile fronds are dry.

ROYAL FERN. One of the stateliest of all ferns. Reddish-pink fronds, lovely in early spring. The fruit is borne in flower-like panicles at the tip of the fronds.

SENSITIVE FERN—Onoclea sensibilis. Coarse and abundant fern of the marshes. Fertile fronds appear in late summer. Stiff, erect habit with terminal fruit.

Fiddleleaf Rubber Plant—Ficus pandurata. Foliage has interesting curves. Place on flat surface to dry, turns brown. Liquid brown shoe polish will improve texture.

Firethorn—Pyracantha crenulata. Dark waxy leaves, brilliant orange-scarlet berries in fall and winter. Let dry in small amount of water. Leaves will fall off, so strip.

Firs—Douglas, Red and Silver. Collect cones in late autumn. Brown upright cones to $4\frac{1}{2}''$ long.

Fittonia, Silverleaf—Fittonia argyroneura. Press or dry hairy white-veined leaves in borax.

Flowering Quince—Cydonia. Place flowering branches lengthwise in borax mixture. Also cut branches in middle of July when has both blossoms and tiny quince, effective and interesting. Dried and combined with thermopsis leaves make a pleasing combination.

Forget-Me-Not—Myosotis. Press flowers and foliage, use for picture in frame.

Forsythia. Use glycerin method. Sprays turn light brown.

Fountain-Grass—Pennisetum ruppeli. Spikes are purple, coppery red and rose. Hang upside down to dry.

Foxglove—Digitalis purpurea. Place white and purple flower bells on stalks lengthwise in borax to dry. Fill bells with borax to preserve shape.

Gaillardia—Blanket-flower. Gather yellow or reddish flowers with purple disks from June until frost, just as petals develop. Hang upside down to dry.

Galax—Shortia galacifolia. Stiff, shiny green leaves, heart-shaped to almost round to five inches across turn a beautiful bronze color in autumn. Pick both green and bronze colors. Cover autumn colored leaves with liquid oxblood shoe polish to enhance their natural color. With glycerin treatment pack leaves close together and do not immerse whole leaf. Glycerin treated skeletonize easily after a few years.

Gas Plant—Dictamnus albus. Fragrant white flowers in terminal racemes. Cut from August to frost. Hang upside down.

Gladiolus. White, cream, yellow, orange, salmon, red and pink flowers. Dry foliage too; put in glycerin or stand in jars. Stems and buds keep well. Use borax method for flowers. Use seed pods.

Globe Amaranth—Gomphrena globosa. White, red, violet and pink flowers in clover-like heads. Hang upside down. Everlasting.

Globe Thistle—Echinops. Dry both the grayish-green leaves and the blue flowers which form in round heads. Hang upside down. Metallic-blue scales give spherical, dense flower head pleasing color effect. Cut August to frost. Leaves rather coarse, white-woolly underneath, effective in a coarse textured arrangement.

Glory-Bower—Clerodendrum trichotomun. Sweet-smelling white flowers with red calyx in summer, showy fruit in autumn. Pink capsules enclose bright peacock-blue fruit. Hang upside down.

Gloxinia. Lay flowers lengthwise in sand or borax to dry. Fill flower with borax mixture to hold shape.

Goldenrain Tree—Koelreutia paniculata. Florida. Fruit a bladder-like 3 valved pod useful in arrangements. Green if picked in July. Brown if picked in late fall.

Goldenrod—Solidago. Cut clustered yellow flowers in fields in dry, sandy places through the summer up until frost. Hang upside down. Also press both flowers and foliage.

Goosefoot—Feather Geranium—Chenopodium botrys. Fragrant foliage even when dried. Hang upside down.

Gourds. Pick after maturity, before frost.

Grape. Cut branches from an old vine for informal arrangement. Just store in box.

Grape Ivy—Cissus rhombifolia. Shellac to preserve and stiffen the leaves. Not necessary to dry. Interesting tendrils. May preserve in glycerin.

Hardhack, Steeplebush—Spirea tomentosa. Grows wild in moist places. Steeple-like panicles of rosy-purple flowers. Cut in August for pink shades. If cut in September and October will dry to the tans. Hang upside down.

Hawthorn—Crataegus. Clusters of berries ripen in September-October; thick, firm, yellow or red. Will keep indefinitely, thorny branches.

Heather—Calluna vulgaris. Cut stems as long as possible and before the young blooms are too fully developed to avoid shattering. Lovely purple. Easy to dry, attractive, hang upside down. Can press flowers and foliage.

Heavenly Bamboo—Nandina domestica. Blossoms may be gathered in June and dried. Hold form well, stay pale cream in color. Upside down or borax method. Red berries excellent, hold shade and color and do not drop as much dried as fresh. Gather when green, salmon and deep orange-red. Hang upside down.

Hemlock—Tsuga canadensis. Gather small cones in late autumn.

Hen-and-chickens—Sempervivum tectorum. Tiny clustered leaf rosettes to 4″ across turn brown when dry. Hang upside down.

Hibiscus. Seed pods are used by arrangers.

Holly—Ilex opaca. Attractive foliage and showy berries. Stand branches in jar or hang upside down. Leaves stay firm and green. Berries dry and turn dark.

Hollyhock—Althaea rosea. Gather when color starts to show in buds. Fine gray-green leaves. Do not use glycerin on them. Hang stalks upside down. Flat flower-like seed heads excellent.

Honesty, Money Plant—Lunaria annua. Sprays of thin, silvery white tissue, like mother-of-pearl, after the seed covering has fallen. Cut when white in late fall, before seeds turn yellow. Hang upside down.

Honey Locust—Gleditsia. Gather seed pods in late autumn. Pods dry naturally.

Honeysuckle. Berries may be black, blue, yellow, red or white, depending upon the species. Gather in fall.

Horse-Chestnut—Aesculus. Gather large spiny nut and burr in late autumn.

Huckleberry—Vaccinium ovatum. Western evergreen huckleberry for sale by florists. Properly applied to species of Gaylussacia. Use glycerin method for foliage.

Husk-Tomato—Physalis pruinosa. Orange-yellow fruit, size of cherry, inside a calyx or husk. Sometimes known as love apple.

Hyacinth Bean—Dolichos lablab. Collect attractive purple or green seed pods in October. Simply store in box.

Hydrangeas. Choice material, easy to dry holding shape and color. Hang upside down or stand in jar. Cut when color is at its best, before frost. Tie single stalk to string to avoid shattering. Blue, pink or white flowers according to the color of the bracts will dry soft blue-greens, pale pink or chartreuse.

H. PANICULATA GRANDIFLORA. Peegee Hydrangea. Cut in early September while green and pink coloring at its best. After frost color changes to beige and brown.

H. HORTENSIS. Florist's hydrangea. Grown outdoors begins to change color early in July. Blue becomes a bluish-green, often with pink edges. Wait until color changes occur. Let flowers season or cure on the bush before picking. Dry this variety slowly.

H. ARBORESCENS. Variety grandiflora. Hills of Snow a hybrid. First white, then chartreuse. Gather in early autumn. Trim out any withered florets.

H. QUERCIFOLIA. Oak leaf hydrangea. Gather long, lacy, pendulous flowers in April-May. Gathered in spring stays pink, in autumn brown.

H. PETIOLARIS. Climbing hydrangea. Glossy foliage and large white flat flower heads attractive after they have turned brown.

H. OPULOIDES. Looks like Queen Annes Lace. Bring indoors in October. Has good form, lacy and attractive, remains olive green.

Immortelles—Xeranthemum annuum. Dainty white, pink and lavender flowers. Use borax or hang upside down. An everlasting.

Iris. All varieties yield interesting seed pods, gather in late fall. Put foliage in glycerin or let dry naturally.

Ironweed—Veronica. Gather showy purple, pink or white sprays in July-August. Hang upside down or use borax method.

Ivy Foliage. Submerge stems and leaves in $\frac{1}{2}$ water, $\frac{1}{2}$ glycerin solution.

Jacaranda. Tropical and sub-tropical tree with broad fruit which looks like a brown bivalve mollusk, being round, flattened, wavy-edged and about 2″ in diameter. Simply store in a box.

Jobs-Tears—Coix lachryma-jobi. Tall ornamental grass. Thick leaves resemble those of maize or Indian corn. Pearly white to gray, hard, shiny seeds to 1½″ across. Seeds often made into necklace. Cut at various stages of coloring.

Joe-Pye-Weed—Eupatorium purpureum. Grows in marshy places. Old rose or lavender flowers in large, open, rounded clusters. Gather in early August in bud stage so won't shatter. Hang upside down.

Jonquil. Place flowers lengthwise in borax. Fill centers with borax to retain shape. Jonquils dry in a few days.

Juniper, Red Cedar—Juniperus virginiana. Small grayish-green leaves which turn light to reddish-brown. Blue or reddish berry-like fruit. Hang upside down or use glycerin. Gather during spring as new growth appears for chartreuse color, may press.

Kale. Leaves dry to lovely shades of warm tans with delicate mauve tints. Cut from garden when size and color you wish.

Lantana. Flat clusters of yellow through orange to red or rosy-lilac flowers, dry well in borax.

Larch—Larix. Spruce-like cones. Gather in late autumn.

Larkspur—(annual). White through pink and blue to deep purple flowers. Blue predominates. Leave foliage on stems as it stays green. In bud form hang upside down. When mature dry in borax.

Laurel. Dark, glossy, shiny green leaves shaped like a lance head, to oval, to four inches long. Turn glossy brown of good leather with glycerin treatment. Easy to do. May gild or silver for holiday season.

Lavender—Lavandula officinalis. Purple flowers. Hang upside down or may press flowers and foliage.

Leatherleaf—Viburnum rhytidophyllum. Leaves remain green or turn brown depending on time left in glycerin. Left in small amount of water to dry, leaves stay green but become brittle.

Leek. The flowers of the leek dry a lovely light gray. Hang upside down or stand in fruit jar. Delicate, so do not box.

Lemon Leaves, Salal—Gaultheria shallon. Gray-green leaves sold by florists. Hang upside down to dry.

Lemon Verbena—Lippia citriodora. Hang upside down. Fragrance of leaves retained when dried. May press flowers and foliage.

Leopards-Bane—Doronicum. Yellow daisy-like flowers. Dry in borax.

Leucothoe. Foliage takes glycerin well, turns greenish-brown. Dry cream colored blossoms in borax.

Lilac—Syringa. Pink, purple and white flowers. Retain fragrance, shape and color. Place lengthwise in borax, cover entire flower. White in time will turn cream.

Lily. Dry flowers in borax 3-5 weeks. Brownish seed pods also useful.

Lily-of-the-Valley—Convallaria majalis. May press flowers and foliage. Flowers dry well in borax. Submerge whole leaf in half glycerin, half water.

Lily-Turf—Liriope variegata. Attractive grass-like foliage with yellow, striped leaves and lilac-purple flower spikes. Use borax for both flowers and leaves.

Loosestrife—Lysimachia. Yellow and white flowers dry well in borax.

Lotus. Bowl-shaped, slate colored pod with flat top dotted with round holes, much in demand by arrangers. May be purchased with or without stems. Leaves 6″ wide 12″ long, dry chartreuse.

Love-Apples—Solanum aculeatissimum. Buy from florist these glossy, shiny, orange-red dried fruits.

Lupine. Blue, purple, pink, rose, red, yellow, orange and white flowers. Place lengthwise in borax. Store flattened pods, often constricted between the seeds, in box or stand in jar.

Magnolia. Valuable for buds, flowers, leaves and seed pods.

M. GRANDIFLORA—Bull Bay. Furnishes 3 types of buds, velvety silver-gray leaf buds in spring, brown in autumn and the white flower buds. Dried branches with gray or brown buds distinctive and establish line in arrangements. Water in fresh arrangement will not hurt dried branches. Gather flower buds or flowers and hang upside down. Collect pods while red seeds are still within. Coat pods with clear shellac or nail polish. Thick shiny leaves to 8″ long. Put leaves in glycerin for satiny finish. Wipe fallen leaves, bleached by nature, with vegetable oil, store in box or arrange. Some leaves are bluish-green, some tan, others brown, some mottled depending upon sun, water and shade tree received. Leaves keep indefinitely.

M. MACROPHYLLA. Large glossy, dark green leaves to three feet long.

M. STELLATA—Starry Magnolia. Blooms in February and March. Branches graceful. Pale pink or white flowers dry nicely. Good in miniature arrangements. Hang upside down.

M. SOULANGEANA—Tulip Magnolia. Blooms early before leaves come. Flowers hold shape and color well when dried. Branches curve gracefully. Hang upside down.

Mallow. Collect flat, wrinkled green fruits in late fall.

Manzanita. Branches from California. Use as they are.

Maple—Acer. Preserve colorful autumn leaves in borax.

Marguerite, Paris Daisy—Chrysanthemum frutescens. White rayed, yellow disked flowers. Flowers and foliage press well. Bury flowers in sand or borax to dry.

Marigold—Tagetes. Yellow and orange flowers. Large, double variety shrinks least. Use upside down method. For singles use borax.

Meadow-Rue—Thalictrum. Rose, lavender or yellow tassel-like flowers bloom in early summer. Delicate attractive foliage. Use upside down method.

Meadowsweet—Spirea alba. Shrub, white flowers in long leafy clusters, grows on banks and rocky places. Hang upside down to dry.

Mescal Bean—Sophora secundiflora. Eight inch long pods liked by arrangers.

Mesquite, Screw Bean—Prosopis pubescens. Fruit is a pod tightly twisted into a cylindric body 1-1½″ long. Much used in arrangements. Grows in southwest, Hawaii.

Mexican Screw-Bean—Prosopis pubescens. Cream-colored, long, oval seed pods much used by arrangers. Use as they are, dry naturally.

Milkweed—Asclepias. Use borax method on bright orange or yellow flowers. Many varieties as A. tuberosa (Butterfly-Weed) which grows in fields and waste places. Pods interesting, vary in shape and texture. Pick during August for attractive gray-green, spiked pods and from August on through winter for grayish-brown. Store in boxes.

Millet, Broom Corn. Seeds small and shiny, grow in drooping, slender sprays. When dried straw-colored or tan to nice browns. Soak in warm water to establish curves.

Mint—Mentha. Many species including apple, orange and spearmint. Hang upside down. Retain fragrance dried.

Montbretia—Tritonia. Yellow or orange-red funnel-shaped flowers. Press or dry in borax.

Moonflower—Calonyction. Greenhouse vine in North. Seedheads interesting.

Morning-Glory—Ipomea. Variety of flower colors. Seed pods when dry resemble small flower, reddish-brown and tan in color. Hang upside down. Excellent for lines and curves.

Morning-Glory—Ipomoea tuberosa. Wood rose of Hawaii.

Mullein—Verbascum. Wild. The long yellow flower spikes and downy leaves are both useful, but best of all, take up the whole rosette of leaves that form the young plant and use it as a focal area. Cut through summer until frost (June-October). Stand in jar.

Narcissus. Dry flowers in sand or borax. Fill center of flower with borax to hold shape.

New Zealand Flax—Phormium tenax. Long narrow leaves, dull red flowers clustered on long stems. Use as they are. One has reddish-purple foliage.

Oak. In July pick oak branches with small acorns just forming, in September and October gather branches with mature acorns for variety in size. On some trees during summer months, oak galls may be found, the little puff balls we liked to pick as youngsters. It is easy to string these, combining the various colors ranging from light tan to dark brown. Vary the size, as well as the color, and make interesting clusters of oak galls to use as center of interest. A small piece of lead will keep the cluster in position.

Oat—Avena. Cut in late summer and stand in jar to dry to a lovely beige.

Oat-Grass—Trisetum pennsylvanicum. Long yellow spikelets. Collect in lowlands or wet places in June-July. Store in box. Good for line.

Okra. Allow ridged pods to mature but pick before frost. Select those with interesting curves in size you want from 4″ to 12″.

Oleander—Nerium. Dark green leathery leaves up to 8″ long. Stand in glycerin.

Onion—Allium. Spreading white or purple ball-like flower clusters. Hang upside down to dry. Small fruit capsules also useful.

Orchard-Grass—Dactylis glomerata. Long green or white spikelets in dense clusters. Attractive grass. Good for line. Hang upside down or stand in jar.

Oregon Grape—Mahonia nervosa. Clusters of yellow flowers in early spring, later long lasting blue berries which dry well, holding color. Use borax method on flowers. In glycerin leaves turn a greenish-brown or light tan, berries gray-blue and shrivel somewhat. May simply shellac to preserve and stiffen leaves.

Painted Daisy, Pyrethrum—Chrysanthemum coccineum. Flowers in red, pink white; single and double in June and July. Press flowers and foliage or dry borax method.

Painted Tongue—Salpiglossis sinuata. Funnel-shaped flowers in many colors. Press flowers and foliage.

Palms. The flowers are as a rule small, but numerous, and borne on a single or multiple, usually branching, spadix enclosed by a spathe or large bract. The leaves are highly decorative and may be used green or dried tan to light brown. Coconut Palm spathe and spadix commonly used in dried arrangements. Palmetto palm, Sabal palmetto, has stiff evergreen fan-shaped leaves, may be cut and trimmed. Use green or dried. Dry to tans and chartreuse. Sago Palm (Cycas) florist material, stiff glossy, long evergreen foliage, more or less fern-like and rolled on edges. Heavy in feeling.

Curled fronds good for rhythmic lines. May paint fronds white, silver or gilt at holiday season. May stand leaves in empty jar to dry or use glycerin.

Palm Drift "Fantazma"—Embryo or unborne palm-leaves, Phoenix. They are the unexpanded or partially expanded leaves of the date palm taken from the terminal bud. The tree is killed in removing these leaves. Come in various sizes. Supplied commercially from California and Arizona.

Palm Flowers—Cocos nucifera. Fruiting calyxes of the coconut palm, expand with the development of the fruit, when fruit is ripe can be removed as a unit, form a whorl of woody scales around an irregularly surfaced center. Use natural or silver or gilt. Seeds may be glued to center to resemble a large flower.

Pampas-Grass—Cortaderia. Tall, handsome, showy, silky white plumes excellent in large decorations. Cut in September when fully developed.

Pandanus. Use long saw-toothed leaves as they are. Will dry naturally.

Pansy—Viola tricolor var. hortensis. Many colors. Bury in sand or borax. Press foliage and flowers for dried pictures.

Partridge-Berry. Dark green, rounded leaves and small red berries featured by florists at Christmas time in glass bowls.

Peach—Prunus persica. Cut sprays before blossoms reach maturity. Place lengthwise in borax. Hold color and shape well.

Pear. In the spring picturesque black branches of the pear tree may be cut and saved for line arrangements. For dining room combine branches with limes made up in threes, five or seven, depending upon the size of the design, use a background of rhododendron leaves for the cluster. Limes, unlike lemons, will dry well.

Peony—Paeonia. Best for drying are double white, pink and red varieties. Use buds too. Hang upside down.

Pepper Tree—Schinus Molle. The hanging fruits or rose colored berries of the California pepper-tree are ornamental. Available in flower shops at Christmas time.

Peppers. Green fruit dries red. Gather in early September. Hang upside down.

Perilla. Attractive colored foliage something like a coleus. Must hang several weeks. Lovely forms and colors.

Philodendron. Furnish many leaves useful in dried arrangements. Treat with glycerin.

Pigeon-Grass, Yellow Fox-Tail—Chaetochloa glauca. Cut long yellow spikelets in July-September. Good for line. Hang upside down or place upright in a jar.

Pincushion Flower—Scabiosa. Hang flowers upside down. Flowers and foliage may also be pressed.

Pines. Cones and needles vary with variety. Collect cones late in autumn. Digger, Longleaf, Pitch, Red, Scotch, Umbrella and White Pine all have interesting cones varying from 2″ to 10″ long. Use for Christmas decorations, plain or spray with silver, gilt or paint or shellac. Cut large cones crosswise to look like flowers. Use in wreaths or plaques. Branches valuable in arrangements, partially trim if too heavy.

Pine-Cone Flowers. The larger cones may be cut crosswise to make various sized cone-flowers, attractive and interesting.

Pink—Dianthus. Press flowers and foliage for flower picture.

Pitcher Plant—Serracenia purpurea. Found in peat bogs in early summer. Purple or greenish flowers 2″ across. Leaves 10″ long. Cut just as it matures in May or June.

Pittosporum tobira. Thick leathery attractive leaves in rosettes. Use glycerin.

Plane Tree, Button Ball Tree—Platanus occidentalis. Ball-like mass of small nutlets form conspicuous fruiting cluster. Just store in box.

Plantain Lily—Hosta. Large conspicuous leaves and blue, lilac or white flowers in spikes. Hang several weeks, use leaves too. Dry to lovely forms and colors.

Plum—Prunus domestica. Put flowering sprays lengthwise in borax. Put leaves in glycerin, do not always dry satisfactorily but sometimes they do.

Pokeberry—Phytolacca. Berries light green before maturity, reddish blue-gray after. Hang upside down. Hold shape well. Dry bare violet-red stalk too.

Poker-Plant—Kniphofia. Autumn blooming with dense cigar-shaped showy spikes in yellow and scarlet. Use borax method to dry.

Polyanthus—Primula polyantha. Hybrid group. Stems topped with flowers of many colors in many flowered umbels, sometimes solitary. Cut in spring. Dry in borax.

Pomegranate—Punica granatum. Gather fruit at various stages for variety in size and form during August-September. Dry buds and lovely rosette calyx by hanging upside down.

Poplar—Populus alba. Found only among old plantings. Roots spread. Leaves white underneath, branches graceful. Cut when hot in summer, stand in jar. Dried leaves dramatic with brown top, very white underneath.

Poppy—Papaver. Perennial and annual types. Seed pods effective, have good sturdy stems, so establish curves and store in boxes. Collect before frost in a variety of sizes.

Princes Feather—Polygonum orientale. Annual of buckwheat family. Dense spikes of bright pink or rose. Good for line in arrangements. Stand upright in jar to dry.

Princess Tree—Paulownia tomentosa. Gather yellow buds which dry well in May-June. Gather attractive pods in early summer while still green, before they get too large, will turn brown. Hang upside down to dry. Large leaves resemble catalpa.

Privet—Ligustrum lucidum. Gather sprays of June blossoms and place lengthwise in borax, stay a pale cream; or hang upside down. Thick glossy leaves turn green and golden brown in glycerin. Try golden and variegated types. Green berries in autumn will remain green. Some varieties have gray-blue, others almost black berries.

Pussy-Toes—Antennaria plantaginfolia. Early everlasting. Gather in late winter or early spring. Found underneath large trees. Delicate green to pale cream color at outer edges. Improves with drying.

Queen Annes Lace, Wild Carrot—Daucus carota. Found in fields or waste places in June-September. Cut just as filmy white flowers mature. Use borax mixture to dry.

Red Gum—Liquidambar stryraciflua. Globular horny fruit. Good for informal fruit or flower arrangements. Attractive gray branches.

Rhododendron. Attractive useful leaves do well treated in glycerin.

Rhubarb. The white flowers dry well and are attractive.

Rice. Slender, graceful plants with rather feathery seed heads somewhat like those of wheat and oats. Stand upright in jar to dry.

Roses. Pink and yellows dry particularly well. Gather when flowers are two-thirds open. Remove foliage and thorns. Red roses dry almost black. Flowers retain fragrance when dried. For double hybrid teas hang upside down tying a single stalk to a string or bury in sand or meal and borax; for singles use borax method only.

Rosa Multiflora. Pick red rose hips in late fall when color is best. Dry naturally.

Rosa Rugosa. Pick red rose hips in late fall when color is best. Dry naturally.

A Christmas tree made of cones, liquidambar and other pods. Fruits are attached to plywood with linoleum cement. Fun to make and many variations are possible.

ARRANGEMENT BY MRS. GORDON ROAF   TALOUMIS PHOTO

An effective decoration shaped like a Christmas tree made of cones and iris pods with red berries. Evergreens may be used in a similar fashion.

ARRANGEMENT BY MRS. GORDON ROAF   TALOUMIS PHOTO

A wreath made entirely of cones. Evergreens are equally popular but for indoor use select evergreens that do not drop their needles readily.

                                                   TALOUMIS PHOTO

Note: Silica gel is a chemical which has been very effective for drying flowers to retain their color. It is sold under trade names such as Flower-Dri and Flor-Ever, with directions for use included. Dorothea Thompson, author of *Creative Decorations with Dried Flowers* originated this process and describes it fully in her book (published by Hearthside Press Inc.).

Rose-of-Sharon—Hibiscus syriacus. When flowers go to seed pick fruit, a five valved capsule containing fifteen or more seeds.

Rosemary—Rosmarinus officinalis. Pinelike bush, light blue flowers, narrow leaves, dark and shiny above, whitish beneath. Hang upside down to dry.

Royal Palm—Roystonea regia. Florida and Cuba. Large, long feathery leaves, handsomely arching. Can buy already dried.

Royal Poinciana—Delonix regia. Florida. Seed pods 2 feet long and 2 inches or more broad, are useful in arrangements.

Rubber Plant—Ficus. Thick, glossy oblong leaves. Plants usually grown in pots or tubs. Cut from house plant if can spare the leaves. Place on flat surface to dry. Turns brown. Rub with brown liquid shoe polish to improve texture.

Rye. Cultivated or wild. Dries to a gray-green beige, attractive for line in arrangements. Stand in jar to dry.

Sage—Salvia bertoloni. Spikes of bright blue, rose and purple flowers in branched racemes. Hang upside down. Can press both flowers and foliage.

Sago Palm—Cycas revoluta. Use as is. Store stiff, glossy, long fern-like foliage in a box.

St. Johns-Bread—Ceratonia siliqua. Flattened leathery 6″-12″ long dark brown pods.

St. Johns-Wort—Hypericum calycium. Yellow flowers. Hang upside down or use borax.

Salsify—Tragopogon porrifolius. Fruit long and stick-like.

Sansevieria—Bowstring-Hemp, Snakeplant. Thick, erect, long, basal leaves, green, variegated or mottled. Excellent for contemporary rooms. Let dry naturally. Lasts a long time untreated.

Sapodilla—Sapota achras. Fruits to $3\frac{1}{2}''$ in diameter, rough, brown with yellow-brown translucent flesh and black shining seeds.

Savory—Satureja nepeta. Use 5-lobed tubular gray calyx. Cut in fields June-September. Store in box to dry.

Scilla. Press flowers and foliage and use in flower pictures.

Scotch Broom—Cytisus scorparius. Gather in spring as tiny leaves come out or in summer when leaves are larger. Dries well staying green. Place on flat surface or store in box. Wire to hanger or tie with string for curves.

Screw Pine—Pandanus. Long saw-toothed leaves. Use as they are.

Sea Grape—Coccolobis uvifera. Tropical and sub-tropical tree native on sea coasts. Leathery, glossy, round leaves to eight inches across, heart-shaped at base. Light tan and pale peach. Use as is.

Sea-Holly—Eryngium maritimum. Pale blue flowers, leaves broadly ovate, three lobed, fleshy and stiff. Found near the seashore. Cut when blue in July to September. Use borax method. Save ovoid seed pods in fall.

Sea Oat—Uniola. Native to the sand dunes near the sea. Dries to lovely tans. Cut in September.

Sedges. Grass-like perennials both wild and cultivated. Grow near ponds and in bogs. Seed heads either in spikes or bunchy clumps. Excellent for line in arrangements.

Sedum spectabile. Numerous small pink flowers and light green foliage. Lovely dried. Cut in late fall.

Silver-Bell Tree—Halesia. Gather clusters of pods in late autumn.

Skunk Cabbage. Found in swampy places along brooks. One of the first flowers of spring. Flower will be found beneath its dark red hood. Soon, large pale leaves unfold. Spadix dries to a lovely purplish-blue slender spike on a chartreuse stem. Looks much like the black lily-of-the-Nile dried. Wonderful in bouquets. Has no odor dried.

Smoke Tree—Cotinus coggygria. Bushy shrub with oval leaves to three inches long, much branched purplish panicles. Cut in June and July. Treat with borax. Hang purplish-brown, kidney-shaped fruit upside down to dry.

Snapdragon—Antirrhinum. Place lengthwise in borax. Dries nicely.

Snowdrop—Galanthus. Press flowers and foliage.

Snow-in-Summer—Cerastium tomentosum. White star-shaped flowers bloom in May and June, leaves silvery-gray. Hang upside down to dry.

Snow-on-the-Mountain—Euphorbia marginata. Press or dry white margined green leaves in borax.

Soapberry—Sapindus saponaria. Small, round, shining orange-brown fruit. Hang upside down to dry.

Sour Wood—Oxydendrum arboreum. Tan capsules like lily-of-the-valley. Gather in autumn, stand in jars and use in mass arrangements.

Spider Flower—Cleome spinosa. Interesting seed pods on stalks. Store in box.

Spindle Tree—Euonymus. Dry colorful leaves in borax.

Spiny Tomato—Solanum aculeatissimum. Decorative detached or on dried branches. Orange-yellow fruit 1-1$\frac{1}{2}$″ in diameter, spiny with golden prickles of the stems and calyx adding to attractiveness.

Spiraea billiardi. Bright pink flowers in pointed clusters. Gather just as they reach maturity. Stand in jar or use borax.

Spruce. Colorado, Blue and Norway Spruce. Gather cones in late autumn. Cones to 4″ to 7″ long.

Star-of-Bethlehem—Ornithogalum. Dry clusters of lily-like flowers in borax.

Star of Texas—Xanthisma texanum. Yellow rayed flowers may be dried in borax.

Statice, Sea lavender—Limonium sinuatum. Flowers in soft shades of rose, blue, lavender, pink and also white. Stand in jars to dry. Flowers and foliage may be pressed.

Stewartia ovata. Fruit a woody, 5-celled capsule. Store pods in box.

Stock—Mathiola incana. White, lavender, rose, pink and purple flowers. Dry in borax.

Strawberry Tree—Arbutus unedo. Fruit strawberry-like; large, warty, orange-red, about ¾" in diameter. Place on flat surface. Will dry nicely.

Strawflowers—Helichrysum bracteatum. White, yellow, orange, pink and red flowers. Cut before completely open. Stand in jar or hang upside down to dry.

Sumac—Rhus. Small greenish flowers covered with red hairs occur in large panicles, followed by dense fruit-heads, often a fine deep red, soft and velvety. Pick at various stages for different colors from June through early September. Dark glossy green foliage becomes brilliant scarlet in the fall. Use flowers, fruit heads and foliage. Bare stalks make striking line arrangements, exotic in appearance. R. schmaltzia crenata, sweet-scented sumac, pick from June through August. Hang upside down or simply store in box.

Sunflower—Helianthus annuus. The flower-heads with yellow rays and yellow, purple or brown centers range from a few inches to huge specimens. They make excellent focal areas. Cut at various stages for variety. Place whole flower in borax or use centers only of yellow and orange flowers and store stems, with centers attached, in box or stand in jar.

Sweet Sultan—Centaurea imperialis. Thistle-like fragrant blooms in white, rose or purple. Hang upside down to dry.

Tansy—Tanacetum vulgare. Cut from August to October. Found along roadsides. Small, tight heads of very small light yellow to orange disk or button flowers. Pungent odor. Hang upside down to dry.

Teasel—Dipsacus. Thistle-like with lavender flowers in dense heads from midsummer until frost. Gather various sizes and colors, throughout the season. Hang upside down. Cut bristly spine-like seed heads in July and August. Dry naturally. Use leaves as they are.

Thermopsis. Spikes of yellow lupine-like blossoms. Hang upside down or dry in borax. Leaves dry to a lovely gray. Pod-like fruit 2"-4" long, also used in arrangements.

Thistle, Plumed—Cirsium. Collect in pastures or fields in July-

November. C. altissimum, tall roadside thistle with light purple flowers. Shear off purple part and dried heads look like powder puffs. Leaves dry well, so do not strip. Hang upside down.

Thyme—Thymus alsinoides. Press leaves, use in flower pictures.

Ti—Cordyline. The colorful leaf from Hawaii. Use glycerin method to dry.

Torch Ginger—Zingiber darceyi. From Hawaii. Hang upside down to dry. Flower remains pink.

Tree-of-Heaven—Ailanthus altissima. Red fruit 1½″ long with one seed in the middle of a paper thin, narrow, oblong, twisted wing.

Trumpet Vine—Campsis radicans. Fruit a long, stalked capsule, interesting in arrangements.

Tulip. To dry place lengthwise in borax. Fill cup with borax to hold its shape. Must be handled carefully, so petals will not drop.

Tulip Tree—Liriodendron tulipifera. Gather buds in May or June. Use borax method to dry. Light cone-like brown fruit to 3″ long has narrow pointed "petals" surrounding a long etched pistil. Hang upside down to dry.

Tumble Weed—Panicum capillare. Collect long spikelets in July-September. Good for large, informal arrangements. Dries naturally.

Umbrella Pine—Sciadopitys verticillata. A Japanese evergreen tree excellent for Christmas decorations. Cones produced near top of the tree difficult to reach. Treat with glycerin.

Unicorn Plant—Proboscidea. Pods resemble birds; hanging, woody, curved and beaked capsules, the body of which is 3″ long. Use as an accessory. Dry naturally.

Verbena hastata—Vervain. Grows wild in damp places and has small, dark-blue flowers, some are lavender, on slender spikes. Dry to a deep blue. Leaves dry well too. Pick in August for green colors and September to frost for brown. Good for height in arrangements. Gather long fruits in fields in July-August. Hang upside down.

Violet—Viola. White, blue or violet flowers. Press or dry in borax.

Wheat. Very effective in arrangements. Bearded sprigs soften the outline. Grow a small quantity in your cutting garden.

White Oak—Quercus alba. Collect branches in April or early May while leaves are small and fuzzy. Hang upside down. Collect large leaves in fall and press. Scarlet oak (Q. coccinea) has lovely flowers, graceful twigs. Hang upside down. Acorns valuable.

Wild Cucumber, Wild balsam apple—Echinocystis lobata. Puffy, rather papery, spiny pods about 2″ long on vines attractive.

Winterberry, Black-Alder—Ilex verticillata. Attractive red berried. Popular at Christmas season.

Wisteria. Lovely with curved, brown tendrils and elongated gray and green seed pods with velvety texture. Useful in formal arrangements. Flowers do not dry well.

Wooden Roses—Ipomoea tuberosa. Come from Hawaii. Seed pods of Morning Glory. Come already dried.

Yarrow—Achillea. Both flowers and finely cut fernlike grayish-green foliage dry well. Small white, pink, yellow or gold flower heads. Common yarrow has red flowers with white centers. Hang upside down or arrange in a container with small amount of water and let dry. Lay foliage on flat surface to dry.

Yucca. Stiff, sword-shaped leaves effective in contemporary rooms. Use glycerin method. Pods in heads or clusters, very effective in arrangements. Fruit of some have dry capsules, others have juicy, berrylike fruit.

Zinnia. Dry type with curled petals. Bury in sand or borax.

DRIED MATERIAL IN COLORS

WHITE:

Ageratum	Honesty
Amaranthus	Hydrangea
Astilbe	Immortelles
Babys-Breath, perennial	Larkspur
Chrysanthemum	Lilac
Daffodil	Pearly Everlasting
Delphinium	Peony buds and blossoms
Deutzia	Poplar leaves, alba
Everlasting	Queen Annes Lace
Globe Amaranth	Shasta Daisy

Snow-in-Summer flowers
Spirea

Statice
Xeranthemum

YELLOW TO ORANGE:

Acacia flowers—yellow
Albizzia seed pods—yellow
Ambrosia—pale yellow
Beech foliage—yellow
Bulbous Buttercup—bright yellow
Celosia flowers—yellow
Chrysanthemums—yellow
Daffodils, in bud and flower, yellow
Elaeagnus leaves—yellow
Goldenrod—yellow
Iris flowers—yellow

Mahonia flowers—yellow
Marigolds—orange
Milkweed, inside pods—yellow
Mullein—yellow
Rose—yellow
Statice—yellow
Strawflowers—yellow, orange
Summer grasses—creamy
Tansy—yellow
Tithonia—orange
Yarrow—yellow
Yucca pods—yellow
Zinnias—yellow

BROWN TO TAN:

Albizzia seed pods—pale yellow to brown
Artichoke
Aspidistra
Aucuba
Beech leaves
Cattails
Dock—tan and brown
Elaeagnus
Fern
Gladiolus leaves
Hickory buds

Hydrangea flowers
Magnolia buds, blossoms and leaves
Palm leaves
Pampas grass
Pine cones
Poplar (P. alba), foliage brown on top, white underneath
Scotch Broom
Strawflowers
Wooden Roses
Zinnias in bronze and rust

PINK AND ROSE PINK:

Astilbe in sprays—pink
Bleeding Heart—rose pink
Celosia—pink and rose pink
Chrysanthemums—pink
Delphinium—rose-pink
Hydrangea—pale pink
Larkspur—rose-pink
Michaelmas Daisy—pink

Peach blossoms—pink
Peony buds and blossoms—pink
Pepper Berries—rose
Pink dogwood blossoms
Roses—pink and rose-pink
Statice—rose-pink
Strawflowers—pink
Zinnias—pink and rose-pink

RED: (Red flowers do not as a rule dry well. These are good.)

Amaranthus "Princess Feather"   Globe Amaranth
Bittersweet berries—red   Holly berries—red
Celosia, Cockscomb—wine   Knotweed, wine and crimson
Fall Maple, foliage—red   Nandina berries—red
Fall Sumac, foliage—red   Strawflowers—red, wine

BLUE:

Ageratum   Larkspur, purple dries blue
Delphinium   Mahonia, dark blue fruit
False Indigo foliage—dark blue Salvia farinacea
Gilia capitata—light blue   Scilla
Hydrangea—light blue   Strawflowers

LAVENDER AND PURPLE:

Alfalfa   Larkspur
Amaranthus   Lilac
Astilbe   Michaelmas Daisy
Cerise Zinnia, dries purple   Statice
Chives—silvery lavender   Xeranthemus

DRIED GREEN FOLIAGE

(Combine with fresh foliage for pleasing results)

GREEN:

Acacia foliage blue-green, gray   Galax
Aspidistra—glycerin treated   Globe Thistle buds—green
Barberry   Hydrangea—chartreuse
Beech leaves—green   Ilex
Bells of Ireland—green   Ivy—glycerin treated
Boxwood   Mullein leaves—gray-green
Dock   Nandina berries
Elaeagnus foliage, gray-green   Orchid foliage
Eucalyptus leaves—pale   Scotch Broom
Fern   Statice

AIDS FOR THE ARRANGER

To Prevent Closing
Drops of wax in center of water lily or passion flower prevent closing, hold tulips or poppies at desired stage, lessen shattering

To Hold Bud For Party
Use collar of wax paper. Fasten with paper clip. Remove just before guests arrive

To Prevent Leaves From Curling
Spray underside only with clear plastic

To Curve Stiff Stems
Place slantwise in container while conditioning. Gladiolus, Delphinium, Lupine, Snapdragons etc.

To Seal Stems
May sear stems with flame - or - dip in boiling water. When using boiling water do not let steam injure foliage or leaves

Good To Remember
While conditioning keep atmosphere humid. Wrap loosely with paper to lessen evaporation. To maintain fragrance, cover with cellophane until ready for use

To Leaf Bamboo Canes
Be sure bottom is even to stand securely with cross section to hold water. Remove top of first section just below node. In lower sections just below each node drill holes large enough to take water. Fill all sections with water. Keep filled. Foliage will last several months

For Rosy Cheeks in Fruit Arrangement
Touch with lipstick

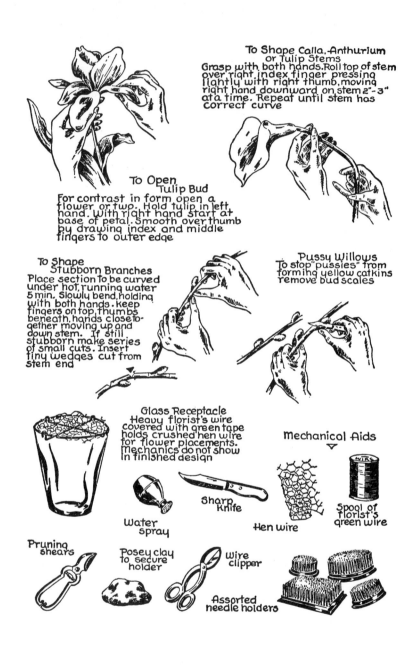

To Shape Calla, Anthurium or Tulip Stems

Grasp with both hands. Roll top of stem over right index finger pressing lightly with right thumb, moving right hand downward on stem 2"- 3" at a time. Repeat until stem has correct curve

To Open Tulip Bud

For contrast in form open a flower or two. Hold tulip in left hand. With right hand start at base of petal. Smooth over thumb by drawing index and middle fingers to outer edge

To Shape Stubborn Branches

Place section to be curved under hot, running water 5 min. Slowly bend, holding with both hands. keep fingers on top, thumbs beneath. hands close together moving up and down stem. If still stubborn make series of small cuts. Insert tiny wedges cut from stem end

Pussy Willows

To stop "pussies" from forming yellow catkins remove bud scales

Glass Receptacle

Heavy florist's wire covered with green tape holds crushed hen wire for flower placements. Mechanics do not show in finished design

Mechanical Aids

Water spray

Sharp Knife

Hen wire

Spool of florist's green wire

Pruning shears

Posey clay to secure holder

Wire clipper

Assorted needle holders

SELECTING PLANTS BY COLOR AND SEASON

(See also page 212 for Dried Material in Colors)

SHRUBS

Blue and Related Hues (Spring and Summer)
Amorpha canescens, July
Buddleia, July
Caryopteris, Hardy Blue Spirea, late August
Clematis
Hibiscus syriacus, Celestial Blue, July
Hydrangea, July
Syringa, President Grevy, spring
Vitex, Chaste Tree, July
Wisteria sinensis, spring
Between Blue and Red (Spring and Summer)
Azalea
Buddleia, July
Cercis, Redbud, spring
Daphne mezereum, spring
Hibiscus syriacus violacea, July
Lespedeza formosa, late fall (Desmodium penduliflorum)
Magnolia, spring
Malus, Flowering Crab Apple, spring
Rhododendron
Syringa, Lilac, spring
Vitex, Chaste Tree, July
Weigela, summer
Wisteria
Pink to Red (Spring and Summer)
Abelia, summer
Albizzia, Hardy Silk Tree, summer
Azalea
Buddleia, July
Chaenomeles, Flowering Quince Japanese Quince
Clematis
Cornus, Pink Flowered Dogwood
Crataegus, Hawthorn
Daphne
Deutzia
Hydrangea, July
Kalmia, Mountain Laurel
Kolkwitzia, Beauty Bush
Lonicera tatarica
Magnolia
Malus, Flowering Crab Apple
Neillia sinensis
Prunus
    Flowering Almond
    Flowering Apricot

Flowering Cherry
Flowering Plum
Rhododendron
Robinia hispida, Rose Acacia
Rose, summer
Syringa, Lilac, spring
Tamarix, Pink Cascade, July
Weigela, summer
Yellow to Orange (Spring and Summer)
Azalea, Flame, late spring
Berberis koreana, spring
Campsis, Trumpet Creeper, late summer
Caragana, Siberian Pea Tree, spring
Cornus mas, spring
Coreopsis, Winter Hazel, spring
Cytisus, Broom, spring
Forsythia, spring
Hypericum, summer
Kerria, summer
Laburnum, Golden Chain Tree, spring
Potentilla fruticosa, summer
Ribes aureum, Golden Currant
Rose
Spartium junceum (Genista juncea)
White (Spring and Summer)
Azalea
Buddleia, July
Clematis
Clethra alnifolia
Cornus florida, Dogwood
Deutzia scabra
Exochorda racemosa, Pearl Bush
Halesia carolina, Silver Bell, spring
Hydrangea, July
Leucothoe catesbaei, spring
Magnolia stellata, spring
Philadelphus virginalis
Pieris (Andromeda), spring
Rhododendron
Spirea
Syringa, Lilac, spring
Autumn and Winter Color
    Mostly Yellow, Orange-Scarlet and Red
Azalea viscosum
Berberis, Japanese Barberry
Caryopteris

Celastrus, Bittersweet
Chaenomeles, Japanese Quince
Chionanthus, Fringe Tree
Clethra
Cornus alba sibirica
Cornus stolonifera var. flaviramea
Cotinus, Smoke Tree
Cotoneaster
Crataegus, Hawthorn
Eleagnus, Russian Olive
Enkianthus
Euonymus
Fothergilla
Ilex, Hollies
Kerria
Leucothoe
Ligustrum, Privet

Lindera, Spicebush
Lonicera periclymenum, Wood-bine
Lyonia
Magnolia grandiflora, Bull Bay
Mahonia, Oregon Holly-Grape
Oxydendrum, Sour Wood
Parthenocissus, Virginia Creeper
Pieris japonica
Pyracantha, Firethorn
Rhus, Sumac
Salix, Golden Weeping Willow
Stewartia
Symphoricarpos
Viburnum
Vitex

ANNUALS

(Most annuals will put on a show far into the fall.)

Blue and Related Hues (Summer)
Ageratum, Blue Perfection
Anchusa capensis
Callistephus chinensis (Aster)
Centaurea cyanus
Cynoglossum amabile
Delphinium ajacis
Lobelia erinus
Nemesia strumosa, Blue Gem
Nemophila insignis
Nigella damascena
Petunia
Salvia farinacea
Salvia patens
Scabiosa, Azure Fairy
Torenia fournieri
Verbena

Between Blue and Red (Summer)
Ageratum, Mauve Beauty
Alyssum, Lilac Queen
Antirrhinum, Snapdragon
Callistephus, China Aster
Centaurea imperialis
Clarkia pulchella
Heliotropium
Iberis
Mathiola, Stock
Petunia
Scabiosa
Verbena
Zinnia

Pink to Red (Summer)
Althaea rosea, Hollyhock
Amaranthus
Callistephus, China Aster
Centaurea
Clarkia
Cosmos
Delphinium
Dianthus
Eschscholtzia, Cal. Poppy
Gaillardia

Godetia
Gypsophila elegans
Iberis umbellata
Impatiens
Mathiola, Stock
Nicotiana
Papaver, Poppy
Phlox
Portulaca
Salvia spendens
Scabiosa
Verbena
Zinnia

Yellow to Orange (Summer)
Althaea rosea, Hollyhock
Antirrhinum, Snapdragon
Asclepias
Calendula
Chrysanthemums
Cosmos
Dimorphotheca, Cape Marigold
Erysimum, Blister Cress
Eschscholtzia, Cal. Poppy
Helianthus, Sunflower
Mathiola, Canary Yellow
Nasturtium, Tropaeolum
Phlox drummondi isabellina
Scabiosa
Solidago sempervirens
Tagetes, Marigold
Tithonia, Mexican Sunflower
Viola cornuta
Zinnia

White (Summer)
Ageratum
Alyssum
Antirrhinum
Callistephus
Iberis
Cosmos
Delphinium
Dianthus

Eschscholtzia
Gypsophila
Mathiola
Nicotiana
Petunia
Phlox
Scabiosa
Viola cornuta
Zinnia
Blue and Related Hues (Spring)
Anchusa
Aquilegia, Columbine
Aster (Michaelmas Daisy)
Iris
Myosotis
Pansies
Phlox
Polemonium reptans
Pulmonaria angustifolia
Tradescantia, Spiderwort
Veronica teucrium
Violets
Blue and Related Hues (Summer)
Aconitum, Monkshood
Ageratum
Anchusa
Aster subcaeruleus
Baptisia australis
Campanula, Bellflower
Centaurea
Delphinium
Echinops, Globe Thistle
Hosta, Plantain Lily
Iris
Lavendula, Lavender
Limonium, Sea Lavender
Linum, Flax
Lobelia
Lupinus, Lupines
Nepeta mussini
Penstemon, Beard-Tongue
Platycodon, Balloon-Flower
Polemonium, Jacobs-Ladder
Salvia
Scabiosa
Veronica, Speedwell
Blue and Related Hues (Fall)
Aconitum, Monkshood
Anemone
Asters, Hardy
Eupatorium, Mist-Flower
Salvia pitcheri
Between Blue and Red (Spring)
Anemone, Pasque-Flower
Aquilegia, Columbine
Aster
Iris
Paeonia suffruticosa
Pansies
Phlox
Viola cornuta
Between Blue and Red (Summer)
Astilbe

Campanula
Centaurea, Knapweed
Delphinium
Digitalis, Foxglove
Echinacea, Purple Cone Flower
Hosta sieboldi
Iberis, Candytuft
Iris kaempferi
Liatris
Lilium martagon (Turks-Cap L.)
Limonium, Sea-Lavender
Lythrum, Purple Loosestrife
Monarda fistulosa
Penstemon ovatus
Phlox
Platycodon, Balloon Flower
Salvia sclarea
Thalictrum, Meadow-Rue
Verbascum, Purple Mullein
Between Blue and Red (Fall)
Aconitum, Monkshood
Anemone hupehensis
Asters in var.
Boltonia
Eupatorium, Mist Flower and Joe
   Pye Weed
Penstemon diffusus
Salvia dichroa magnifica
Pink to Red (Spring)
Armeria, Sea Pink
Aquilegia, Columbine
Aster
Bellis perennis, English Daisy
Dianthus, Garden Pink
Dicentra, Bleeding Heart
Iris
Lychnis alpina
Paeonia, Peony
Papaver, Poppy
Phlox
Pink to Red (Summer)
Achillea, Yarrow
Anemone
Aquilegia, Columbine
Astilbe
Campanula, Bellflower
Centranthus ruber
Chrysanthemum, Pyrethrum
Dianthus, Garden Pink
Digitalis, Foxglove
Echinacea
Filipendula palmata (Astilbe)
Gaillardia aristata
Geum coccineum
Helenium autumnale rubrum
Heuchera, Coral-Bells
Hibiscus moscheutos
Iris kaempferi
Kniphofia, Red Hot Poker-Plant
Lilium, Lilies
Lobelia, Cardinal Flower
Lupinus, Lupines
Lychnis

Monarda, Bee Balm
Montbretia, Tritonia
Paeonia, Peony
Papaver, Poppy
Penstemon, Beard-Tongue
Phlox
Physostegia, False Dragonhead
Salvia
Pink to Red (Fall)
Anemone
Aster, New York
Boltonia
Chrysanthemum
Helenium autumnale rubrum
Yellow to Orange (Spring)
Adonis
Alyssum, Basket-of-Gold
Anemone
Aquilegia, Columbine
Doronicum, Leopards Bane
Euphorbia, Yellow Spurge
Hemerocallis flava
Iris germanica
Iris pumila excelsa
Pansies
Primula vulgaris superba
Primula veris superba
Ranunculus, Buttercup

Yellow to Orange (Summer)
Achillea
Centaurea macrocephala
Chrysanthemum
Coreopsis
Delphinium nudicaule luteum
Digitalis, Foxglove
Geum
Helenium
Helianthus, Sunflower
Heliopsis
Hemerocallis
Hypericum, St. Johns Wort
Iris ochroleuca gigantea
Kniphofia, Tritoma
Lathyrus
Lilies
Linaria dalmatica
Montbretia, Tritonia
Oenothera, Evening Primrose
Papaver orientale
Rudbeckia, Coneflower
Scabiosa
Solidago, Goldenrod
Thalictrum, Meadow-Rue
Thermopsis
Tritoma, Kniphofia
Trollius, Globe Flower
Verbascum

PERENNIALS

Yellow to Orange (Fall)
   (Many summer per-
   ennials last until
   frost.)
See summer list.
White (Spring)
   Aquilegia
   Aster
   Bellis perennis
   Campanula
   Dicentra
   Iris
   Linum
   Paeonia, Peony
   Papaver, Poppy
   Phlox
   Statice
   Violets
White (Summer)
   Althea rosea alba
   Anemone
   Anthericum

Astilbe japonica
Aster
Campanula
Centaurea
Centranthus
Chrysanthemums
Delphinium
Dianthus
Dictamus
Digitalis
Echinacea
Euphorbia
Filipendula hexa-
   petala
Gypsophila
Heuchera
Hosta
Iberis sempervirens
Iris
Liatrus
Lilies
Lupinus

Lychnis
Oenothera
Penstemon
Phlox
Physostegia
Platycodon
Polemonium
Scabiosa
Thalictrum
Verbascum
Veronica
White (Fall)
Anemone
Artemesia, Worm-
   wood
Aster
Boltonia
Chrysanthemums
Eupatorium
Hibiscus moscheutos
   alba

FLOWERING BULBS

Bulbs are available in a wide range of colors. Pages 110 ff. list Spring
Flowering Bulbs. Pages 121 ff. list Summer Flowering Bulbs. Pages 132 ff.
list Late Summer and Fall Flowering Bulbs.

INDEX

A CATALOGUE OF
SELECTED DOVER BOOKS
IN ALL FIELDS OF INTEREST

A CATALOGUE OF SELECTED DOVER BOOKS IN ALL FIELDS OF INTEREST

CELESTIAL OBJECTS FOR COMMON TELESCOPES, T. W. Webb. The most used book in amateur astronomy: inestimable aid for locating and identifying nearly 4,000 celestial objects. Edited, updated by Margaret W. Mayall. 77 illustrations. Total of 645pp. 5⅜ x 8½.
20917-2, 20918-0 Pa., Two-vol. set $10.00

HISTORICAL STUDIES IN THE LANGUAGE OF CHEMISTRY, M. P. Crosland. The important part language has played in the development of chemistry from the symbolism of alchemy to the adoption of systematic nomenclature in 1892. ". . . wholeheartedly recommended,"—Science. 15 illustrations. 416pp. of text. 5⅝ x 8¼. 63702-6 Pa. $7.50

BURNHAM'S CELESTIAL HANDBOOK, Robert Burnham, Jr. Thorough, readable guide to the stars beyond our solar system. Exhaustive treatment, fully illustrated. Breakdown is alphabetical by constellation: Andromeda to Cetus in Vol. 1; Chamaeleon to Orion in Vol. 2; and Pavo to Vulpecula in Vol. 3. Hundreds of illustrations. Total of about 2000pp. 6⅛ x 9¼.
23567-X, 23568-8, 23673-0 Pa., Three-vol. set $32.85

THEORY OF WING SECTIONS: INCLUDING A SUMMARY OF AIRFOIL DATA, Ira H. Abbott and A. E. von Doenhoff. Concise compilation of subatomic aerodynamic characteristics of modern NASA wing sections, plus description of theory. 350pp. of tables. 693pp. 5⅜ x 8½.
60586-8 Pa. $9.95

DE RE METALLICA, Georgius Agricola. Translated by Herbert C. Hoover and Lou H. Hoover. The famous Hoover translation of greatest treatise on technological chemistry, engineering, geology, mining of early modern times (1556). All 289 original woodcuts. 638pp. 6¾ x 11.
60006-8 Clothbd. $19.95

THE ORIGIN OF CONTINENTS AND OCEANS, Alfred Wegener. One of the most influential, most controversial books in science, the classic statement for continental drift. Full 1966 translation of Wegener's final (1929) version. 64 illustrations. 246pp. 5⅜ x 8½.(EBE)61708-4 Pa. $5.00

THE PRINCIPLES OF PSYCHOLOGY, William James. Famous long course complete, unabridged. Stream of thought, time perception, memory, experimental methods; great work decades ahead of its time. Still valid, useful; read in many classes. 94 figures. Total of 1391pp. 5⅜ x 8½.
20381-6, 20382-4 Pa., Two-vol. set $17.90

YUCATAN BEFORE AND AFTER THE CONQUEST, Diego de Landa. First English translation of basic book in Maya studies, the only significant account of Yucatan written in the early post-Conquest era. Translated by distinguished Maya scholar William Gates. Appendices, introduction, 4 maps and over 120 illustrations added by translator. 162pp. 5⅜ x 8½.
23622-6 Pa. $3.00

THE MALAY ARCHIPELAGO, Alfred R. Wallace. Spirited travel account by one of founders of modern biology. Touches on zoology, botany, ethnography, geography, and geology. 62 illustrations, maps. 515pp. 5⅜ x 8½.
20187-2 Pa. $6.95

THE DISCOVERY OF THE TOMB OF TUTANKHAMEN, Howard Carter, A. C. Mace. Accompany Carter in the thrill of discovery, as ruined passage suddenly reveals unique, untouched, fabulously rich tomb. Fascinating account, with 106 illustrations. New introduction by J. M. White. Total of 382pp. 5⅜ x 8½. (Available in U.S. only)   23500-9 Pa. $5.50

THE WORLD'S GREATEST SPEECHES, edited by Lewis Copeland and Lawrence W. Lamm. Vast collection of 278 speeches from Greeks up to present. Powerful and effective models; unique look at history. Revised to 1970. Indices. 842pp. 5⅜ x 8½.   20468-5 Pa. $9.95

THE 100 GREATEST ADVERTISEMENTS, Julian Watkins. The priceless ingredient; His master's voice; 99 44/100% pure; over 100 others. How they were written, their impact, etc. Remarkable record. 130 illustrations. 233pp. 7⅞ x 10 3/5.   20540-1 Pa. $6.95

CRUICKSHANK PRINTS FOR HAND COLORING, George Cruickshank. 18 illustrations, one side of a page, on fine-quality paper suitable for watercolors. Caricatures of people in society (c. 1820) full of trenchant wit. Very large format. 32pp. 11 x 16.   23684-6 Pa. $6.00

THIRTY-TWO COLOR POSTCARDS OF TWENTIETH-CENTURY AMERICAN ART, Whitney Museum of American Art. Reproduced in full color in postcard form are 31 art works and one shot of the museum. Calder, Hopper, Rauschenberg, others. Detachable. 16pp. 8¼ x 11.
23629-3 Pa. $3.50

MUSIC OF THE SPHERES: THE MATERIAL UNIVERSE FROM ATOM TO QUASAR SIMPLY EXPLAINED, Guy Murchie. Planets, stars, geology, atoms, radiation, relativity, quantum theory, light, antimatter, similar topics. 319 figures. 664pp. 5⅜ x 8½.
21809-0, 21810-4 Pa., Two-vol. set $11.00

EINSTEIN'S THEORY OF RELATIVITY, Max Born. Finest semi-technical account; covers Einstein, Lorentz, Minkowski, and others, with much detail, much explanation of ideas and math not readily available elsewhere on this level. For student, non-specialist. 376pp. 5⅜ x 8½.
60769-0 Pa. $5.00

THE SENSE OF BEAUTY, George Santayana. Masterfully written discussion of nature of beauty, materials of beauty, form, expression; art, literature, social sciences all involved. 168pp. 5⅜ x 8½.   20238-0 Pa. $3.50

ON THE IMPROVEMENT OF THE UNDERSTANDING, Benedict Spinoza. Also contains *Ethics, Correspondence*, all in excellent R. Elwes translation. Basic works on entry to philosophy, pantheism, exchange of ideas with great contemporaries. 402pp. 5⅜ x 8½.   20250-X Pa. $5.95

THE TRAGIC SENSE OF LIFE, Miguel de Unamuno. Acknowledged masterpiece of existential literature, one of most important books of 20th century. Introduction by Madariaga. 367pp. 5⅜ x 8½.
                                                        20257-7 Pa. $6.00

THE GUIDE FOR THE PERPLEXED, Moses Maimonides. Great classic of medieval Judaism attempts to reconcile revealed religion (Pentateuch, commentaries) with Aristotelian philosophy. Important historically, still relevant in problems. Unabridged Friedlander translation. Total of 473pp. 5⅜ x 8½.   20351-4 Pa. $6.95

THE I CHING (THE BOOK OF CHANGES), translated by James Legge. Complete translation of basic text plus appendices by Confucius, and Chinese commentary of most penetrating divination manual ever prepared. Indispensable to study of early Oriental civilizations, to .modern inquiring reader. 448pp. 5⅜ x 8½.   21062-6 Pa. $6.00

THE EGYPTIAN BOOK OF THE DEAD, E. A. Wallis Budge. Complete reproduction of Ani's papyrus, finest ever found. Full hieroglyphic text, interlinear transliteration, word for word translation, smooth translation. Basic work, for Egyptology, for modern study of psychic matters. Total of 533pp. 6½ x 9¼. (USCO)   21866-X Pa. $8.50

THE GODS OF THE EGYPTIANS, E. A. Wallis Budge. Never excelled for richness, fullness: all gods, goddesses, demons, mythical figures of Ancient Egypt; their legends, rites, incarnations, variations, powers, etc. Many hieroglyphic texts cited. Over 225 illustrations, plus 6 color plates. Total of 988pp. 6⅛ x 9¼. (EBE)
                            22055-9, 22056-7 Pa., Two-vol. set $20.00

THE STANDARD BOOK OF QUILT MAKING AND COLLECTING, Marguerite Ickis. Full information, full-sized patterns for making 46 traditional quilts, also 150 other patterns. Quilted cloths, lame, satin quilts, etc. 483 illustrations. 273pp. 6⅞ x 9⅝.   20582-7 Pa. $5.95

CORAL GARDENS AND THEIR MAGIC, Bronsilaw Malinowski. Classic study of the methods of tilling the soil and of agricultural rites in the Trobriand Islands of Melanesia. Author is one of the most important figures in the field of modern social anthropology. 143 illustrations. Indexes. Total of 911pp. of text. 5⅝ x 8¼. (Available in U.S. only)
                                                        23597-1 Pa. $12.95

CATALOGUE OF DOVER BOOKS

THE PHILOSOPHY OF HISTORY, Georg W. Hegel. Great classic of Western thought develops concept that history is not chance but a rational process, the evolution of freedom. 457pp. 5⅜ x 8½. 20112-0 Pa. $6.00

LANGUAGE, TRUTH AND LOGIC, Alfred J. Ayer. Famous, clear introduction to Vienna, Cambridge schools of Logical Positivism. Role of philosophy, elimination of metaphysics, nature of analysis, etc. 160pp. 5⅜ x 8½. (USCO) 20010-8 Pa. $2.50

A PREFACE TO LOGIC, Morris R. Cohen. Great City College teacher in renowned, easily followed exposition of formal logic, probability, values, logic and world order and similar topics; no previous background needed. 209pp. 5⅜ x 8½. 23517-3 Pa. $4.95

REASON AND NATURE, Morris R. Cohen. Brilliant analysis of reason and its multitudinous ramifications by charismatic teacher. Interdisciplinary, synthesizing work widely praised when it first appeared in 1931. Second (1953) edition. Indexes. 496pp. 5⅜ x 8½. 23633-1 Pa. $7.50

AN ESSAY CONCERNING HUMAN UNDERSTANDING, John Locke. The only complete edition of enormously important classic, with authoritative editorial material by A. C. Fraser. Total of 1176pp. 5⅜ x 8½. 20530-4, 20531-2 Pa., Two-vol. set $16.00

HANDBOOK OF MATHEMATICAL FUNCTIONS WITH FORMULAS, GRAPHS, AND MATHEMATICAL TABLES, edited by Milton Abramowitz and Irene A. Stegun. Vast compendium: 29 sets of tables, some to as high as 20 places. 1,046pp. 8 x 10½. 61272-4 Pa. $17.95

MATHEMATICS FOR THE PHYSICAL SCIENCES, Herbert S. Wilf. Highly acclaimed work offers clear presentations of vector spaces and matrices, orthogonal functions, roots of polynomial equations, conformal mapping, calculus of variations, etc. Knowledge of theory of functions of real and complex variables is assumed. Exercises and solutions. Index. 284pp. 5⅝ x 8¼. 63635-6 Pa. $5.00

THE PRINCIPLE OF RELATIVITY, Albert Einstein et al. Eleven most important original papers on special and general theories. Seven by Einstein, two by Lorentz, one each by Minkowski and Weyl. All translated, unabridged. 216pp. 5⅜ x 8½. 60081-5 Pa. $3.50

THERMODYNAMICS, Enrico Fermi. A classic of modern science. Clear, organized treatment of systems, first and second laws, entropy, thermodynamic potentials, gaseous reactions, dilute solutions, entropy constant. No math beyond calculus required. Problems. 160pp. 5⅜ x 8½. 60361-X Pa. $4.00

ELEMENTARY MECHANICS OF FLUIDS, Hunter Rouse. Classic undergraduate text widely considered to be far better than many later books. Ranges from fluid velocity and acceleration to role of compressibility in fluid motion. Numerous examples, questions, problems. 224 illustrations. 376pp. 5⅝ x 8¼. 63699-2 Pa. $7.00

CATALOGUE OF DOVER BOOKS

THE AMERICAN SENATOR, Anthony Trollope. Little known, long un-available Trollope novel on a grand scale. Here are humorous comment on American vs. English culture, and stunning portrayal of a heroine/villainess. Superb evocation of Victorian village life. 561pp. 5⅜ x 8½.
23801-6 Pa. $7.95

WAS IT MURDER? James Hilton. The author of *Lost Horizon* and *Goodbye, Mr. Chips* wrote one detective novel (under a pen-name) which was quickly forgotten and virtually lost, even at the height of Hilton's fame. This edition brings it back—a finely crafted public school puzzle resplendent with Hilton's stylish atmosphere. A thoroughly English thriller by the creator of Shangri-la. 252pp. 5⅜ x 8. (Available in U.S. only)
23774-5 Pa. $3.00

CENTRAL PARK: A PHOTOGRAPHIC GUIDE, Victor Laredo and Henry Hope Reed. 121 superb photographs show dramatic views of Central Park: Bethesda Fountain, Cleopatra's Needle, Sheep Meadow, the Blockhouse, plus people engaged in many park activities: ice skating, bike riding, etc. Captions by former Curator of Central Park, Henry Hope Reed, provide historical view, changes, etc. Also photos of N.Y. landmarks on park's periphery. 96pp. 8½ x 11. 23750-8 Pa. $4.50

NANTUCKET IN THE NINETEENTH CENTURY, Clay Lancaster. 180 rare photographs, stereographs, maps, drawings and floor plans recreate unique American island society. Authentic scenes of shipwreck, light-houses, streets, homes are arranged in geographic sequence to provide walking-tour guide to old Nantucket existing today. Introduction, captions. 160pp. 8⅞ x 11¾. 23747-8 Pa. $7.95

STONE AND MAN: A PHOTOGRAPHIC EXPLORATION, Andreas Feininger. 106 photographs by *Life* photographer Feininger portray man's deep passion for stone through the ages. Stonehenge-like megaliths, forti-fied towns, sculpted marble and crumbling tenements show textures, beau-ties, fascination. 128pp. 9¼ x 10¾. 23756-7 Pa. $5.95

CIRCLES, A MATHEMATICAL VIEW, D. Pedoe. Fundamental aspects of college geometry, non-Euclidean geometry, and other branches of mathe-matics: representing circle by point. Poincare model, isoperimetric prop-erty, etc. Stimulating recreational reading. 66 figures. 96pp. 5⅝ x 8¼.
63698-4 Pa. $3.50

THE DISCOVERY OF NEPTUNE, Morton Grosser. Dramatic scientific history of the investigations leading up to the actual discovery of the eighth planet of our solar system. Lucid, well-researched book by well-known historian of science. 172pp. 5⅜ x 8½. 23726-5 Pa. $3.50

THE DEVIL'S DICTIONARY. Ambrose Bierce. Barbed, bitter, brilliant witticisms in the form of a dictionary. Best, most ferocious satire America has produced. 145pp. 5⅜ x 8½. 20487-1 Pa. $2.50

CATALOGUE OF DOVER BOOKS

HISTORY OF BACTERIOLOGY, William Bulloch. The only comprehensive history of bacteriology from the beginnings through the 19th century. Special emphasis is given to biography-Leeuwenhoek, etc. Brief accounts of 350 bacteriologists form a separate section. No clearer, fuller study, suitable to scientists and general readers, has yet been written. 52 illustrations. 448pp. 5⅝ x 8¼.   23761-3 Pa. $6.50

THE COMPLETE NONSENSE OF EDWARD LEAR, Edward Lear. All nonsense limericks, zany alphabets, Owl and Pussycat, songs, nonsense botany, etc., illustrated by Lear. Total of 321pp. 5⅜ x 8½. (Available in U.S. only)   20167-8 Pa. $4.50

INGENIOUS MATHEMATICAL PROBLEMS AND METHODS, Louis A. Graham. Sophisticated material from Graham *Dial*, applied and pure; stresses solution methods. Logic, number theory, networks, inversions, etc. 237pp. 5⅜ x 8½.   20545-2 Pa. $4.50

BEST MATHEMATICAL PUZZLES OF SAM LOYD, edited by Martin Gardner. Bizarre, original, whimsical puzzles by America's greatest puzzler. From fabulously rare *Cyclopedia*, including famous 14-15 puzzles, the Horse of a Different Color, 115 more. Elementary math. 150 illustrations. 167pp. 5⅜ x 8½.   20498-7 Pa. $3.50

THE BASIS OF COMBINATION IN CHESS, J. du Mont. Easy-to-follow, instructive book on elements of combination play, with chapters on each piece and every powerful combination team—two knights, bishop and knight, rook and bishop, etc. 250 diagrams. 218pp. 5⅜ x 8½. (Available in U.S. only)   23644-7 Pa. $4.50

MODERN CHESS STRATEGY, Ludek Pachman. The use of the queen, the active king, exchanges, pawn play, the center, weak squares, etc. Section on rook alone worth price of the book. Stress on the moderns. Often considered the most important book on strategy. 314pp. 5⅜ x 8½.
                                                        20290-9 Pa. $5.00

LASKER'S MANUAL OF CHESS, Dr. Emanuel Lasker. Great world champion offers very thorough coverage of all aspects of chess. Combinations, position play, openings, end game, aesthetics of chess, philosophy of struggle, much more. Filled with analyzed games. 390pp. 5⅜ x 8½.
                                                        20640-8 Pa. $5.95

500 MASTER GAMES OF CHESS, S. Tartakower, J. du Mont. Vast collection of great chess games from 1798-1938, with much material nowhere else readily available. Fully annotated, arranged by opening for easier study. 664pp. 5⅜ x 8½.   23208-5 Pa. $8.50

A GUIDE TO CHESS ENDINGS, Dr. Max Euwe, David Hooper. One of the finest modern works on chess endings. Thorough analysis of the most frequently encountered endings by former world champion. 331 examples, each with diagram. 248pp. 5⅜ x 8½.   23332-4 Pa. $3.95

THE COMPLETE BOOK OF DOLL MAKING AND COLLECTING, Catherine Christopher. Instructions, patterns for dozens of dolls, from rag doll on up to elaborate, historically accurate figures. Mould faces, sew clothing, make doll houses, etc. Also collecting information. Many illustrations. 288pp. 6 x 9. 22066-4 Pa. $4.95

THE DAGUERREOTYPE IN AMERICA, Beaumont Newhall. Wonderful portraits, 1850's townscapes, landscapes; full text plus 104 photographs. The basic book. Enlarged 1976 edition. 272pp. 8¼ x 11¼. 23322-7 Pa. $7.95

CRAFTSMAN HOMES, Gustav Stickley. 296 architectural drawings, floor plans, and photographs illustrate 40 different kinds of "Mission-style" homes from The Craftsman (1901-16), voice of American style of simplicity and organic harmony. Thorough coverage of Craftsman idea in text and picture, now collector's item. 224pp. 8⅛ x 11. 23791-5 Pa. $6.50

PEWTER-WORKING: INSTRUCTIONS AND PROJECTS, Burl N. Osborn. & Gordon O. Wilber. Introduction to pewter-working for amateur craftsman. History and characteristics of pewter; tools, materials, step-by-step instructions. Photos, line drawings, diagrams. Total of 160pp. 7⅞ x 10¾. 23786-9 Pa. $3.50

THE GREAT CHICAGO FIRE, edited by David Lowe. 10 dramatic, eye-witness accounts of the 1871 disaster, including one of the aftermath and rebuilding, plus 70 contemporary photographs and illustrations of the ruins—courthouse, Palmer House, Great Central Depot, etc. Introduction by David Lowe. 87pp. 8¼ x 11. 23771-0 Pa. $4.00

SILHOUETTES: A PICTORIAL ARCHIVE OF VARIED ILLUSTRATIONS, edited by Carol Belanger Grafton. Over 600 silhouettes from the 18th to 20th centuries include profiles and full figures of men and women, children, birds and animals, groups and scenes, nature, ships, an alphabet. Dozens of uses for commercial artists and craftspeople. 144pp. 8⅜ x 11¼. 23781-8 Pa. $4.50

ANIMALS: 1,419 COPYRIGHT-FREE ILLUSTRATIONS OF MAMMALS, BIRDS, FISH, INSECTS, ETC., edited by Jim Harter. Clear wood engravings present, in extremely lifelike poses, over 1,000 species of animals. One of the most extensive copyright-free pictorial sourcebooks of its kind. Captions. Index. 284pp. 9 x 12. 23766-4 Pa. $8.95

INDIAN DESIGNS FROM ANCIENT ECUADOR, Frederick W. Shaffer. 282 original designs by pre-Columbian Indians of Ecuador (500-1500 A.D.). Designs include people, mammals, birds, reptiles, fish, plants, heads, geometric designs. Use as is or alter for advertising, textiles, leathercraft, etc. Introduction. 95pp. 8¾ x 11¼. 23764-8 Pa. $4.50

SZIGETI ON THE VIOLIN, Joseph Szigeti. Genial, loosely structured tour by premier violinist, featuring a pleasant mixture of reminiscences, insights into great music and musicians, innumerable tips for practicing violinists. 385 musical passages. 256pp. 5⅝ x 8¼. 23763-X Pa. $4.00

CATALOGUE OF DOVER BOOKS

TONE POEMS, SERIES II: TILL EULENSPIEGELS LUSTIGE STREICHE, ALSO SPRACH ZARATHUSTRA, AND EIN HELDEN-LEBEN, Richard Strauss. Three important orchestral works, including very popular *Till Eulenspiegel's Marry Pranks*, reproduced in full score from original editions. Study score. 315pp. 9⅜ x 12¼. (Available in U.S. only)
23755-9 Pa. $8.95

TONE POEMS, SERIES I: DON JUAN, TOD UND VERKLARUNG AND DON QUIXOTE, Richard Strauss. Three of the most often performed and recorded works in entire orchestral repertoire, reproduced in full score from original editions. Study score. 286pp. 9⅜ x 12¼. (Available in U.S. only)
23754-0 Pa. $8.95

11 LATE STRING QUARTETS, Franz Joseph Haydn. The form which Haydn defined and "brought to perfection." (*Grove's*). 11 string quartets in complete score, his last and his best. The first in a projected series of the complete Haydn string quartets. Reliable modern Eulenberg edition, otherwise difficult to obtain. 320pp. 8⅜ x 11¼. (Available in U.S. only)
23753-2 Pa. $8.95

FOURTH, FIFTH AND SIXTH SYMPHONIES IN FULL SCORE, Peter Ilyitch Tchaikovsky. Complete orchestral scores of Symphony No. 4 in F Minor, Op. 36; Symphony No. 5 in E Minor, Op. 64; Symphony No. 6 in B Minor, "Pathetique," Op. 74. Bretikopf & Hartel eds. Study score. 480pp. 9⅜ x 12¼.
23861-X Pa. $10.95

THE MARRIAGE OF FIGARO: COMPLETE SCORE, Wolfgang A. Mozart. Finest comic opera ever written. Full score, not to be confused with piano renderings. Peters edition. Study score. 448pp. 9⅜ x 12¼. (Available in U.S. only)
23751-6 Pa. $12.95

"IMAGE" ON THE ART AND EVOLUTION OF THE FILM, edited by Marshall Deutelbaum. Pioneering book brings together for first time 38 groundbreaking articles on early silent films from *Image* and 263 illustrations newly shot from rare prints in the collection of the International Museum of Photography. A landmark work. Index. 256pp. 8¼ x 11.
23777-X Pa. $8.95

AROUND-THE-WORLD COOKY BOOK, Lois Lintner Sumption and Marguerite Lintner Ashbrook. 373 cooky and frosting recipes from 28 countries (America, Austria, China, Russia, Italy, etc.) include Viennese kisses, rice wafers, London strips, lady fingers, hony, sugar spice, maple cookies, etc. Clear instructions. All tested. 38 drawings. 182pp. 5⅜ x 8.
23802-4 Pa. $2.75

THE ART NOUVEAU STYLE, edited by Roberta Waddell. 579 rare photographs, not available elsewhere, of works in jewelry, metalwork, glass, ceramics, textiles, architecture and furniture by 175 artists—Mucha, Seguy, Lalique, Tiffany, Gaudin, Hohlwein, Saarinen, and many others. 288pp. 8⅜ x 11¼.
23515-7 Pa. $8.95

THE CURVES OF LIFE, Theodore A. Cook. Examination of shells, leaves, horns, human body, art, etc., in "*the* classic reference on how the golden ratio applies to spirals and helices in nature . . . ."—Martin Gardner. 426 illustrations. Total of 512pp. 5⅜ x 8½.   23701-X Pa. **$6.95**

AN ILLUSTRATED FLORA OF THE NORTHERN UNITED STATES AND CANADA, Nathaniel L. Britton, Addison Brown. Encyclopedic work covers 4666 species, ferns on up. Everything. Full botanical information, illustration for each. This earlier edition is preferred by many to more recent revisions. 1913 edition. Over 4000 illustrations, total of 2087pp. 6⅛ x 9¼.   22642-5, 22643-3, 22644-1 Pa., Three-vol. set **$28.50**

MANUAL OF THE GRASSES OF THE UNITED STATES, A. S. Hitchcock, U.S. Dept. of Agriculture. The basic study of American grasses, both indigenous and escapes, cultivated and wild. Over 1400 species. Full descriptions, information. Over 1100 maps, illustrations. Total of 1051pp. 5⅜ x 8½.   22717-0, 22718-9 Pa., Two-vol. set **$17.00**

THE CACTACEAE,, Nathaniel L. Britton, John N. Rose. Exhaustive, definitive. Every cactus in the world. Full botanical descriptions. Thorough statement of nomenclatures, habitat, detailed finding keys. The one book needed by every cactus enthusiast. Over 1275 illustrations. Total of 1080pp. 8 x 10¼.   21191-6, 21192-4 Clothbd., Two-vol. set **$50.00**

AMERICAN MEDICINAL PLANTS, Charles F. Millspaugh. Full descriptions, 180 plants covered: history; physical description; methods of preparation with all chemical constituents extracted; all claimed curative or adverse effects. 180 full-page plates. Classification table. 804pp. 6½ x 9¼.
23034-1 Pa. **$13.95**

A MODERN HERBAL, Margaret Grieve. Much the fullest, most exact, most useful compilation of herbal material. Gigantic alphabetical encyclopedia, from aconite to zedoary, gives botanical information, medical properties, folklore, economic uses, and much else. Indispensable to serious reader. 161 illustrations. 888pp. 6½ x 9¼. (Available in U.S. only)
22798-7, 22799-5 Pa., Two-vol. set **$15.00**

THE HERBAL or GENERAL HISTORY OF PLANTS, John Gerard. The 1633 edition revised and enlarged by Thomas Johnson. Containing almost 2850 plant descriptions and 2705 superb illustrations, Gerard's *Herbal* is a monumental work, the book all modern English herbals are derived from, the one herbal every serious enthusiast should have in its entirety. Original editions are worth perhaps $750. 1678pp. 8½ x 12¼.
23147-X Clothbd. **$75.00**

MANUAL OF THE TREES OF NORTH AMERICA, Charles S. Sargent. The basic survey of every native tree and tree-like shrub, 717 species in all. Extremely full descriptions, information on habitat, growth, locales, economics, etc. Necessary to every serious tree lover. Over 100 finding keys. 783 illustrations. Total of 986pp. 5⅜ x 8½.
20277-1, 20278-X Pa., Two-vol. set **$12.00**

CATALOGUE OF DOVER BOOKS

GREAT NEWS PHOTOS AND THE STORIES BEHIND THEM, John Faber. Dramatic volume of 140 great news photos, 1855 through 1976, and revealing stories behind them, with both historical and technical information. Hindenburg disaster, shooting of Oswald, nomination of Jimmy Carter, etc. 160pp. 8¼ x 11.   23667-6 Pa. $6.00

CRUICKSHANK'S PHOTOGRAPHS OF BIRDS OF AMERICA, Allan D. Cruickshank. Great ornithologist, photographer presents 177 closeups, groupings, panoramas, flightings, etc., of about 150 different birds. Expanded *Wings in the Wilderness.* Introduction by Helen G. Cruickshank. 191pp. 8¼ x 11.   23497-5 Pa. $7.95

AMERICAN WILDLIFE AND PLANTS, A. C. Martin, et al. Describes food habits of more than 1000 species of mammals, birds, fish. Special treatment of important food plants. Over 300 illustrations. 500pp. 5⅜ x 8½.
20793-5 Pa. $6.50

THE PEOPLE CALLED SHAKERS, Edward D. Andrews. Lifetime of research, definitive study of Shakers: origins, beliefs, practices, dances, social organization, furniture and crafts, impact on 19th-century USA, present heritage. Indispensable to student of American history, collector. 33 illustrations. 351pp. 5⅜ x 8½.   21081-2 Pa. $4.50

OLD NEW YORK IN EARLY PHOTOGRAPHS, Mary Black. New York City as it was in 1853-1901, through 196 wonderful photographs from N.-Y. Historical Society. Great Blizzard, Lincoln's funeral procession, great buildings. 228pp. 9 x 12.   22907-6 Pa. $8.95

MR. LINCOLN'S CAMERA MAN: MATHEW BRADY, Roy Meredith. Over 300 Brady photos reproduced directly from original negatives, photos. Jackson, Webster, Grant, Lee, Carnegie, Barnum; Lincoln; Battle Smoke, Death of Rebel Sniper, Atlanta Just After Capture. Lively commentary. 368pp. 8⅜ x 11¼.   23021-X Pa. $11.95

TRAVELS OF WILLIAM BARTRAM, William Bartram. From 1773-8, Bartram explored Northern Florida, Georgia, Carolinas, and reported on wild life, plants, Indians, early settlers. Basic account for period, entertaining reading. Edited by Mark Van Doren. 13 illustrations. 141pp. 5⅜ x 8½.   20013-2 Pa. $6.00

THE GENTLEMAN AND CABINET MAKER'S DIRECTOR, Thomas Chippendale. Full reprint, 1762 style book, most influential of all time; chairs, tables, sofas, mirrors, cabinets, etc. 200 plates, plus 24 photographs of surviving pieces. 249pp. 9⅞ x 12¾.   21601-2 Pa. $8.95

AMERICAN CARRIAGES, SLEIGHS, SULKIES AND CARTS, edited by Don H. Berkebile. 168 Victorian illustrations from catalogues, trade journals, fully captioned. Useful for artists. Author is Assoc. Curator, Div. of Transportation of Smithsonian Institution. 168pp. 8½ x 9½.
23328-6 Pa. $5.00

SECOND PIATIGORSKY CUP, edited by Isaac Kashdan. One of the greatest tournament books ever produced in the English language. All 90 games of the 1966 tournament, annotated by players, most annotated by both players. Features Petrosian, Spassky, Fischer, Larsen, six others. 228pp. 5⅜ x 8½. 23572-6 Pa. $3.50

ENCYCLOPEDIA OF CARD TRICKS, revised and edited by Jean Hugard. How to perform over 600 card tricks, devised by the world's greatest magicians: impromptus, spelling tricks, key cards, using special packs, much, much more. Additional chapter on card technique. 66 illustrations. 402pp. 5⅜ x 8½. (Available in U.S. only) 21252-1 Pa. $5.95

MAGIC: STAGE ILLUSIONS, SPECIAL EFFECTS AND TRICK PHO-TOGRAPHY, Albert A. Hopkins, Henry R. Evans. One of the great classics; fullest, most authorative explanation of vanishing lady, levitations, scores of other great stage effects. Also small magic, automata, stunts. 446 illustrations. 556pp. 5⅜ x 8½. 23344-8 Pa. $6.95

THE SECRETS OF HOUDINI, J. C. Cannell. Classic study of Houdini's incredible magic, exposing closely-kept professional secrets and revealing, in general terms, the whole art of stage magic. 67 illustrations. 279pp. 5⅜ x 8½. 22913-0 Pa. $4.00

HOFFMANN'S MODERN MAGIC, Professor Hoffmann. One of the best, and best-known, magicians' manuals of the past century. Hundreds of tricks from card tricks and simple sleight of hand to elaborate illusions involving construction of complicated machinery. 332 illustrations. 563pp. 5⅜ x 8½. 23623-4 Pa. $6.95

THOMAS NAST'S CHRISTMAS DRAWINGS, Thomas Nast. Almost all Christmas drawings by creator of image of Santa Claus as we know it, and one of America's foremost illustrators and political cartoonists. 66 illustrations. 3 illustrations in color on covers. 96pp. 8⅜ x 11¼. 23660-9 Pa. $3.50

FRENCH COUNTRY COOKING FOR AMERICANS, Louis Diat. 500 easy-to-make, authentic provincial recipes compiled by former head chef at New York's Fitz-Carlton Hotel: onion soup, lamb stew, potato pie, more. 309pp. 5⅜ x 8½. 23665-X Pa. $3.95

SAUCES, FRENCH AND FAMOUS, Louis Diat. Complete book gives over 200 specific recipes: bechamel, Bordelaise, hollandaise, Cumberland, apricot, etc. Author was one of this century's finest chefs, originator of vichyssoise and many other dishes. Index. 156pp. 5⅜ x 8. 23663-3 Pa. $2.75

TOLL HOUSE TRIED AND TRUE RECIPES, Ruth Graves Wakefield. Authentic recipes from the famous Mass. restaurant: popovers, veal and ham loaf, Toll House baked beans, chocolate cake crumb pudding, much more. Many helpful hints. Nearly 700 recipes. Index. 376pp. 5⅜ x 8½. 23560-2 Pa. $4.95

ILLUSTRATED GUIDE TO SHAKER FURNITURE, Robert Meader. Director, Shaker Museum, Old Chatham, presents up-to-date coverage of all furniture and appurtenances, with much on local styles not available elsewhere. 235 photos. 146pp. 9 x 12.   22819-3 Pa. $6.95

COOKING WITH BEER, Carole Fahy. Beer has as superb an effect on food as wine, and at fraction of cost. Over 250 recipes for appetizers, soups, main dishes, desserts, breads, etc. Index. 144pp. 5⅜ x 8½. (Available in U.S. only)   23661-7 Pa. $3.00

STEWS AND RAGOUTS, Kay Shaw Nelson. This international cookbook offers wide range of 108 recipes perfect for everyday, special occasions, meals-in-themselves, main dishes. Economical, nutritious, easy-to-prepare: goulash, Irish stew, boeuf bourguignon, etc. Index. 134pp. 5⅜ x 8½.
                23662-5 Pa. $3.95

DELICIOUS MAIN COURSE DISHES, Marian Tracy. Main courses are the most important part of any meal. These 200 nutritious, economical recipes from around the world make every meal a delight. "I . . . have found it so useful in my own household,"—N.Y. Times. Index. 219pp. 5⅜ x 8½.   23664-1 Pa. $3.95

FIVE ACRES AND INDEPENDENCE, Maurice G. Kains. Great back-to-the-land classic explains basics of self-sufficient farming: economics, plants, crops, animals, orchards, soils, land selection, host of other necessary things. Do not confuse with skimpy faddist literature; Kains was one of America's greatest agriculturalists. 95 illustrations. 397pp. 5⅜ x 8½.
                20974-1 Pa. $4.95

A PRACTICAL GUIDE FOR THE BEGINNING FARMER, Herbert Jacobs. Basic, extremely useful first book for anyone thinking about moving to the country and starting a farm. Simpler than Kains, with greater emphasis on country living in general. 246pp. 5⅜ x 8½.
                23675-7 Pa. $3.95

PAPERMAKING, Dard Hunter. Definitive book on the subject by the foremost authority in the field. Chapters dealing with every aspect of history of craft in every part of the world. Over 320 illustrations. 2nd, revised and enlarged (1947) edition. 672pp. 5⅜ x 8½.   23619-6 Pa. $8.95

THE ART DECO STYLE, edited by Theodore Menten. Furniture, jewelry, metalwork, ceramics, fabrics, lighting fixtures, interior decors, exteriors, graphics from pure French sources. Best sampling around. Over 400 photographs. 183pp. 8⅜ x 11¼.   22824-X Pa. $6.95

ACKERMANN'S COSTUME PLATES, Rudolph Ackermann. Selection of 96 plates from the Repository of Arts, best published source of costume for English fashion during the early 19th century. 12 plates also in color. Captions, glossary and introduction by editor Stella Blum. Total of 120pp. 8⅜ x 11¼.   23690-0 Pa. $5.00

CATALOGUE OF DOVER BOOKS

THE ANATOMY OF THE HORSE, George Stubbs. Often considered the great masterpiece of animal anatomy. Full reproduction of 1766 edition, plus prospectus; original text and modernized text. 36 plates. Introduction by Eleanor Garvey. 121pp. 11 x 14¾. 23402-9 Pa. $8.95

BRIDGMAN'S LIFE DRAWING, George B. Bridgman. More than 500 illustrative drawings and text teach you to abstract the body into its major masses, use light and shade, proportion; as well as specific areas of anatomy, of which Bridgman is master. 192pp. 6½ x 9¼. (Available in U.S. only) 22710-3 Pa. $4.50

ART NOUVEAU DESIGNS IN COLOR, Alphonse Mucha, Maurice Verneuil, Georges Auriol. Full-color reproduction of *Combinaisons ornementales* (c. 1900) by Art Nouveau masters. Floral, animal, geometric, interlacings, swashes—borders, frames, spots—all incredibly beautiful. 60 plates, hundreds of designs. 9⅜ x 8-1/16. 22885-1 Pa. $4.50

FULL-COLOR FLORAL DESIGNS IN THE ART NOUVEAU STYLE, E. A. Seguy. 166 motifs, on 40 plates, from *Les fleurs et leurs applications decoratives* (1902): borders, circular designs, repeats, allovers, "spots." All in authentic Art Nouveau colors. 48pp. 9⅜ x 12¼. 23439-8 Pa. $6.00

A DIDEROT PICTORIAL ENCYCLOPEDIA OF TRADES AND INDUSTRY, edited by Charles C. Gillispie. 485 most interesting plates from the great French Encyclopedia of the 18th century show hundreds of working figures, artifacts, process, land and cityscapes; glassmaking, papermaking, metal extraction, construction, weaving, making furniture, clothing, wigs, dozens of other activities. Plates fully explained. 920pp. 9 x 12. 22284-5, 22285-3 Clothbd., Two-vol. set $50.00

HANDBOOK OF EARLY ADVERTISING ART, Clarence P. Hornung. Largest collection of copyright-free early and antique advertising art ever compiled. Over 6,000 illustrations, from Franklin's time to the 1890's for special effects, novelty. Valuable source, almost inexhaustible.
Pictorial Volume. Agriculture, the zodiac, animals, autos, birds, Christmas, fire engines, flowers, trees, musical instruments, ships, games and sports, much more. Arranged by subject matter and use. 237 plates. 288pp. 9 x 12. 20122-8 Clothbd. $15.00

Typographical Volume. Roman and Gothic faces ranging from 10 point to 300 point, "Barnum," German and Old English faces, script, logotypes, scrolls and flourishes, 1115 ornamental initials, 67 complete alphabets, more. 310 plates. 320pp. 9 x 12. 20123-6 Clothbd. $15.00

CALLIGRAPHY (CALLIGRAPHIA LATINA), J. G. Schwandner. High point of 18th-century ornamental calligraphy. Very ornate initials, scrolls, borders, cherubs, birds, lettered examples. 172pp. 9 x 13. 20475-8 Pa. $7.95

GEOMETRY, RELATIVITY AND THE FOURTH DIMENSION, Rudolf Rucker. Exposition of fourth dimension, means of visualization, concepts of relativity as Flatland characters continue adventures. Popular, easily followed yet accurate, profound. 141 illustrations. 133pp. 5⅜ x 8½.
23400-2 Pa. $2.75

THE ORIGIN OF LIFE, A. I. Oparin. Modern classic in biochemistry, the first rigorous examination of possible evolution of life from nitrocarbon compounds. Non-technical, easily followed. Total of 295pp. 5⅜ x 8½.
60213-3 Pa. $5.95

PLANETS, STARS AND GALAXIES, A. E. Fanning. Comprehensive introductory survey: the sun, solar system, stars, galaxies, universe, cosmology; quasars, radio stars, etc. 24pp. of photographs. 189pp. 5⅜ x 8½. (Available in U.S. only)
21680-2 Pa. $3.75

THE THIRTEEN BOOKS OF EUCLID'S ELEMENTS, translated with introduction and commentary by Sir Thomas L. Heath. Definitive edition. Textual and linguistic. notes, mathematical analysis, 2500 years of critical commentary. Do not confuse with abridged school editions. Total of 1414pp. 5⅜ x 8½.   60088-2, 60089-0, 60090-4 Pa., Three-vol. set $19.50